Early Praise for Heali

Healing Noelle is a you're-going-to-stay-up-too-. ......g page-turner, full of powerful spiritual lessons. From page one to the bombshell ending, the message in this engaging work of Christian fiction is as razor sharp as a surgeon's scalpel: It's not about us, it's all about God.

—David Stevens, MD, MA (ethics)
Executive Director, Christian Medical and Dental Associations

Real characters...a gripping plot with unexpected developments...I could hardly put it down! This novel graphically illustrates how far nanotechnology can go astray if, in our aspirations to save the human race, we are willing to sacrifice humanity.

—John F. Kilner, PhD, President,
Center for Bioethics and Human Dignity

Michael's new novel challenges us to consider the horrific implications of science gone too far. Healing Noelle perhaps foretells the last great battle for life as we know it. An entertaining and thought-provoking novel.

—Kay Orr, former Governor of Nebraska

An intriguing admixture of themes involving spirituality, medicine and small town American life...Fascinating characters artfully woven into a unique story of drama, mystery and intrigue. This is a great novel to be enjoyed by a wide audience of readers.

—David P. Asprey, PhD, PA-C, Former President,
Association of Physician Assistant Programs
Associate Professor and Program Director,
The University of Iowa Physician Assistant Program

Healing
NOELLE

Michael J. Huckabee

Michael J. Huckabee

Paul & Kathy,
So many find memories!
Blessings to you & may you
experience the healing
touch of Jesus!
Psalm 103:3

Dageforde Publishing, Inc.

ISBN 0-9753031-0-4
Cover design by MDirect, Omaha,Nebraska

Dageforde Publishing, Inc.
128 East 13th Street
Crete, Nebraska 68333

www.dageforde.com
1-800-216-8794

Printed in the United States of America
10 9 8 7 6 5 4 3 2 1

*To Bailey and Nancy, who together
have taught me the most about healing.*

Acknowledgments

*T*he lifeblood of any story comes from the heartbeat of many. My opportunity to observe healings, whether by medicine or by the supernatural, is only due to the many patients who trusted me enough to share in this intimate aspect of life and sometimes death.

The encouragement I received from those reading early versions of this story helped expand my understanding of the effect of health and healing on the soul. Thanks to April, Bailey, Barb, Bonnie, Boyd, Cindy, Dan, David, Jeff, Jennifer, John, Kay, Kathy, Laurie, Nancy, and Tyler.

My family must be credited for so often restoring my own soul.

The support of Amy, Linda and Barbara at Dageforde Publishing was never-ending. Dan at Parsons Public Relations, Inc. was instrumental in getting this book into the readers' hands.

The ongoing work of my dear friends in undergirding the production of this novel has been and will continue to be vital: Kevin and Kathy, Gary and Bonnie, Gary and Cindy, and Tim.

And most of all, we are all in incomparable debt, whether we acknowledge it or not, to the One who promises to heal all our diseases (Psalm 103). If the reader is interested in speaking to someone about beginning a personal relationship with Jesus Christ, please call 1-888-NEED HIM, or visit www.needhim.org.

Chapter 1

"*J*eno! Come back!"

Noelle shuddered as the ugly thud of tires rolled over the cat. She screamed as the small, mangled, gray-streaked body flew out from behind a car obliviously speeding down the road.

Kneeling beside Jeno, the young girl was hesitant to stroke its fur. The animal made a slow gasp, its head falling back to the pavement.

"Wake up, Jeno!" She gently nudged the cat.

"Please, Jeno, wake up," she sobbed. "God, don't let him die, pretty please?"

It was her first encounter with death. The putrid odor of blood and bowels violated her undefiled five-year-old senses. Carefully lifting Jeno to her arms, she swallowed the odor with her agony, cradling the carcass like a doll.

"Why'd you have to go chasin' a car?" she sniffled, trying to reason in her little mind. "Why'd you have to get runned over?"

"Can I help?" A young, blond-haired boy sat on a tree stump across the street.

Her privacy shattered. Choking back tears stifled her response.

The boy stepped closer. "Is your cat hurt?" Bending down, he laid a small hand on Jeno's head.

"Yes, bad." Noelle took one hand to stroke her brunette hair behind her ear and quickly returned it to support her pet.

"I think I can help." He raised his head to the sky and lifted a small hand upward.

Her sorrow dammed by confusion, Noelle watched the boy close his eyes, whispering words she could not hear. They were not meant for her.

A moment later she sniffed at a cool breeze sweeping past her. Something like sweet lilacs saturated her senses. Fur brushed against her arms and she glanced down, Jeno's ebony eyes shining back at her. The kitty almost held a smile as he gently crawled up, his sandpaper tongue licking her chin.

Noelle was dumbstruck. Her young mind could barely conceive death, let alone life afterward. Astonished, she gazed at the young boy.

He simply smiled. "God loves cats. He loves you too." He pressed his glasses to his nose, turned and walked down the road.

Unrehearsed with common courtesies, Noelle stared in wonder. As an afterthought she yelled to him. "What's your name?"

He turned his head for just a moment, not stopping his stride. "Jonathon."

Seven years later

"You look great!" Jonathon exclaimed at the bedside of Manny Lewis. "Are you faking it?"

Manny gave a tired smile. "I'm so much better than I was. Just having that hunk of tumor whacked out of my leg is a good feeling."

"The doctors said he's one-hundred-percent cured," Noelle announced, sitting on the edge of her older brother's bed.

"I'm very thankful," Manny sighed, appearing weak despite a precocious muscular build for a fourteen-year-old. "It was great to have you pray for me, Jonathon. You're the only one who did that. I keep thinking something happened then. To think my little sister's friend prayed for me."

"Gotta put things in God's hands. He really cares about you, Manny."

"Yeah, I keep thinking about that."

"God wants you to keep thinking." Jonathon turned serious. "He wants you to reach out to Him. He wants you to trust Him for the life He has given back to you."

"Well, you look awfully tired," Noelle interrupted. "We better let you get your rest." She stood up from the bed, moving right in front of Jonathon. "It was great of you to stop by, Jon."

She only called him Jon when she was peeved. A quick goodbye and he was ushered out of the room.

"You can't keep this up, Jon." She slammed Manny's bedroom door, accenting her words.

"Keep what up?" His calm reply bred her anger.

"Can't you see it's crazy? How could you ever believe that you healed him?"

"Noelle, even you said your brother was going to die. You told me the cancer was raging."

"I didn't mean to make you pull out your magic."

"It's not magic." Jonathon turned away.

She bit her lip. "Look, I'm sorry. But you've got to come back to reality some time. I thank God my brother's alive. The doctors said the operation removed the whole melanoma. I can't let you take credit for it."

"I don't want the credit; you know that. But you've gotta believe that God is moving. Moving all around you. He's alive, working His miracles."

"But why you, Jonathon? Why do you think He'd want you to be 'the healer'?"

She'd heard it all before at least a dozen times. She knew better than to ask again. God was not some mystical cure-all. When would Jonathon understand?

He wasn't answering. Good. She was tired of arguing. It would be a great friendship if it wasn't for this.

"I gotta go do the dishes," she said more tenderly, stroking a few strands of her brunette hair. "Tomorrow after school let's go to McDee's. As long as you promise no more healin' talk."

"Okay," he relented. "Only if you bring it up."

"Good. No grudges held." She really did want to spend time with him.

"I am glad your brother's going to make it." He bumped his glasses up on his nose. "He's a great guy."

Three years later

Her pale face matched the white sheets of her hospital bed. The only contrasts were her wrinkles of age against the starched pillow. Jonathon hated to see her so frail.

"Aunt Emma, please let me pray for you." His pleadings made his eyes wet.

"No, Jonathon," her voice croaked softly. "I know your heart. This you cannot change."

One at a time she had asked to see her relatives. Jonathon, the fifteen-year-old nephew, paced the waiting room while her two grown sons and their families had visited. He was the last one following his mother, his aunt's

3

only sister. Despite the exhaustion on his dear aunt Emma's face, he still had to try.

"But why? You're the only one who understands, Aunt Emma. Why won't you seek healing?"

"Your youth blinds you." Her speech was thick and dry. "It is my time. You cannot heal what God chooses not to, Jonathon."

He peered out the window, avoiding her stare. Though her body was frail and dying, her eyes still penetrated his heart.

"I don't know what I'll do when you're gone," he whispered.

"Remember the first time?" she asked, taking short breaths between every few words. "Remember what I said?"

He was only five then, but he remembered it like it was yesterday. "You said this was of God, and that He alone controls it. You told me few would understand, that I should not expect any different. You said to be sure the glory went to God."

Breathing with less effort, her lips curled into a slight smile as she closed her eyes.

"Good, Jonathon...now remember this also. You have been chosen. Your gift will not depart. Keep your eyes...on Jesus Christ. You will fall...if you don't do this. Heal as He directs. No more, no less."

She spoke with difficulty. He wondered if he should call the nurse, yet he clung to every word. This was eternity speaking.

"Jesus will never...fail you."

Her eyes closed and her breaths diminished.

Jonathon grabbed her limp hand. "God, please heal—" His words were choked by tears. Like a balloon squeezed too tight, his emotions suddenly burst as he beheld his aunt's evaporating life.

Three years later

"You want me to take Latin with you? I can't even say 'quesadilla taco platter' without stuttering."

"Come on, Jonathon. I have to take it for college. I'll help you."

"Noelle, who's going to talk to you in all the *e pluribus* stuff? Let's look for something else." He walked away from the curb to his '88 once-silver-now-graying Chevette.

4

"I've looked at everything. It's the only possible class we could have together. Everything else I need conflicts with your requireds."

"How about that life skills class? TC or something. Now there's a practical class."

She rolled her eyes at him. "You mean TIC. It's 'Teens in Crisis.' You gotta be either pregnant or under arrest to take it. I wish you wouldn't have to take Government over. Then we could do Economics together."

"You always bring up that gov class like it was all my fault. You know I don't do well in any class after lunch. It's insane. Who can think clearly after eating? It should be illegal."

Noelle laughed. "Yeah, and let's cancel any class that requires you to write."

"I can't do Latin." He leaned over the car's rooftop, setting his chin in his hands. His blond hair had matured into variegated colors resembling broadly grained oak. No comb could tame the wavy mix of golds and browns left by the summer sun.

"But we'll never see each other. Our senior year and we won't have a single class in common."

"Then you're going off to college anyway," he pouted. "For ten years probably, if you stay pre-med."

His sulking wounded her. "You could too. You really need to get away from home. There's a big world outside of Windwood, you know."

"Don't 'big world' me, Noelle. You're the one in the closet."

"Oh yes, everyone is so close-minded but you." Her sarcasm bit. "But you're afraid to move on. Always hiding. Hiding behind your ideas of God."

"It's not hiding. It's called obeying. It's called following the path God has laid out for me."

"Is it? Or is it called security, afraid to branch out and try something new?" She had the upper hand and gloated. "Go ahead. Tell me about your big spiritual world. Tell me about how much God wants me to surrender everything to Him. Tell me about how you hear God speak. How you just— know what God wants you to do. Jonathon Edward Peters, you fry me!"

There. That should shake his tree.

She turned her back to him, allowing her brunette locks to fly before landing again across her shoulders.

How could I call him my friend? Life-long friends, my parents brag. He's impossible! Cute maybe, but impossible.

His voice was quiet, apologetic. "So you think I could handle Latin?" She turned around.

Yes, definitely cute, in his own way. But I'm still mad at him.

"And you promise you'll help me?" he asked.

What choice do I have?

"Yes," she spoke with exasperation. "I promise to help you. But remember, God helps those who help themselves."

"Ah, yes. Sage words from the Gospel of Noelle, chapter forty-five." He smiled.

She melted. Again.

Six months later

"Do you ever wonder about us?" she asked him bluntly.

"What do you mean?" Jonathon replied.

Noelle had this conversation thought out. While he drove the thirty miles to the movies in Rollings, she would have to ask him. She had to know.

"You know—us. Do you think we have a future?"

"I uh, I guess I didn't know you were thinking of...a future."

"But Jonathon, we've had too many years together. Everybody thinks we're a couple. We're the ones who deny it, all the time." She fidgeted with the blonde leather clutch purse on her lap.

"I thought we'd been through that, Noelle. You said you didn't want anything serious. Just friends. That was fine with me."

"That was two years ago. Haven't you changed at all since then? I know I have."

His hands gripped the steering wheel, eyes glued to the road. "Well, sure. I just didn't consider...I thought it was special to have this kind of friendship with you. Hasn't it been great not feeling any pressure with dating? I thought that was the whole idea."

"But we are dating. What do you think this is? You're driving me to Rollings to a movie. We'll probably have some ice cream or something afterward, right?"

"Probably."

"So what's the difference?"

For the first time, he glanced at her before he spoke. His chocolate-brown eyebrows contrasted against the bronze waves of his bangs. "I don't call this dating for a bunch of reasons. We have our differences."

"Like what?" Her face tightened. "Oh, I know...." She'd tread this water many times before. "You mean religion, don't you? You still feel like you need to save me."

"Noelle, come on now. I know you're religious. It's more than that. You and I think very differently in lots of ways."

"I don't think we're as far apart as you think. It's just that you go overboard."

"Such as?"

She started to shoot back a response but thought better of it. "No, I won't do it, Jonathon. I won't let you drag me into another fight. Just forget I said anything. Let's enjoy our night."

"Your choice, Noelle. I'm always ready to talk when you are."

His patronizing air burned her. "No, Jonathon. You're just always ready to talk about what you want to. I can't believe the way you can turn our conversation around to your healing stuff."

"Who said anything about healing?"

"Don't. Just don't start."

The rest of the car ride was more quiet. They made small talk about friends and school. Safe topics. Noelle pretended well. Inside she was crying.

The movie went smoothly, a romantic comedy. They laughed together in the same spots, and both had tears in their eyes when the lights came back on. After discussing the movie over ice cream, Noelle looked forward to the car ride home.

"So did you hear from St. Louis University?" he asked, turning onto the freeway.

"Yes." She was surprised, but hid it. He never asked about her college plans. "Their catalog looks good. Getting into the med school would be tough, but it would help if I did my undergrad there."

"So it's that or Creighton?"

He remembered. He actually remembered.

"I think so. I've got a few months to think about it, but yes, those are the places I applied."

7

The darkness of the night seemed to mellow both of them. He was caring, and she was warmed by it. She wished the ride could linger on forever.

"Would you consider college?" she asked gently.

"I don't think so. I've prayed about it, Noelle, but I just don't see God leading me that way. I've got an idea of something else. Want to hear it?"

"Sure. What is it?"

"I'm applying at the hospital, a patient aide. They have a job that I can work now during school. Then next summer it could turn full-time. Maybe work my way up the ladder."

"It would be a foot in the door."

She was disappointed. He needed to set his sights higher. She just didn't feel like pushing him on it tonight. It was a beautiful drive. "At least we're both interested in medicine."

"More than you realize, Noelle."

She glanced at him, expecting to catch his gleaming eyes smiling at her. Instead, his face turned stern as his gaze narrowed into the rear-view mirror.

"That van's really flying."

Over her shoulder she saw headlights racing up behind them. "Pull over a bit, Jonathon. Give them some room."

Just as he pulled to the shoulder, the van swerved widely around them. Gravel flew across the road as its wheels sharply hit the opposite shoulder and began to skid.

"They're losing it!" Jonathon yelled and braked hard as Noelle braced herself against the dashboard.

As they watched in horror, the van veered into the median ditch, violently bulldozing a path through the tall grass. In the dark, twin red tail lights bounced into the air and chased each other in slow wide arcs; a macabre crimson dance that signaled its end by blackness.

Gunning his engine, Jonathon sped forward on the vacant highway. "We gotta help them!"

The only light was their own headlamps. Noelle peered in the darkness to identify the van.

"Have we missed them?" He kept swerving toward the median to shine his lights into the grass.

"We couldn't have. They must have kept rolling."

Finally a shape came into view.

"There it is!" Noelle grabbed Jonathon's shoulder.

He pulled into the grass and grabbed a flashlight from the backseat before they raced to the van. It laid on its side, every window shattered. An eerie silence hung in the chilled air.

Jonathon climbed up the front axle to the door, shining his flashlight inside. "The driver's here!"

Noelle was afraid to ask the obvious. Jonathon answered before she had to.

"He's breathing!" The shaking light beamed on a man in his thirties, his body dangling from the driver's seat down to the passenger side. Jonathon reached through the broken window. "Hey, mister!" he spoke into the van. "Are you awake?"

"Careful, Jonathon. He might have a head injury." Noelle tried her best to remember elementary first-aid.

"He's slumped over," Jonathon shouted down. "His shoulder's all bloody."

It was then Noelle heard a sound behind her—someone moaning.

"Stay with him, Jonathon. Make sure he keeps breathing. I need your light. There's somebody else over here."

Noelle took Jonathon's flashlight and made broad steps through the weeds. The crisp night air left goosebumps as it tingled her skin. Squinting, she shined her light into the shadows created by the high beams shooting across the median from Jonathon's car.

It was a woman sprawled out in the grass. One leg was bent unnaturally behind her at the knee.

Noelle felt a wave of nausea but was still able to reflexively ask, "Are you okay?" She flinched at the idiocy of her question.

The lady moaned again. She was saying something.

"Ba—by...my ba—by."

Shivers coursed down Noelle's spine, worsening the nausea. "You have a baby? Where? In the van? In a car seat?"

The lady slowly moved her head sideways. Noelle couldn't see her eyes, but the lady raised a hand and pointed away from the van further down the median.

"Jonathon!" she screamed. "Come over here!" She moved hesitantly in the direction the lady pointed. Her heart throbbed in her chest as she stepped gingerly. Jonathon jumped through the tall weeds to her side.

"There's a baby. The lady said it's over here." Noelle's voice shook. "Jonathon, I don't think I can do this!"

"We have to find it."

He took a couple of steps in front of her as they both strained their eyes in the darkness. Noelle's ears tensed to hear any noise.

Over at the highway median, a car pulled over. A man's voice yelled out, "Do you need any help?"

Noelle cried, "Yes! There's a baby out here somewhere!"

"And a man is in the van over there," Jonathon shouted. "He's hurt pretty badly."

Car doors opened and slammed. It sounded like at least three.

"Hurry!" Noelle was fighting anxious tears, hoping to find the baby—hoping she wouldn't see it first.

But she did.

A little bundle, it had to be it. Jonathon heard her gasp and was at her side. "I'll get it," he stepped over and picked it up.

"Is it...?"

"Noelle, it's not breathing! What do I do?"

The flashlight illuminated a tiny ashen arm limply falling out of the bundle. "You've got to breathe for it. Now!" She was frozen but forced herself to speak. "Put your mouth over its mouth and nose. Puff into it!"

Jonathon quickly bent his head over the baby's face and breathed once, then again.

"I don't think it's doing anything!"

"Help us!" Noelle screamed. "Over here! We need CPR!" Someone walking toward them broke into a run. "Please! Do you know CPR?"

As the figure came closer he was shaking his head. "But we called on our cellular. Help is on the way."

"We don't have time!" she sobbed. "It's a baby! Doesn't anyone know CPR?"

She turned back to Jonathon but was unprepared for what she saw.

He was kneeling with his back to her, the baby still cradled in his arms. He rocked on his knees in the tall grass, his head tilted upward.

Grabbing her head in disbelief, she shrieked, "Jon!"

He rose from his knees and turned to her. In the darkness, his black figure moved in slow motion.

"It's okay."

10

As he stepped forward, her light shined on a small hand outside of the bundle. Its color had turned from gray to pink. Jonathon held the blankets tightly, tears tracing his smiling cheeks.

A gentle coo sounded.

She looked into his wrapped arms to find the eyes of a smiling baby staring sweetly up at its holder. Doll-like fingers wiggled and grasped Jonathon's thumb.

On the heels of relief, Noelle began to burn with anger. "Jon! I can't believe...."

Her words died out in the peel of sirens careening toward them. Exhaustion consumed her defeated emotions. She turned her back and walked to the car alone.

Chapter 2

*T*hey hadn't seen each other for the rest of the summer. Now he stood at the door, suddenly looking very young. "Heard tomorrow's your last day around here. I wanted to come by to wish you well."

"That's kind of you, Jonathon. I heard you got the job at the hospital. How's it going?" Noelle stood inside the opening of the screen door and didn't invite him in.

"Between you and me, the mop buckets are too small." His lips curled into the smile she used to love.

"Well, maybe they'll promote you to the kitchen soon. Those bonnets would look great on you."

"Yeah, maybe." He pushed his glasses up on his nose. "Noelle, I hope things go well for you in St. Louis. I really do."

"It should be a challenge, but I'm ready," she replied distantly.

There was an uncomfortable pause that she couldn't stand.

"Well, I better get back to my packing. We leave early in the morning. It was nice of you to stop by."

"Okay. Uh, I'll be praying for you, Noelle."

"Thanks. Maybe I'll see you during Christmas break." She let the door close before he had a chance to say more.

Walking into the kitchen where the octagonal window faced the driveway, she watched until he returned to his car and drove a block away. Her mother called from upstairs, but she told her she needed to go to the bathroom. She didn't come out for twenty minutes.

*****

The fever returned, this time shooting past one hundred and four degrees in under an hour. Henry Smitherton fought his hospital sheets and gown, banging arms and legs against the side rails. In a delusion, he was swimming

12

through steaming oils, his body spinning in a vortex. With open eyes, the room twirled like a nauseating carnival ride. To avoid the dizzying sight, he kept his eyes closed, stuck in the boiling furnace. Everywhere his mind looked, he saw marbled hues of crimson flowing into each other. No flames were in sight, but the heat had to mean a fire was close by.

I'm burning up. Someone's got to help me!

"Nurse! Nurse!" He screamed twice but the sound caused the waves to ripple up around him, trickling into his throat. He batted himself more violently, not noticing the IV needle ripping out of his left arm.

I'm going to suffocate. They're trying to kill me!

He cracked his eyes for a moment to see if any help was at hand. The blur of the room swept around him, causing him to retch. Tightly closing his eyes, he fought the urge to vomit and descended back into the hell pit of sulfur.

Isn't there anyone out there? Can't let them get an old man.

He yelled for his daughter, "Denise!" But as his mouth opened to scream, he felt himself sink deeper in the grisly red oils. There was still no response. Surely someone would hear him; for God's sake, he was dying!

He tried to turn onto his stomach, still tied by the thin sheets binding his arms. Wrestling free, he cast himself up on his knees in bed, his gown slipping off his shoulders. He felt an opportunity of escape. Gripping his nausea, he braced himself to open his eyes. With surprising clarity, he prepared to move toward the door of his room.

The moment Henry's eyes opened, the room raced around in a surreal blur. Briefly holding an image of bloody sheets near his left wrist, he began spinning and clenched his eyes shut, tipping back into the whirlpool of the unctuous abyss. He lurched over the bed rail and crashed to the linoleum, his fragile body crumpling into a fetal position on the floor. On the way down, his forehead crashed against the side table, slashing the skin above his right eye. A vase of chrysanthemums followed after him, hitting his shoulder before tipping over to the floor. Reaching for the pain at his eyebrow, he felt the sticky fluid of his own blood. Naked on the bare floor, his mind reeled and his stomach heaved. Fighting his relentless, feverish nightmare, he slipped into unconsciousness. No one yet heard.

It might have been minutes or an hour when he woke again. His first sensation was his own movement, his whole body shaking uncontrollably. Then he felt cold. Bitterly cold. The smell of stale blood filled his nostrils.

Opening his eyes, he found his head against the icy floor. For a moment it seemed like a dream, but the clotted blood stuck on his wrist reminded him of his fall out of bed. At least the dizziness had subsided. He eyed the call button dangling by the side rail. Head throbbing, he pulled himself to the bed frame and hit the red button.

A voice from the wall sung, "May we help you?"

Attempting to speak, only a guttural cough came out. Seconds later the door opened.

"Mr. Smitherton!" Jonathon rushed to his side, hitting the call button again. When the voice answered he yelled, "Mr. Smitherton's fallen out of bed. He's bleeding. I need help right away." He reached for his wrist to check a pulse and noticed the lost intravenous site. Fresh blood still oozed around a three-inch laceration at Smitherton's right eyebrow. Pulling sheets from the bed, Jonathon covered the frail body.

"Mr. Smitherton, can you hear me?"

Henry moaned.

"Where do you hurt?"

Henry pointed a finger to his temple and moaned again.

Two other nurses entered the room. They quickly checked for injuries and strapped a blood pressure cuff to his arm.

"Do you think you can stand?" Jonathon asked.

Henry nodded and reached an arm around the nurse. He wanted nothing but to get off the floor.

With two nurses, Henry stood and shuffled to the side of the bed. His senses were returning and he tried to speak. "Didn't...anyone...hear?"

"I'm so sorry, Mr. Smitherton," Jonathon said. "What happened?"

In a whisper only Jonathon could hear, he responded, "You're...killing... me."

"Looks like he tried to climb out of bed," the nurse in charge declared.

"What'd you say, Mr. Smitherton?" Jonathon asked again.

Smitherton wearily glared at Jonathon with eyes that said, "you heard me."

"Okay, let's get you warmed up and back to bed."

Clean gowns and sheets started flying. Warm moist towels gently rubbed his wrist and forehead. Henry closed his eyes.

At least it's over for now.

*****

"Honey, the phone's for you. It's the hospital."

In response to his wife's call, Dr. Jack Mittlestedt picked up the phone from beside his black leather easy chair. "Dr. Mittlestedt here...Does he have any injuries?...What's his vital signs?...Okay, set up a suture tray, I'll be right up."

He turned to his guest. "I'm sorry but I have to interrupt our dinner. Why don't you come up to the hospital with me? There's a patient I need to sew up; fell out of bed or something."

"I'd love to," Noelle responded with enthusiasm. When she was invited to the Mittlestedts for dinner, she had no idea she might get to see some actual medical work.

"Well, let's go. Someday this might be your call to take." He turned to his wife in the kitchen. "Barb, I'm taking Noelle up to the hospital to see a patient. Should just be a short one. Can you hold dinner for us?"

"What else is new, honey? Call if you're going to be late."

"She's a great woman," he said to Noelle.

"I'm sure. Very understanding."

"Hope you can find a man like that someday, Noelle."

Fat chance. "So what do you know about SLU, Dr. Mittlestedt? I can't believe I will be there tomorrow."

They got into his Viper before he answered. Noelle was filled with adrenalin just closing the car door.

"St. Louis? It's a fine city and school. Just what you need. My question for you is, how badly do you really want medical school?"

"Oh, there's no question. I'll do whatever it takes," she answered, getting into the black leather bucket seat.

*****

Jonathon was setting the chrysanthemums back in their vase when Dr. Mittlestedt walked in.

"Henry, what happened here?" Dr. Mittlestedt ushered the lady in behind him, ignoring Jonathon. "Looks like you took a little tumble."

Jonathon stepped back toward the sink as Noelle passed by him to the patient's bedside. She didn't even see him.

"Nasty cut on your forehead, Henry. That's going to need a few stitches."

Henry didn't even offer the doctor eye contact. Jonathon didn't know if he was still in a delusion or if he always treated his doctor this way. But he didn't care either. He was wondering what Noelle was doing there.

"Can someone tell me what happened?" Dr. Mittlestedt spoke without looking away from Henry's forehead.

"Uh, yes, doctor," Jonathon stammered. Noelle heard his voice and turned with a stunned look on her face. Jonathon pushed his glasses up and tried to continue. "When I came in, he was on the floor and barely responsive. He'd pulled out his IV and must have hit his head on the table as he went down. He'd broken out in a sweat and his temp was—"

"One hundred and two point four," Dr. Mittlestedt interrupted. "Okay, let's stitch him up. Are you going to help me?" It was a demand, not a question. Problem was, Jonathon was just an aide.

"I'll go get someone, Dr. Mittlestedt."

As he left, he caught Noelle's eyes one more time. Her look of disappointment didn't faze him. He just smiled. "Nice to see you again, Noelle."

"You know him?" Dr. Mittlestedt asked Noelle as Jonathon left the room.

"Just a guy from high school."

He nodded. "Well, Henry here has longstanding chronic obstructive pulmonary disease. Too many years of those coffin nails in your lips, right Henry?" He didn't wait for a response; he'd never get one. "We put him in for a little tune-up, but with this fever it looks like we've got an infection going on, maybe pneumonia. With the shape of Henry's lungs, he can't take much of this. So now he topples out of bed. You're not helping us much here, Henry. You're supposed to be getting better, not worse." Dr. Mittlestedt gave Noelle a wry smile. His patient ignored him.

A nurse came into the room and Noelle, enamored with the majesty of medicine, stepped back as they prepared the sterile suture tray. She glanced one more time out the door. No sign of Jonathon. Moving closer to the bed to watch the needlework, she determined not to give him another thought.

*****

Jonathon shut off his car lights before he drove into the garage. If he was quiet enough, he might not wake his mother.

16

It was a cool September midnight, the cloudless sky glimmering in the solitude. The house was dark, and he hesitated before going in the door. Instead, he walked into the backyard and found his childhood swing. The chains were slightly rusty now and the seat didn't fit right at all, but he sat anyway. Rocking back and forth a few times seemed to hold him so he cast his feet out to climb in the air. Throwing his head back, the nippy air blew across him. With the half moon as his only witness, he thought and prayed.

Minutes passed; a dog barked in the distance interrupting the silent night. Stepping out of the swing, he entered the house, twisting the doorknob quietly. It didn't help.

"Jonathon, what were you doing swingin' out there?"

"Hi, Mom. Why aren't you asleep?"

"Couldn't. Too much goin' around in my head."

"Mind if I turn on a light?" Jonathon slipped his hand over the switch on the kitchen wall and the room was lit by a plastic diamond chandelier. "If you'd go to bed I bet you could sleep, Mom."

His mother sat at the kitchen table fingering the rim of an empty ceramic mug that boasted a raised relief of Mt. Rushmore. She'd never been there, but paid a dime for it at last year's community garage sale. "Don't you be preachin' to me, son. I'll sleep when I'm ready. So how was your shift tonight? Everybody okay at pill hill?"

"Sure. Quiet evening, mostly. A guy fell out of bed, gashed his head. But he's fine." Jonathon paused, remembering his uninvited and under-appreciated visit with Noelle. *Guess it wasn't any worse than our goodbye scene.*

"Don't tell me you did your sparkle to him."

"No, Mom. Not today. I promised you I'd tell you each time, didn't I?"

"That's right. And I appreciate that, dear. You're only nineteen and I don't want you bearing all that responsibility yourself. It's just too much. Well, what's troubling you then? I've never seen you swingin' since you were ten." Her cheeks sagged less than expected for fifty-four years, but her dusky gray hair betrayed her age more honestly.

"C'mon, Mom. It's a beautiful night. I just wanted to enjoy the peacefulness. No big deal. I'm going to bed."

"Good, dear. Don't forget about our greetin' in church tomorrow. We need to be there by at least nine."

Jonathon rolled his eyes before he caught himself. "Can't you take care of that by yourself, Mom? Those folks don't want to see me."

"None of it, Jonathon. They love seein' you. And since your daddy's gone, I'm not standing there like a lone widow or somethin'. You're my best man."

Her smile went cheek to cheek, and he couldn't resist it. He gave her a hug and kissed her forehead.

"You're right, Mom. I'm your man. Don't want any of those old coots chasing you around the pews. We'll see you in the morning."

"That's right, dear."

*****

The next morning he donned his black slacks and a gray crew neck wool sweater over a white open-collared shirt, and drove his mother to the First Congregational Church, a ritual that was seldom missed. She commented on the way that she wished he'd put on a tie, and he replied that he would if she'd buy a new dress for herself.

"You've worn the blue daisies for two years, Mom."

"There's nothing wrong with this dress," she replied smartly, no more offended than a cat that avoided petting.

After standing in the foyer shaking hands with about a hundred folks that knew him by name, Jonathon and his mother took their usual seats in the fifth pew on the left, half way in. Mr. and Mrs. Wittenburg sat to his right, always the first to leave immediately after the service. He felt sure they never lingered so that no one would ask about their son. Something about him going out to California five years ago with a band, but he had never come back to Windwood. Word was he'd never made contact with his folks since.

Marvel Woodruff, a single mom, regularly sat behind them. She spent every Sunday morning wrestling Bullet, her two-year-old boy, all through the service. Jonathon once asked his mother why they didn't sit somewhere else so that the Woodruffs wouldn't be such a distraction. His mom just said, "Someone has to sit here, might as well be us." It didn't matter that there were plenty of seats around the sanctuary.

After the service, he drove his mom to the Country Inn where they had chicken-fried steak and the salad bar. They spent most of the meal nodding and waving at his mother's acquaintances who followed the same ritual. It was a great meal, as always.

He took his mom home for her Sunday afternoon nap, changed, and went down to Harrison Elementary to the only soccer fields in town. The goals were rusted and the nets ripped, but there was always a pick-up game, even on cold fall days like this, mostly among middle school kids. They loved seeing Jonathon come down, and more than once there'd be dog piles with him at the bottom.

By four o'clock he was back at Windwood Memorial Health Center, wiping out bed pans and making beds. On top of it all, Martha Chandler was on charge.

"Thompson!" When she yelled, two charts fell off the nursing station desk.

"Right here, Miss Chandler." He was two steps behind her, wheeling a patient back from the bath.

"128's messed himself—," she barked.

"Got it." Jonathon pushed the wheelchair down the hall.

The smell of excrement hit him as he entered room 128. Mr. Smitherton was upright in bed, wrists wrapped in lambs wool and tied with cloth belts to the bed rails. The call button was pinned to the sheets at his right hand.

"Good evening, Mr. Smitherton. It's Jonathon here. Looks like we didn't make it in time. Let's get you cleaned up, okay?"

Henry stared at the foot of the bed. Two bandage strips stretched across his eyebrow from last night's fall.

"Looks like you're doing a little better than yesterday," Jonathon offered. He released one of the wrist restraints and pulled the covers back. The rank smell made him blink several times. "Roll to your left, Mr. Smitherton, and let's clean things up."

Henry didn't move. Jonathon leaned over to break into his line of vision. "C'mon, Mr. Smitherton, help me out here."

Smitherton's lips flinched.

"What? Say that again, Mr. Smitherton."

The words came at a whisper, but clearly. "You're killing me."

"Not at all, Mr. Smitherton. Just here to help you." Jonathon gave him a little nudge to help him roll, but Smitherton remained rigid.

"Don't let me die," the whisper was barely intelligible.

"Not in my plans, Mr. Smitherton. C'mon, just roll to your side."

On his own, Smitherton leaned to the left and Jonathon quickly donned disposable gloves. Discretely wiping up what he could with warm moist towels, he moved the sheets around him off the bed. "Thanks, Mr. Smitherton. That should feel a lot better."

For the first time Henry looked at Jonathon. There was still no sense of trust, but Jonathon took it as a dare.

"So do you feel better tonight?" Jonathon rolled Henry back to the right and replaced the soiled sheets with fresh ones. Henry gave no answer.

"Mr. Smitherton, I want to help you. We're here to get you better, but we have to know how you feel. We gotta hear from you. Can you give me a little something to go on here?"

The whisper was barely audible. "They're killing me."

Jonathon took a moment and sat on the bed. "Mr. Smitherton, no one's trying to kill you. You've been sick and your doctor wanted to get you some special medicine and treatment here in the hospital. It's our job to keep you alive." He reapplied the wrist restraint and tied the belt to the guard rail.

Smitherton shook his head twice while staring at Jonathon. Then he took his gaze away.

"Listen, I've got to take care of your linens, and then I'll come back. You can tell me a little more about how you're feeling. Okay?"

Smitherton looked out the window in answer.

"See you in ten."

Jonathon left the room and found Sandy Carruthers, the medications nurse for the hall.

"Sandy, do you know much about Mr. Smitherton in 128?"

"Sweet guy. He's been really down the past few days; he's usually pretty chipper."

"Is he playing with a full deck?"

"Oh yeah. He's pretty clear. Why?"

"Last night he hit his head. Seems like it kind of took it out of him. Just wondered if he usually makes sense. Why is he in wrist restraints?"

"He's yanked out his IV three times; that's why. But he does fine. Hey, what's that smell? Smells like—you know..."

"Oh, it's these sheets. I gotta go dump 'em."

"Do it, Jonathon. That's bad stuff." She wrinkled her nose.

"Okay, okay." Jonathon took the linens all wrapped together and went straight to the laundry, down in the basement. When he came back up, he had to fill water pitchers for five patients, clean pudding off the floor from the peds patient in 134, and help another aide lift a lady in 112 into her Geri-chair. Then he got back to 128.

When he walked in the room, he was surprised to see Martin Feddersen, the hospital administrator in the room. Henry's back was to the door, lying on his left side. Both wrist restraints were now tied to the same guard rail on the far side of his bed.

"Oh, excuse me, Dr. Feddersen. I was just coming to visit Mr. Smitherton."

Martin Feddersen was something of a godsend to the hospital. He'd practiced medicine on the East coast for ten years before discovering his keen interest in health care management. After adding an MBA to his MD, he joined Windwood a year and a half ago, providing his medical background and strong hospital administration skills at a time of financial crisis. Now the hospital was back in the black, and everyone was in awe of the dramatic change led by this man. Dr. Feddersen would often be found wandering the halls of the hospital, visiting equally with staff and patients alike.

"Hello, Jonathon. No problem, I'm just leaving. You take care now, Henry." Dr. Feddersen patted Henry's hand. "We'll stop by and see you again tomorrow." As he stepped away, Feddersen put his hand on Jonathon's shoulder. "Take good care of him; he's a special man."

"Sure will, Dr. Feddersen. That's kind of you to come visit him. Are you related or something?"

"No, just good friends."

As Feddersen left, Jonathon walked around the bed. Henry's eyes were open, tears streaking his cheeks. "Hey, c'mon Mr. Smitherton, it's not that bad. Let's have that visit now. There's lots I'd like to hear from you."

"You don't get it." His voice was soft and coarse, but at least it wasn't a whisper.

"But I want to try. Tell me how you're doing." Jonathon sat on the bed.

"What's your name?"

"Jonathon."

"You gotta believe me."

"Sure, anything you say, Mr. Smitherton."

"This hospital, these doctors. They're killing their patients."

This time Jonathon stayed quiet.

"I don't know how, but I think I know why. Most of what I know is just that they are." Henry slid his hand along the side rail bar.

"Why do you think someone's trying to hurt you, Mr. Smitherton?"

"It's why I'm in here. I wasn't that sick." Henry's voice dropped to a raspy whisper, his eyes looked to the ceiling. "Once I got here, then I got bad."

"Sometimes that just happens, though."

"I've been in here enough times." He closed his eyes. "I know how it goes."

The hall speakers suddenly interrupted, "Code Blue, ER. Code Blue, ER." A rush of feet sounded outside the door.

"I gotta go to that call, Mr. Smitherton."

"Don't tell anyone." Henry's hands grabbed Jonathon's jacket sleeve tightly. He coughed twice. "Promise me."

"Okay, Mr. Smitherton. I'll be back."

"Promise me, Jonathon. Promise?" He still held tight to his sleeve, his voice hoarse.

"Sure, I won't say a word. But we've got to talk some more. I gotta go."

Jonathon moved to the door and ran down the long hall to the back of the hospital where the four-bed emergency room was housed. There was not a lot for him to do, but it was a rule that all nurse aides should report to any code. He didn't feel the anxiety of the rest of the workers because usually he was an onlooker and a go-for. Reaching the room, a crowd of five nurses, including Chandler; two respiratory techs; and a physician assistant circled the ER bed. All he could see of the patient were two old and dusky bare feet. Jonathon stepped up and looked over the shoulder of a nurse writing on a clipboard. "What's going on?"

"Lady passed out at home. When the unit got there she'd come around, complaining of chest pain. They got her here but as soon as she hit the door we lost her. Mark says it looks like asystole. They've given her an amp of epi already, but no response yet."

"That's Mrs. Wittenburg."

"You know her? She's in tough shape right now. Go grab another IV pole, would you?"

"Sure." Jonathon moved two steps back. One of the respiratory techs was pumping his fists on Mrs. Wittenburg's bare chest and the other was getting ready to intubate her. Jonathon turned to find the IV pole just as Dr. Samson, the doctor on call, came into the room.

Jonathon felt a tingle in his spine. Not an electrical shock, but more like a warm glow of pulsing twinkle lights along the length of his spinal column. It was unmistakable as the sensation throbbed from his neck down to his tail bone. The warmth migrated around to his chest as usual, becoming an intense and steady burn beneath his sternum.

It was time.

He moved back to the bed. Tubes and adhesive pads were being placed all around Mrs. Wittenburg's body, and no one was distracted as he crept back into the bustling circle. He had to step sideways, reaching out his hand, barely able to touch her.

He found her shoulder; it felt chilled and clammy.

"Stop CPR for a minute, let Dr. Samson see the rhythm," Nurse Chandler barked. The tech stopped the compressions so the EKG tracing could be clearly seen.

"Still asystole. Okay, resume CPR and give an amp of atropine."

Jonathon watched Dr. Samson shrugging his shoulders as he eyed Mark, the physician assistant. He could read the lips of Mark's response, "I think it's over."

"How long has it been?" Dr. Samson asked.

The nurse with a clipboard responded. "She's been here fifteen minutes. We estimate she collapsed probably about thirty-five minutes ago."

"Not good," he said, but no one let up in their duties, breathing for her, giving chest compressions, providing medication, or gaining more access for other treatments if needed.

Jonathon's hand rested on Mrs. Wittenburg's shoulder unnoticed. He felt a familiar, yet astounding hotness, in his fingers, while smelling the pungent odors of alcohol and death.

"Where's another IV pole?" Chandler shouted from behind him.

"I told Jonathon to go—" the clipboard nurse caught view of him. "Jonathon, I thought you were getting another pole."

He quickly withdrew his hand.

"What are you doing?" she asked.

"Nothing, I'll go get it right now."

Dr. Samson interrupted everyone. "Hold on. I see something. Stop CPR for a minute."

All eyes moved to the heart monitor as the strong spikes of the external compressions disappeared from the screen, replaced by a small but natural peaked wave of a heart beating.

"We have a rhythm, folks. She's back," Dr. Samson announced.

No one moved except the rhythmic bagging of the respiratory tech breathing for Mrs. Wittenburg.

"It looks like it's staying," Mark said. "It's stronger!"

"I feel a pulse," Chandler said, her hand on Mrs. Wittenburg's wrist.

"Okay, everyone. Let's keep some epi handy, but get her back to ICU as quickly as we can. Nice work, all." Dr. Samson turned to speak to Mark.

The clipboard nurse glared at Jonathon. "We still need that IV pole. What happened to you?"

"I dunno, got wrapped up in the excitement, I guess. That was so cool!" Rubbing his hands as he raced out of the room, he breathed deeply the odd fragrance of lilacs and wore a big smile across his face.

Chapter 3

*O*ver the next few days, Mrs. Wittenburg remained stable in the hospital. Jonathon sat with her during her cardiac catheterization. Two significant blockages were found, and she was transferred to Rollings for surgery. He wanted to say something about the healing, but it didn't seem right at the time.

Mr. Smitherton was dismissed from the hospital a week later. Jonathon had not been scheduled to work on his hall, and he was just as happy. Out of curiosity, he found and reviewed Smitherton's hospital record during one of his shifts. It looked like a straightforward treatment of the old man's chronic bronchitis. Too many years of smoking. The report said his laceration was healing well, and he was dismissed with no new medications.

Two weeks later, Mrs. Wittenburg was back in church, sitting with her husband right behind Jonathon and his mother. They all stood together, recited the prayer of forgiveness together, sang the hymns together, and quietly fidgeted around Bullet Woodruff's tantrum during the sermon. Things were back to normal.

Immediately after the service, Mrs. Thompson pushed her son to catch up with the usual hasty departure of the Wittenburgs.

"Esther, Esther, wait up," Elaine hollered down the sidewalk just outside. "Jonathon wants to talk at you. Why are you always in such a scoot after church, gal? Now here, listen to the boy; he's got somethin' to tell ya."

"Hi, Mrs. Wittenburg." Jonathon had his hands in his pockets, rolling back and forth on his heels. "Mom and I were talking, and, well, we're sure glad you're feeling better."

"That's sweet of you, Jonathon. You gave me great care in the hospital."

"I just wanted you to know that we were—well, actually, I was—praying for you."

"Oh, you dear. That's so sweet. It must've done some good—"

"No, I mean I, uh…I prayed for you in the emergency room. That first day. I think you were really about, um…gone, really." Jonathon fumbled for words and pushed his glasses up on his nose. He saw Mrs. Wittenburg staring precariously.

"Yes, well, I think God healed you right there in that room. I think He spared your life, Mrs. Wittenburg."

Mr. Wittenburg had been quiet, but entered in. "Well, thank you, Jonathon. Like Esther said, the care we received at the hospital was excellent. I think we'd better go now, but we are thankful to God for every day we have."

"Now don't cha understand what he's sayin'?" Elaine jumped in. "He's sayin' God healed ya, Esther. It's a miracle, that's what it is. And we need to give credit where credit is due."

Esther looked to her husband as he corralled her with his arm. "Yes, Elaine, I know what you're saying. And again, we thank you for your prayers. Now really, Esther needs her rest. But, thanks for all you've done." With that, they turned and quickly moved to their car.

"Mom—" Jonathon started.

"Don't say it, son. It's not your fault their faith is weak."

"No, Mom. I just don't think we should…be preaching like that."

He walked her to the car. As soon as they were in, he got an earful.

"Preachin'! Preachin'! Is that what you think this is? My goodness gracious, here the Lord of all heaven's given you a gift so that He can be glorified, and you think tellin' the Wittenburgs that God healed them is preachin'? Where'd I go wrong with you, Jonathon Edward Thompson?"

"I don't mean that, Mom. I just don't know if the time was right."

"You think there's a right time to bring God glory, do ya? How long didja want to wait? It's been two weeks already. You remember what your Aunt Emma said. You gotta be sure to bring God the glory, that's what she said. Don't 'cha think that's why God's not healing much these days? He's not getting any glory out of it."

"I know. I'm just not sure that always means telling everyone about it. Especially like this. They weren't ready to hear it, Mom."

"And when would they be ready, Jonathon? Ya gotta be bold, son. God won't see His gift used if He don't get no glory, you know that, don't 'cha? So don't feel guilty now. You did your job, now it's up to the Wittenburgs on what they gonna do with it."

"Mom, you've got to let me make that decision. I know God deserves the glory. I just wish you would let me tell people in my own way. I've gotta have some room."

They drove up to the Country Inn for lunch. They were both silent, but he was glad he got in the last word. It rarely happened.

*****

October blew into Windwood, literally. The community celebrated the month as it heralded its namesake. The wind gusted fiercely most days, bringing out the smell of burnt leaves, orange and red home flags, the annual hospital jog-for-cancer, and the community chili cook-off. High school football games crowded already packed schedules, but folks found their sweaters and winter coats to not miss a one.

And the season was unmistakably marked by the tradition of girls wrapped in guys' arms. Jonathon attended homecoming at his alma mater only to long for Noelle. In high school they had never found themselves in the public cuddle, but having her near made him warm and content on chilly nights. Tonight, he tired of the questions from his graduated classmates.

"You still at the hospital?" "Still living at home?" "Heard from Noelle?"

Then somebody behind him accidentally dumped hot chocolate down his back. He left the game before half-time was over, dying of loneliness.

"You back already, Jonathon?" his mom asked from her chair in the living room the moment he opened the door.

"Yeah, the game's pretty much a blowout. We'll never make it, same as usual." He raced through the room, hoping to bypass any other questions.

"See any of your friends?"

"No, Mom." He knew where she was going with this. "But I'm fine."

"Noelle there?"

"No."

"Jonathon, you gonna get some friends?"

"Mom, I'm fine." He headed down the hall to his bedroom.

"But, Jonathon, you've gotta—"

"Leave it, Mom. I'm fine." Before his last words were out, he shut the door. He stripped off his shirt, sprawled out on his bed, grabbed his pillow in his arms. *I gotta get out of this.* Rolling back and forth, he wrestled whether he should pray. What he really wanted was a talk with Noelle. A nice long talk.

27

At his desk, he flicked on the small bulb of the gooseneck and found a blank sheet of paper. He wrote swiftly and easily, the pen scribbles soothing his emotions. Twenty minutes later he rose and walked across the room, passing the dresser mirror and pausing. Standing full in front, he grimaced at his skinny shoulders and thin chest, looking more deeply for answers. *Something's gotta change.*

He cracked the door.

"Mom, I'm sorry I slammed the door on you," he yelled down the hall.

"I understand, honey. Just tryin' to help. You know me."

"Yeah, Mom. I appreciate it too. Don't change."

"Not on your life. You comin' out?"

"I'm writing a letter. I'll come out when I finish."

"Do that. We can watch *Star Trek* if you want."

"Great. See you in a bit."

*****

The first of November was accompanied with a full house at the hospital. The flu had hit town the past week. As Jonathon looked at the folks he was assigned to, one name jumped off the page: Henry Smitherton, room 122. He made a point to head there at his first chance.

"Mr. Smitherton, remember me?"

The head was turned away.

"Mr. Smitherton?"

No sound. Just the rise and fall of respirations moving the bed sheets.

Jonathon walked around the bed. He caught his breath.

Smitherton's face was dark blue and purple, heavy bruising across his cheeks and forehead. There was a small place on the chin that was flesh colored. Otherwise his face was surrounded in livid crimson blotches extending into his scalp. Jonathon raised the top sheet to look further. The patchy discoloration continued along Smitherton's neck and down his chest as far as Jonathon could see. Both arms bore the same marks; a couple of raised areas on the left arm resembled large blood blisters.

"What happened?" Jonathon exclaimed to no one.

Smitherton's eyes suddenly opened, death come to life. His eyes were freakishly bloodshot. Jonathon took a step back.

"Mr. Smitherton, can you hear me?"

28

Licked by a pink tongue, the purplish lips parted. "I tried…to tell you."

"Yes, I remember. What happened?"

"Can't…talk here." His voice dropped to a whisper. "They're giving me… shots. Shots."

"What can I do for you? Are you in pain?"

"It's not bad." He closed his eyes. Tears soaked through to each corner.

"This is horrible. I'll find out what's going on, Mr. Smitherton."

Henry's head bobbed slightly, and his shoulders began to shudder. He was sobbing.

"Can I pray for you?" Jonathon asked.

Henry's blood red eyes opened again and stared pleadingly at Jonathon. The tears magnified their ruby color as they overflowed. He turned his face into his pillow.

Laying a hand on Henry's shoulder, Jonathon entered a silent prayer. While he sought healing, God had not led him to heal. Yet. Jonathon asked for answers instead.

Only moments into the prayer, a knock came at the door and a lady stuck her head in. "May I come in?" she asked.

"Uh, I suppose. Mr. Smitherton's not feeling very well. Are you family?"

"I'm his daughter."

"Well, of course," Jonathon smiled sheepishly. "Come on in."

The woman immediately came to her elderly father's bedside and took his hand. "I'm here, Daddy," she said quietly. Jonathon admired her tender composure with her father's ill state. She looked about forty, dressed with apparent affluence, but the way she stroked her father's arm was like a young girl petting her golden retriever. "How's he doing today?" Her eyes never left her dad.

"I can't really say," Jonathon answered. "I just came on, and when I saw Mr. Smitherton was in, I wanted to see him right away before I got started with my shift. He's become kind of special to me. How does he look to you?"

"About the same as yesterday. It all happened so fast."

"What did happen, Mrs., uh, Mrs.—?"

"I'm sorry. My name is Denise Harrison. My dad's been in and out of the hospital. His health's not ideal. But lately they've been having a hard time figuring out what's going on. He broke out with a rash a couple of days ago, but it turned like this yesterday. The doctors don't know what it is for sure; they think now it might be an allergic reaction."

The door opened again and Dr. Feddersen entered. "Good afternoon, Denise. And Jonathon, good to see you again. I just wanted to stop by and see how Henry was doing."

"Well, this is enough of a crowd for one patient. I better go check on some others." Jonathon said. "I'll be back here in an hour or so. Mrs. Harrison, don't hesitate to call me if you need anything."

Jonathon left the room, but he couldn't help hearing Dr. Feddersen comment to Mrs. Harrison, "That young man is one of the best things we have going for us here at the hospital."

*****

"Hey, Noelle, we're all going out for pizza after the chem exam. Are you in?"

"I don't think so."

"C'mon, you need a break." Dave was yelling at her from outside in the hall while she made a dilute mixture of sulphuric acid in the lab. Looking up at him through her goggles, she saw again his quarterback frame, piercing brown eyes, and tight dark hair—Oakley shades perched at his thick neck-line.

"No, I don't."

"Hey, hey, what's this about?" He stepped into the lab.

She backed away to the sink with her flask in hand.

"What's going on, Noelle? Why don't you come with us?"

She messed with a hose clip attached to a jug of distilled water, ignoring him.

"Noelle? What's up?"

With a moment of courage, she turned to face him. "You really don't know, do you?" She moved back to her chemistry bench, leaving him at the sink.

"Oh." He looked around the lab. The only other person in earshot was the lab assistant in the department office next door. "You mean last weekend."

She pretended to read something in her lab manual.

"Noelle, I thought it was great."

Her flask hit the floor and shattered.

Dave reflexively reached for her arm. "Let me help."

"Just get away!" she shouted, ready to burst like the glass on the floor.

The lab assistant rushed into the room and grabbed a squirt bottle of neutralizer. "It's no big deal, Noelle. If you guys got something to settle, why don't you step out. I'll get this."

Noelle's hands were shaking as she clutched a handful of paper towels. "I'm fine. I'll do it."

"Noelle, come here," Dave insisted.

She ripped off her goggles and grabbed her notebook before rushing out into the hall. Dave quickly followed.

"Really, Noelle. I know it was your first time. It was perfect."

"Great, just great." She swore under her breath. "Get away from me."

She felt his fingers on the back of her shoulder.

"Don't touch me!" Her scream echoed in the tiled walls as she ran the long hall to the women's bathroom. Inside, she slammed her notebook on the counter and took one look in the mirror before sinking to her knees.

"Oh God, what have I done?" Her bottled tears broke.

The afternoon sun disappeared into darkness before she got up. Picking up her notebook, she pulled papers together that had flown out, among them an unopened envelope postmarked from Windwood the day before. The return address said, "Jonathon." She stuffed the letter in with her other papers.

Outside, Dave was gone. She took the long, lonely walk back to her apartment.

Chapter 4

*T*he next Sunday, Jonathon couldn't believe his eyes.

He and his mom had entered the little sanctuary as usual, right on time at 10:55 for the eleven o'clock service. They took their seats, fifth pew on the left, halfway down. They nodded to Mrs. Woodruff right behind them. Elaine mussed Bullet's dark hair and Jonathon received his little high- five slap. Same as always.

The organ began the routine call to worship and everyone stood. Elaine started to sing with the others, turning her head casually but far around to both sides to take her personal attendance record. That's when Jonathon felt her grab his arm.

He looked at his mom and saw the horrified expression on her face. The squeeze on his arm tightened. He looked just beyond her and saw why.

Behind them on the right side of the sanctuary, the opposite side, there they sat: Mr. and Mrs. Wittenburg. For years they had always sat behind the Thompsons.

His mom maintained her grasp of him through the first hymn. She was shaking, and he thought she was going to faint. Thankfully it was a short hymn and they sat down. Elaine moved her hand down to Jonathon's, and he held her with his other arm through the whole service. Neither of them could have said what the service was about. They dutifully stood for the closing hymn, but neither could sing. After the service, Jonathon embraced his mom while he watched the Wittenburgs make their quick exit without a glance.

Lunch was fairly quiet. Finally, Elaine said, "Twenty-five years."

"I know, Mom. A long time."

"So what happened?"

They both picked at their chicken-fried steak.

"I don't know," Jonathon replied.

"Yeah, you do."

He ate another bite so he wouldn't have to answer right away. "C'mon, Mom. It doesn't matter."

"You sparkled on her, Jonathon. She'd be dead as a door nail if it weren't for you."

"Mom, I didn't do it. You know that. This is God's problem, not yours."

"How come? How come He healed her? She don't even believe it. What kind of glory is He gettin'? Why, He'd be better off touching those little kids with fat bellies in Africa. I bet those tykes would believe. Why waste time on Esther when this is all He gets?"

"It's not up to us, Mom. You remember how much I wished I could have healed Aunt Emma. She deserved to live if anyone did. It's His call."

She put her fork down and crossed her arms, looking away.

"It was a great service," he lied. "Bullet was better than usual, right? He only threw his ball over the pew twice." Cracking a smile, he caught his mom's eye.

"Remember when he pitched his pacifier, and it bounced into my c'munion cup?"

"The pew cushion still shows the stain. You ought to try to get that out, Mom."

"You run me up there later today and I'll work at it."

"I'll take you when I go to play soccer, okay?"

"Great steak today, ya think?"

"Yeah, Mom. Great steak."

*****

The next day Jonathon pulled the evening shift again. At his first chance, he nosed into room 122 at the far end of the hall.

"Good evening, Mr. Smitherton."

"Hello," came the dull reply.

"Well, look at you. You're doing much better." In fact, Henry was sitting up in a chair, his facial coloring remarkably improved.

"Yes, thanks. You must have been one of my nurses when I came in. I heard I was quite a sight."

"You were, Mr. Smitherton. We've had a couple of visits actually. Don't you remember me—Jonathon?"

"I'm sorry; I haven't been feeling very well. I can't recall the last few days."

"But how about the last time you were in, when you fell out of bed. Do you remember that?"

"Not very well, actually. Did you help me then?"

"Yes, I found you on the floor. You surprised all of us. Anyway, it's great to see you doing so much better."

"Thanks, I'm really feeling good. Might go home tomorrow. Got to hand it to you folks. I sure get great care."

"Really…? I mean, that's great. So you're happy with your doctor and all?"

"Dr. Mittlestedt? He's the best. Been my doctor for years. I only wish he'd let me smoke in here. Can't wait to be dismissed. Why do you ask?"

"No…no reason. He is very good. And look at you—it's proof he knows what he's doing. Well, I better go. Hope you have a great night."

"I expect to. Thanks for stopping, uh…Jonathon, right?

"Right. I'll stop in a little later." He reached for the door.

"That'd be great."

Jonathon stepped into the hall, amazed at what he just saw. Only a couple of small bruises on his face and his arms looked virtually normal. Three days ago he looked like death warmed over. Jonathon had never seen anyone improve that quickly. He recalled his short time of prayer for Henry.

He was sure God had not led him to heal. It was always so clear, just like Aunt Emma said it would be. If he was to heal, he'd feel it first in his spine, a tingle. Then there'd be a definite warmth in his chest, followed by a burst of lilacs. There was never any confusion.

Ever since he was four years old he had known the feeling. He remembered only a few images, like the smell of baking chocolate chip cookies and Legos scattered over the floor. His mother filled in the blanks of the whole scene.

He was sitting on the living room floor, playing all by himself. A song played on the radio from a Christian music station his mother always had on. The lyrics told of how Jesus Christ had died and how his blood was shed for all people. The sacrifice was for him, even him.

He didn't really understand the song. All he remembered was that it was so sad. Even at that young age, he felt the agony of what Jesus Christ had to go through. He started crying. That's what brought his mother in.

Elaine found her son sitting on the floor, weeping young tears of remorse. "It's so sad, Mommy. He shouldn't have died."

"Yeah, Jonathon. He don't deserve it."

"But He died for me?"

"Yep. Fer you and me both."

"He really...loves us, doesn't He, Mommy?"

"Sure does. You want to tell Him?"

And with that, Jonathon prayed for the first time. Sure, he'd said his bedtime prayers before, but this was different. He knew, for the first time, that he was praying to Someone who loved him so much that He would give everything up. That prayer changed everything.

The next day, Jonathon was out in the backyard, playing by the swing. It was a sunny spring morning, tulips blooming near the house with a crop of daffodils sprouting up thick along the back fence. Aunt Emma had come over to gather the daffodils for the church altar. While he was swinging, he remembered seeing Aunt Emma on her hands and knees, cutting the daffodils with her butcher knife.

She suddenly screamed, "Lordy, have mercy!" as loud as the heavens crashing.

His mom came running out the back door. That's when Jonathon saw it. Aunt Emma held up her hand with the little finger dangling from the end like a dead worm on a baited hook. Blood was dripping off the finger and running down her arm as she grabbed the loose finger, held by just a piece of flesh. He was ignored in all the excitement, his mom running back inside to call an ambulance.

He walked over to his aunt, not completely understanding. "Should I pray for you, Aunt Emma?"

"Yes, boy, yes. Be praying for me!"

He put his little chubby hand on his aunt's and closed his eyes. "Jesus, fix my aunt's finger. I still love You." His hand suddenly tightened and Aunt Emma had said his eyes popped open as big as croquet balls. He felt a tingle in his spine. A wonderful warmth spilt across his chest. The sweet odor of lilacs flooded his senses.

Aunt Emma held up her hand. There was still blood covering the finger and arm but it was not actively bleeding. The little finger stood right up where it should. Aunt Emma flexed her hand, and all her fingers worked together. The next thing he knew, she scooped him up and ran into the house screaming to her sister.

*****

"Jonathon?" Nurse Chandler's voice pierced the air like a chainsaw in a peaceful forest.

"Right here."

"We're short tonight. Any chance you can stay on?"

"Guess so. I'll get off at eight?"

"That'd be perfect. I'll let Jenni know. She's on charge for the night."

He thought one favor deserved another. Martha Chandler was one of the smartest people he knew.

"Hey, Martha, could I ask you something?"

"Shoot."

"Do you know much about what Henry Smitherton had? I saw him a couple of days ago and I thought he was a goner. Now he looks great."

"On rounds today Dr. Mittlestedt was really surprised too. He really made a turn around. They were thinking he'd had an acute episode of ITP—idiopathic thrombocytopenia. Clotting factors, like platelets, stop functioning. It sometimes happens without reason, but I've never seen it that bad. Dr. Mittlestedt loaded him up with steroids and we transfused him some fresh platelets. It really took hold."

"Those bruises healed so fast. Have you ever seen that?"

"I guess it was the steroids. Sometimes they work like a miracle."

"Yeah, a miracle."

"You better claim the dinner trays before the kitchen gets on us, Jonathon. Thanks for staying late."

"No problem, Martha. Thanks for the education."

*****

It still bothered him into the night. Did he miss God's voice on a healing? Could God have used his prayer and he didn't even know it? Was he out of touch? It just didn't seem like he was as close to God anymore. He knew he wasn't praying as much. Used to be he'd find himself praying all through the day.

Am I unplugged from you, God? Did I miss Your move?

He stopped by room 122 about 2:45 in the morning. He just had to see him again. He was sound asleep, the roar of a restful snore filling the small room.

Jonathon went to the far side of the bed and sat in the guest chair. Only the bathroom night light was on, shining through the crack in the door so that the beam just creased the face of Mr. Smitherton. In the darkness, Jonathon thought perhaps his face even looked better. The dark bruise over the cheek had receded even further, if that was possible. Or maybe it was the lighting.

Jonathon closed his eyes and sat back. "Oh, Lord, help me know Your voice. Did You touch Mr. Smitherton? Did I miss Your call to heal? I want to be used by You, Lord. I'm sorry that I've been away from You. I've been more confused lately. You know, stuff with Mom, the Wittenburgs…Noelle, maybe. But I need You, Lord. Help me follow You. Guide me, Lord, so I may be Your servant."

Jonathon's prayer was interrupted by the sound of the door closing. The room was pitch black except for the slit of light coming from the bathroom doorway. Someone had stepped in and shut the door to the hall.

His eyes had adjusted to the dark, so he could see it was Larry Crenshaw from the laboratory. His hair was always shaggy, long bangs constantly hanging in his eyes. Must be a late night-timed test, maybe a serum drug level. He felt guilty sitting there, so he tried not to make a sound. If he startled Larry now, he might wake up Mr. Smitherton's sound rest. Better to just stay quiet and let Larry do his work.

Larry sat his tray on the bedside table and silently fiddled with its contents. Reaching for the IV tubing running into Mr. Smitherton's veins, he shined a miniature flashlight back and forth between the tubing and a syringe he held. The syringe was full. Rather than the usual white plastic syringes for blood draws, this was a shiny silver in the light.

Hold it, Larry's not drawing blood for a test. He's putting something in. That's not the lab's job. Medications are to be given by the med nurse. But maybe this is some new test. Maybe it requires a dose of some testing solution. They'll check it later.

The flashlight clicked off.

Not a sound was heard, except for the slow, snoring inhalations of Mr. Smitherton. Jonathon grimaced from holding his teeth tightly together. He heard Larry lift the tray off the table and crack the door to leave. Jonathon couldn't resist.

"Nice work, Larry," he whispered.

Larry spun around, hair flopping with him. He clicked on the flashlight, shining it directly into Jonathon's eyes.

"What are you doing here?" Larry harshly whispered back.

"I work here, remember?" Jonathon smiled at catching the phlebotomist by surprise.

"You can't. Oh man, you couldn't have." He was still whispering, not appreciating the humor. "I gotta get out of here."

Jonathon stood from his chair and followed him out the door. Larry exited but accidently banged his tray on the way out. The silver syringe, its bare needle still attached, flew off the tray to the floor just outside in the hall. Jonathon bent over and picked it up.

"This must be some new test, right? I'm surprised you don't have to dispose of these in the room like everything else."

"Oh, it's nothing really."

Larry wanted to get out of there. He brushed his brown bangs out of his eyes and reached for the syringe, almost grabbing it from Jonathon. But Jonathon knew he wasn't following universal precautions. This was wrong; the whole thing was wrong.

Jonathon pulled his hand back, protecting Larry from getting stuck with the exposed needle. "Here, Larry. Let me just lay it back on your tray, okay?"

"Sure, of course. Just put it there, thanks."

Jonathon placed it back in the tray, again noticing the bright chrome coloring. An emblem on the side of the syringe read in black letters, "NanoMed." Almost before the name registered, Larry was off down the hall.

Almost.

Chapter 5

Back in the lab, Larry closed the door and locked it. Taking the silver syringe, he wrapped it in a blue foam pad and inserted it into a metal cylinder. After lids were screwed onto either end of the cylinder, he rolled it in bubble packing and placed it in a small but thick cardboard carton. Carefully sealing the carton with strapping tape on all sides, he slid the entire package into a zippered insulated bag. Red lettering across the side of the pouch read, "NanoMed." He laid the bag in the laboratory courier box and shut the lid. A metal padlock was worked through the latch of the box and he spun the dial. Glancing at the clock, he noted that the courier would be by to pick up the parcel in two hours, at five o'clock.

Beads of sweat rippled on his forehead as he sighed. Moving over to the lab director's office, a room he never entered during daytime hours unless invited, he sat in the high-back chair and eyed the clock. With sweaty palms he rubbed the leather arms while rocking back and forth. At 3:10 he opened the lower desk drawer and pulled out a cell phone. Laying it on the desk, he alternated between staring at it and the clock. His hands rummaged through his thick hair, making the long bangs fold tightly back against his scalp.

He reached for the phone. Lightly fingering the numbered buttons in order, he pretended to dial over and over again.

3:12. He got up from the chair and paced.

3:15. He called.

"Injection occurred at three sharp. It's ready to be picked up. Uh, yes, maybe a little problem. Someone saw me…It was no big deal, I'm sure they won't suspect." Larry started pacing. "I don't want to say. I don't want any trouble."

After holding the phone for another minute, he turned it off and put it back in the drawer. He fell back into the leather chair, exhausted.

*****

Before leaving the hospital the next morning, Jonathon made one more visit.

"Do you know if you're going home yet, Mr. Smitherton?"

"Well, hello, Jonathon. Yup, Dr. Mittlestedt gave me the go-ahead."

"You look amazingly better." He truly did. He sat in the side chair, completely dressed in a blue plaid shirt and khaki slacks, grasping the handle of his black overnight bag. The bruising was completely gone from his face, with just a hint of redness in his cheeks.

Jonathon knew steroids couldn't do that in a few days.

"I'm just waiting for my daughter, Denise. Then we're out of here."

"Yes, I met your daughter the other day. She really cares about you."

"She sure does. Don't know what I'd do without her."

"You take care of yourself now. We don't want to have to see you back here for a while."

"I've stopped trying to make those predictions, Jonathon. But I'm with you. I hope it's a long time."

"I've got to ask you one more thing, Mr. Smitherton."

"Sure, what is it?"

"You are really clear mentally, so much better than a couple of times when I cared for you in your last hospitalizations. Both of those times you said something to me that was a little peculiar. I know you weren't feeling well, but I just wanted to be sure. You're really okay with how you're feeling now? Everything's okay?"

As Jonathon was talking, he couldn't help but notice Mr. Smitherton grabbing his bag more tightly. His cheeks seemed suddenly pale. Or was it nothing?

"Everything's fine, even great, Jonathon. Why? What did I say?"

"Oh, it's nothing. Just wanted to be sure."

Mr. Smitherton's knuckles were white against the handle of his bag. "You've got my curiosity now. Would you mind filling me in on what I said?"

"It's nothing, Mr. Smitherton." He turned to leave. "Glad you're feeling so much better."

"Wait." Smitherton stood. "I need to know what I said—at least, what you think I said. Won't you please tell me?"

"You know, I hardly remember. Just something about how you thought someone was killing you. But really, I know you were feeling badly. Forget it."

Mr. Smitherton came close to Jonathon and eyed him directly. "Please. You mustn't tell anyone what you heard." His voice was a whisper.

"No problem. It's forgotten. And you take care of yourself, Mr. Smitherton." Jonathon quickly walked out the door.

When he came home at 8:30 that evening, Jonathon gave his mom a hug before she left to man the local Casey's gas mart. He downed two frosted strawberry Pop Tarts, untoasted, and headed for bed. It had been a long night.

He was lazy the next morning, sleeping late and doing little else besides flipping through old soccer magazines. At mid-afternoon he heard the doorbell. Yelling for his mom, he remembered she was at work. Whoever was at the door might have heard him shout, so he jumped off his bed, still in his pajama pants, and snuck out to the living room, peeking out the glass pane alongside the front door.

There stood a slender girl, maybe eighteen, with blonde, shoulder-length hair. She couldn't see him sneaking a look as she reached to the other side of the door to ring the doorbell again.

Dashing back to his room, he found a Kansas City Chiefs jersey laying in a heap behind his bedroom door and threw it on. Back at the front door in an instant, he looked out the window again to see her walking away down the sidewalk.

He pulled the door wide open. "Uh, hello?"

She didn't hear him.

He yelled louder. "Did you need something?"

She turned with a surprised smile and then frowned with concern. "Oh, I'm sorry. I must have woken you up."

He ran a hand threw his hair, feeling it standing on end. "No, really, it's okay. Is there something you need?"

She walked a few paces closer, yet avoiding the front step. "Well, I was just passing out this flyer."

"Hey, don't I know you from school?"

"Uh, maybe. I'm not sure I've seen you."

The frumpled way he looked, no one would recognize him. He ignored her quizzical stare at his hair and asked, "What's your name?"

"Hillary. Hillary Wells. Who are you?"

"Jonathon Thompson. Yeah, I know you. Your dad's a doctor, right?"

"That's my claim to fame. What year are you?"

"I graduated last year, but I know I've seen you around there. Man, you've really changed though. Like, your hair, or your face, or something."

"I'm a junior. Can't say I recognize you, but your name's familiar. Maybe you look a little different too." She seemed ready to leave.

"No, I didn't mean that badly. I mean, I look bad. But you—" he stumbled again.

"Anyway, I go to Windwood Community Church, just down the street. We're doing a musical this weekend and we're just passing these flyers around to invite folks." She stepped up to hand him a blue postcard and looked over his shoulder into the house. "Do you live here with your parents?"

"Just my mom. My dad left us a while ago."

"Oh, I'm sorry." She stepped back off the front step.

"It's no big deal. Anyway, thanks for the invite, Hillary. You know, I might just surprise you and come."

She took a couple more steps back and looked to her right. Only then did he see a blue Intrepid parked at the curb. A man in an olive trench coat stood at the rear, looking his way. Jonathon knew his intentions were being mistaken.

"Yeah, well, I better go. Thanks for stopping, Hillary. It was great looking at you—er—you know, you look great—no, I mean—the musical sounds great."

She said goodbye with her back to him, moving to the next house around the corner. As he died at the door, she turned and offered a cute smile again, if only briefly, before disappearing out of view.

The postcard read:

Thankful to God?
Celebrate a new way of telling Him.
Join us for a special worship concert,
Friday, November 8, 7:00 PM
at Windwood Community Church

Jonathon usually would have tossed it by now. Instead, he carried the card to his bedroom and laid it prominently on his dresser.

*****

Noelle sat at her computer in a downtown St. Louis studio apartment, sifting through her e-mail. She was up on the fourth floor of a century-old building and enjoyed the privacy, despite the traffic and siren sounds through the night. It was nightlife, something she never experienced in Windwood.

The radiator began popping as heat invaded the chilly room. The first few nights that noise was terrifying, but she was proud of herself for quickly adjusting, now even able to ignore the sounds in her sleep. Her small kitchen table served as a work station, and she sat surrounded by the rest of her furniture: a twin bed; a four-drawer, white dresser; and a lavender upholstered chair; all from the Goodwill. Hot cinnamon filled the air from her brewed tea; coffee was still disagreeable but she was working on it. For now, sweet tea was like a warm hug from home.

There were two General Biology assignments with attached files on her computer screen; she still needed to download those. Instead, she read an e-mail from her mom, usual stuff about the cold weather at home and the football team's homecoming loss. Everything calm and boring.

There was an e-mail from hawkman@aol.com. That'd be Dave. She deleted it with an angry poke of her mouse and reached for a handful of Cheetos.

Scrolling down old e-mails, she ran through several from her brother, Manny. He passed forwarded messages to her like candy canes at Christmas. Most were silly, boring, or both. She really needed to write him about those. Licking the orange salt off her fingers, she scrolled some more.

Then there were six e-mails from jon4jc@juno.com. She paused at each one, reading the short texts again. Jonathon sent them every few days the first couple of weeks, but she never replied. It was just too risky. No reason to lead him on. But right now, it was a balm that soothed her pain, if ever so slightly.

He would never desire her now. It was over—it never had a chance. Not after Dave. So stupid.

But maybe just a little note to Jonathon. Just let him know she got his mail. She hadn't heard from him in a week. He would probably give up soon.

She hit "reply" and the screen came up. Every e-mail he had sent had to come from his trek to the Windwood library. The guy was so backward he didn't even have a computer of his own. He'd said, "Why buy one when I can use one for free?" It was his way of protecting himself; he hid behind so much. Such potential, but he never would escape Windwood.

That wasn't for her. She had to get away.

She cancelled the reply and hit "shut down." It was over. The computer made the sound of a flushed toilet as it closed. Fitting.

*****

Jonathon was back to work the next afternoon. He was still behind on his sleep from the double shift, but he'd make it. When he hit the door, all the action was in the emergency room. The red crash cart was in the hall just outside the double doors; a small crowd of strangers and police stood in the ER lobby. The doors banged open and Dr. Mittlestedt, dressed in greens covered by a long, white jacket, raced down the hall.

Dodging him, Jonathon turned into the nurses' lounge to hang up his coat. Wilbur, the hospital's custodian and longest running employee, filled him in.

"Some guy got hit out in the country. He was a jogger or something," the grizzled old man said. "Must have been a nut about it during this cold snap. Anyway, these kinds are always a mess in the ER. No one understands what it takes to clean it up. I'll probably have to stay a couple of hours after my shift, and you know how much the hospital hates overtime. Hit and run, they said. Probably some punks in their pop's farm truck. They'll find them, that's for sure. Who was it? The body was so banged up, they couldn't identify him. He was still breathing when he hit the door, but they didn't think he'd make it." He pulled a water bottle out of a locker and banged the door shut.

"I don't have the stomach for this stuff. Besides, they don't need me in there now. My job's comin'."

Jonathon wandered down to the ER to check it out, just to be sure he couldn't be of help. He approached a small huddle of lab folks and a couple of nurses. Dr. Martin Feddersen was in the center of them, his arm around one of the lab ladies. Eyes were noticeably reddened as they turned to him.

"It's Larry," Martha Chandler offered without being asked. "Larry Crenshaw. He's dead, Jonathon."

Chapter 6

*J*onathon's night was slow. The hospital census was low, and they'd offered to let some staff go home. He stayed so another aide with two girls at home could have the night off. Most of the talk was about Larry: nice guy, always there to help, big future ahead of him, family down in Kansas. Was he dating anyone? No one knew. How could anyone hit someone and drive away? Jonathon offered what Wilbur had told him, "probably some punks."

Maybe not.

It bothered him that he had just seen Larry the day before he died. Death rarely gives a warning. While he didn't know Larry well, he knew he was a likable guy. Last night he was a bit distracted, whatever that was about, but he was usually very helpful.

To try to move the night along, he patrolled the darkened hallways of the hospital. *Lord, is there anybody I can touch tonight?*

He'd never prayed that way before. It was always clear. But that was before this whole Mr. Smitherton thing; somehow he missed it. Was he healed?

Would You use me without me knowing, God? I mean, that's okay. I just want to be sure I'm doing what You want.

He needed to visit Mr. Smitherton again. Aunt Emma had said to be sure God got the glory. Mr. Smitherton didn't have a clue. He'd better tell him. But for now he wondered if there was anyone else the Lord wanted him to touch.

*****

The next day he went down to the library in the morning to get online. After school and in the evenings, lines were long. One could rarely get on the Internet for more than fifteen minutes. Mornings were wide open to at least one of the three terminals.

"Morning, Mrs. Davis," he said as he took a chair beside the gray-haired lady pounding away on her own keyboard. She smelled like the bad potpourri his mother kept in the bathroom. "How are the auctions looking today?"

"Hello, Jonathon. I'm bidding on a blue-and-white teacup and saucer. 1820s transferware. The color is extraordinary, a floral design in a deep vivid blue. We're up to fifty dollars. Two more minutes and it's mine."

"Way to go." He entered his screen name on another keyboard and found his e-mail account.

"Heard from your friend?" Mrs. Davis asked casually.

"Guess not today."

"Might as well try her again, right?"

He paused. "Yeah, might as well."

"Oh no, someone has bid me up."

"Go for it, Mrs. Davis."

Clicking on the address book, he selected Noelle's name.

Okay, but now what do I say? Here I am again, the guy you love to hate.

He typed in the subject line, "Me again," and clicked onto the message screen. "Hi, Noelle. I hope you're getting these. How's SLU treating you? What's happening with school? Not much happening hereeeeeeeeeeeeeeeeeeeee." His finger weighed on the *e* key. *This sounds like a letter to my dog.*

Mrs. Davis grunted beside him, "They raised me five bucks."

"You can do it," he replied.

"It's a fantastic piece. Maybe just once."

Her computer screen started the two-minute countdown again. If a counter-bid surfaced, the clock would restart and the new bid would be highlighted where Mrs. Davis' bid now blinked at sixty dollars.

Jonathon returned to his screen and typed, "Hey, let me ask you this. Ever heard of NanoMed? It may be some kind of medical business around here. If you have any info on it let me know. Well, better go, I'm sure you're busy. Love to hear from you—"

"They raised me again, blast it!" Mrs. Davis fumed, her thinning, silver hair starkly contrasted against the angry blush of her face.

"Calm down, Mrs. Davis." He patted her shoulder. "Do you really want it?"

"You don't understand, Jonathon. It's a blue-and-white. The flowers in that design are so real you can almost smell them."

He pulled out his wallet. "Here then. Go up another ten dollars. It's on me." He placed two fives in her bony palm.

"Oh no, I couldn't."

"C'mon, Mrs. Davis. You're minutes away from owning it. I want to help—let me."

He leaned over to her screen, reached for her mouse, and clicked on bid again. "Ten bucks. Do it."

Her blue eyes danced into a smile. She typed in her new bid. He clicked her mouse to enter it. "It's gotta work."

Her two-minute countdown began again.

As he sought something more than small talk about the weather, Jonathon returned to his screen. His fingers sat on the keys without moving.

"Don't make small talk, son. Tell her how you feel," Mrs. Davis whispered while staring at her bid.

He gritted his teeth and whispered back, "Okay."

"Actually, Noelle, I'm frustrated that I have not heard from you," he typed. "I still care about you, and not a day goes by that you don't cross my mind. I miss you. I miss our talks. I miss your smile. I miss your wisdom. And I miss your hand in mine. I just wanted you to know that. So when I say I'd love to hear from you, please understand what that second word means. —Jonathon."

"I got it!" The word "SOLD" flashed in bold letters on her screen. She grabbed Jonathon around the neck for a hug.

"That's great, Mrs. Davis."

"Couldn't have gotten it without your help, Jonathon."

"Glad to do it. You give me a call when you get your teacup. I want to see it."

"I'll call you the moment it comes in. After all, we own it together, right?"

"Nope, it's all yours, Mrs. Davis. I was just here to nudge you along."

"As I am for you, my boy." She turned back to her screen to complete her purchase. "As I am for you."

He clicked on "send" and logged off. "Gotta go, now. You take care, Mrs. Davis."

"I always do. It'll work out, Jonathon." Her eyes twinkled like sapphires. She was a woman rich with experience and wisdom. He hesitated, questioning whether he should seek more of her advice.

Instead, he left and said a prayer that Noelle would respond to his note.

*****

At Jonathon's hospital shift later in the day, he found a folded note hanging on the nurses' lounge door with his name hand-printed on it. It was from Nurse Chandler. Notes on lockers announcing nurse meetings were not untypical, but a personal note from the director of nursing was peculiar. Unfolding the paper, he read that he was to report to Mr. Feddersen's office as soon as he clocked in.

He went to the administrative offices and walked past the carpeted dividers to a rear office where Joni Carruthers sat in front of her brass nameplate, "Administrative Assistant." She was working away on her keyboard, chewing gum as fast as she typed.

"Hi, Joni. I guess Dr. Feddersen wanted to see me?"

"Yes, Jonathon. I'll let him know you're here."

"What's it about, Joni, do you know?"

"He's just talking to everyone who recently worked with Larry Crenshaw. The police are still trying to get some clues, I guess. No big deal." She chewed right through her speech.

The door behind her opened and Dr. Feddersen appeared, taller than ever in a charcoal gray Armani suit with matching shirt and tie.

"Jonathon, good to see you. Thanks for stopping by right away. Come in, come in." He gave a strong handshake that lasted a moment longer than average and smiled broadly. "I know you need to get on with your work, but Nurse Chandler was kind enough to let me borrow you for just a minute." He gestured for him to sit.

Jonathon was still taking in the sight. He entered a beautifully spacious office, nearly the size of the nurses' entire report room. Oak Wainscoting lined the lower walls on all sides, with a deep blue, marbled wallpaper on the top half. Lighthouses were scattered around the room on shelves and in wall hangings. Jonathon sat on a navy blue, suede love seat while Dr. Feddersen relaxed in a matching armchair in front of his large cherry wood desk.

"Let's get right to it, Jonathon. I don't mean to intrude on your day." He nodded reassuringly at Jonathon with his classic smile that raked in millions for the hospital and won political friends across the community. He then turned serious. "The police are investigating Larry Crenshaw's death. A horrible thing. They asked me to visit with our staff about it. Just those who knew Larry, or worked with him in the last couple of days. As I've told everyone else I've talked with, in no way are they suspecting you or anyone up here. If they were, they'd be talking with you directly." His eyes winked with a slight grin. Then he flipped to serious again. "So don't worry about anything you might say. Was there anything peculiar going on with Larry over the past few weeks?"

Right before he answered, Jonathon glanced away and his eyes landed on a peculiar paperweight on Dr. Feddersen's desk, right beside a lighthouse statue. It was a three-inch tall block of black and silver sparkling granite, with a now familiar logo sandblasted across it in polished raised letters: NanoMed.

"Uh, you know, Dr. Feddersen, I didn't know Larry very well."

"Yes, of course. But just from your work with him, did he ever seem disturbed about anything?"

Something wasn't right.

"No, Dr. Feddersen. Nothing I can think of. I really didn't know Larry very well. We weren't really friends."

"Yes, I see. Well, how about his last shift up here? We've been talking with everyone who worked with him. Just wondering if there was anything he might have said to you that night. Did you see him at all?"

"Didn't even know he was working. It was a quiet night as I recall. Why? Did something happen?"

"No, no." That smile flashed back on and he stared into Jonathon's eyes a second too long. "Well, that's all I need from you, Jonathon. Thanks so much for visiting with me. Listen, I've heard recently from a patient that you helped them the other day. I think it was Mrs. Tracy, when she was in last week. She praised you. Thanks for helping make Windwood Community Hospital what it is."

"No problem, Dr. Feddersen. And I hope the police find whoever did this to Larry."

"Yes, of course. The whole situation is in our prayers, isn't it?" His hand was thrust forward for another power shake. "Thanks again."

Jonathon left the office calmly, careful not to draw any attention to himself.

*****

The Windwood Community Church parking lot was nearly full when Jonathon showed up Friday night. It was a great crowd—he had no idea it would have this kind of a draw. Parking his car far off in the north lot, he

---

wrestled whether he should still go. His mom would not approve. "You don't go to other church's functions," she would say.

It wasn't like he was leaving First Congregational. He was just making a new friend in Hillary. Certainly his mother wasn't against that.

He walked across the length of the parking lot and entered the front doors. An older man and woman that he'd never met greeted him as if he were a long-lost nephew.

Stepping into the church was like entering another world. Spinning in a slow circle, he felt the uneven dimples of the rock tile beneath his feet as unknown people rushed past in every direction across the expansive foyer. Fresh flowers—gold chrysanthemums, white daisies, and burgundy roses—filled his senses before he noticed the four-foot bouquet adorning a central, white marble table. He glanced at his clothes in comparison to the many suits on other, older, gentlemen in the room. Smoothing down his navy blue sweatshirt, he pushed the long sleeves up his forearms.

Maybe this wasn't such a good idea, he thought. He looked for a side exit as he wandered across the foyer, passing three entrances to the sanctuary. Light jazz sounds came from within, in addition to the noise of the surrounding crowd.

He felt very alone. Finding a hallway heading to the restrooms, he eyed a side door at the end of the hall that could provide an inconspicuous exit. *Let's work on a new friend later*, he told himself.

Sneaking past the restrooms, one of the doors opened. The young woman that stepped out was just as surprised as he.

"Oh! Hi. You're the guy—when I was delivering flyers."

"Uh, hello, Hillary. Yes, it's Jonathon."

"Jonathon, right. So you made it."

"Yeah, I guess I did."

"Did you find a place to sit yet?"

"Uh…well, no."

"Come with me then. Sit with our gang. It's a bunch from our youth group."

"Well—" he thought one more time about escaping out the side door. "Sure."

They turned and started to go back up the hall. Then Hillary stopped. "Oh, were you heading to the restroom? I can wait."

"No, I'm fine."

She remained hesitant. "Really?"

"I'm okay." At least she didn't push it.

She brought him into one of the sanctuary side doors and down to the first row. He felt like he was entering a giant movie theater, minus the screen. Row after row of lavender upholstered seats surrounded him, with a balcony overhead that was nearly half as large as the main floor. She introduced him to her friends, and he recognized a few from school last year. He hated being so close to the front. If the service became crazy, it'd be hard to escape. Sitting beside Hillary, he had just a moment to get his bearings before the lights went low.

Faintly through the darkness, he saw more than fifty adults in robes entering down the aisles and marching onto the platform, filling the front stage. Lights came up on the floor over to the left, revealing six musicians with guitars, assorted drums, and two keyboards.

When the music started, the air was suddenly ethereal. There was an intensity to their music that immediately made Jonathon anticipate something unique. He adjusted himself in his seat, and his mind was removed from his mother, church, the hospital, Larry Crenshaw, Mr. Smitherton, Noelle, and even Hillary.

Moments into the song, the young people he was sitting with all stood and began to clap their hands in unison to a song they all knew. Jonathon turned to see the whole sanctuary rise and begin clapping. They all joined with the beat of the music in a thunderous percussion.

He felt like he was participating in some primeval ritual; nevertheless, he stood and clapped like the other neanderthals.

Floodlights flashed across the stage as the choir burst into song, robes flapping as they clapped enthusiastically. But their singing! It was the sound of a magnificent instrument. A single note sung by all shot through the air, moving across the musical register with precision. Words communicated the highest praise at an intellectual level, but the melody carried the message deeply and deliberately into the soul. Soon the sounds became perfectly complicated with elaborate harmonies. The imagination of the sense of hearing was stretched beyond measure. Jonathon didn't only hear, but actually felt the music move him. Shouting to his very heart, the jubilant chorus broke a shell of stiffness and formality. He caught himself with a smile on his lips, and, unaware of his own voice, he sang the new song. Blending with the choir and the voices around him, he discovered an abandonment he had never before experienced.

When the song ended, the choir's hands were lifted high. Those in the sanctuary began clapping wildly, but the applause was interrupted by the electric guitar segueing to the next song. Some around him continued clapping without concern, as they were not applauding the music, but the heavens. A worship leader came in front of the choir and nodded, his finger pointing straight up. He turned to the choir and gave them a downbeat to start singing the next song.

Jonathon leaned over to Hillary. "Those guys are great!"

"I thought you'd like it." She grinned as they both kept clapping.

Jonathon felt something coming out of himself, an emotion he had not experienced for a long time, if ever. It was as if he had been wrapped too tight, and this music somehow cut through the surface of his pretension. He felt unencumbered as he reached out for his relationship with his Creator. Yet it was risky, going into unknown mysteries such as God.

Swelling across the sanctuary, the music encompassed the large population, a perfect blend of vocals and band. Jonathon had to keep catching himself for fear he would get swallowed up in the moment. When he felt almost mesmerized, he would step back and look around him, curiously noticing how others would be caught up in a dreamworld of the music. Early on, he would always catch Hillary's eye and get a nod from her, but toward the end of the third song, she herself had her eyes closed and hands raised, lost in the ambience.

He'd heard about this stuff. He had to be careful.

Chapter 7

A t first, Hillary's thoughts couldn't get past this guy. He acted oddly when she dropped off the flyer at his house. Now, she believed, God allowed her to bump into him this night, even sit together. Watching him at the start of the worship service reminded her of the first time she came to Windwood Community, wide-eyed as a kid stepping onto a roller coaster. Jonathon was honest with his emotions, not trying to hide them like other guys. Fitting the mold wasn't important to him. Even his hair, longer, blond locks that fell onto his glasses if he moved too fast, didn't meet today's standard. He wasn't a game-player.

Maybe she liked that.

After the second song she returned to her purpose for coming, to worship. She needed this, and her God deserved it and so much more. The sincerity of expressing her feelings to her God brought a relationship she had longed for all her life. It was one of her highest joys.

In the middle of the concert, a woman in a wheelchair came out of the choir to sing a solo. Hillary shivered in anticipation. Melinda Camelson had an incredible voice, but more so, she had literally saved Hillary's life a year ago. To hear her sing now brought back a wash of memories that flooded her mind; tears formed in her eyes even as the music started.

One hand on a microphone, Melinda gave the audience an engaging smile as the musical introduction played. She looked stunning in a simple black turtleneck, her long coffee brown hair pulled back in a braid. A forest green paisley lap blanket draped her legs. Placing her other hand over her heart as she touched her first note, worship happened again. It was a powerful lyric of how God was in control of all things, all the time, with a perfect plan. Her eyes were drawn upward, and for the rest of the song she was clearly not singing to any human crowd.

Hillary stole one more look at Jonathon. He was bent forward, elbows on his knees, completely engrossed. She stared for a moment longer to catch his eye, but he didn't flinch. Closing her eyes, she turned forward and allowed the melody to quietly wander through the passages of her soul. This was God ministering to her.

*****

The service's ending was uncomfortable. Jonathon knew well enough to be cautious, and he supposed it could have been worse. The music had been simply amazing; he'd never heard such energy. The closing song moved into an intense prayer session. There were people on their knees around where he sat, even in the aisles. No one forced it to happen, and the church locals seemed used to it. There were many people kneeling together, arms around each other as they prayed, and lots of crying. The only thing missing was a preacher shouting over the top of it to keep everyone riled up. This wasn't good.

Jonathon felt a heaviness, an oppressive manipulation, forcing him into a corner where he didn't want to go. Even the air was dense and his breathing fast. Had they released some form of mind-altering vapor? Looking around, no one paid any attention to him, but something peculiar was moving through this place.

Tapping Hillary's arm, he interrupted her prayer. "Thanks, Hillary. I've gotta go. Maybe I'll see you around." Before getting a response from her—he assumed she'd return to her meditation, or mantra, or whatever—he got up and stepped over a sea of legs all lined up along the front steps of the sanctuary.

This is crazy!

Moving up the aisle, he eyed an usher at the door. Fearing they wouldn't let him out, he looked at his wristwatch, pretending he was late for something. The usher completely ignored him, and he escaped the sanctuary.

Breaking out the front door was like bursting out of water after being held under. He took large gulps of the chilly night air, stepping onto a grassy hill around the side of the building.

Hillary had to follow him. He had raced in a beeline to the door, but she couldn't reach him. The usher asked her if everything was okay, sincerely concerned about her friend. That short delay slowed her down just enough. When she reached the door, she knew he was probably gone. Looking across the front lawn and parking lot, she couldn't see any sign of his skinny frame. Her breath clouded the air in front of her and she shivered. Turning to walk back in, she glanced to her side.

There he was, standing twenty yards away, hands tight in his pockets with his back to her.

"Jonathon!" she burst out without thinking.

He looked around and cracked a half smile before hanging his head. She stepped over to him.

"I know how you feel," she offered.

"Yeah, well. It's just not my thing."

"That's okay. It's not for everyone."

There was a lengthy gap that she wished he would fill. Nothing came.

"So, besides the end, was it alright?"

"Yeah." He raised his head, pushing his glasses up. "That was awesome. Especially that lady in the wheelchair. I couldn't believe the power of her song."

"She's an incredible lady."

Another lapse. Both wondered what to say.

"Would you like to meet her? She's a friend of mine."

"You know, I really think I would, but maybe another time. Except..."

She waited for him.

"Except when she sang, I felt something."

"I know. It happens every time. It's incredible."

"No, not that. I mean, maybe about her wheelchair." His voice was soft, thoughtful. He looked away, acting like he wished he could be somewhere else.

"What do you mean?"

"It's nothing," but he continued. "Has she been in the wheelchair long?"

"She's paralyzed. I know that. Some kind of accident when she was young. Why?"

"It's nothing. I just felt something peculiar when she was singing, a tingle in my spine." He was talking more to himself than to her. "Maybe I could meet her sometime."

"I know she's still inside. Let's go back in and I'll introduce you. She'll enjoy it, and you'll like her."

"Thanks, Hillary, but I should go."

Hillary bristled, flustered at herself and hurt that Jonathon wasn't accepting her invitation. She nervously pushed her hair behind her ears. Not knowing exactly what to say, she had to try again.

"Look, I know you're a bit shook up, just like I was the first time I came to this church. But it's not phoney, Jonathon. I think it may be hard for you to come back if you leave now. Why don't you just seize the moment and let me introduce you to Melinda?" She pleaded with him with her eyes. "Then you can be done, go home, and forget all about it."

"Did you ever know Noelle Lewis?" he asked.

She was taken aback by his change of direction. "No. Who's that?"

"Just a friend of mine. She'd talk to me that same way. I guess I just bring that out in people."

"Being bossy, you mean?" She laughed for the first time.

"Maybe I need it." He smiled back. "Okay, let's meet the lady."

They walked back into the church and Jonathon followed her to the east side of the lobby.

"The worship here is so awesome, Jonathon. I know it can overwhelm a person, but really, God is moving here. Do you believe in angels?"

"Sure."

"Well, you won't believe this, but sometimes during our worship, we'll even hear singing that comes from angels."

"Just like tonight?"

"No, I don't mean us singing. I mean real angels. Singing."

"Oh. I see." *Yup, this church is on the fringe.* Suddenly, his own First Congregational seemed like a great little church.

"Here they are." Hillary approached a woman in the wheelchair coming down from a back hallway. Behind her pushing the chair was a tall, lanky man. They were both in their forties, and Jonathon thought he had seen the man on the platform earlier. "Melinda, John, I want you to meet a friend of mine."

The Camelsons both stopped, and John offered a firm handshake. Melinda's outstretched hand was gentle and warm. Jonathon was surprised at the strength of her grasp.

"I really enjoyed your song," Jonathon said, star-struck but sincere.

"She can really move your heart, can't she?" her husband said.

"That's for sure. It was a great concert tonight."

"John's the worship leader here," Hillary said.

"I wondered who put all this together." Jonathon responded. "I never saw anyone directing the choir. How do you do it?"

"All with mirrors, Jonathon. It's our secret." Hillary and Melinda laughed with him. "John just doesn't like to be out front," Melinda responded. "He trains us so well, we can do it blindfolded."

"Yeah, you guys don't need me. I better look for a new job." John said.

"Well, however you do it, it was great." Jonathon felt removed from an inside joke. He wanted to speak directly to Melinda. "Your song really meant a lot to me. While you were singing, I had a weird thought. Like, that maybe I should talk with you. Has that ever happened to you before?"

Everyone was suddenly quiet. "Not really," Melinda replied, puzzled.

"I'm sorry, I don't mean to be difficult. Sometimes I get impressions of people, and I'm able to help them. Maybe it doesn't make sense, but I think I had one about you…that maybe I could help you."

Melinda stammered, "Well, sure. I mean, I'm not sure—"

"I think we should get together," John interrupted. "Jonathon, you're not being difficult. At least, we're used to weird things around here. Anyway, let's make a time when we can visit. We'd like to hear more about what you're thinking."

"Hey, I'm sorry to come off so abrupt with you all, but I would like to get together. It's important."

"It's settled. Call me tomorrow, Jonathon, here at the church. We'll set a time. Now tell us, how'd you meet Hillary here?"

"Oh, she and another guy were delivering those flyers to my house."

"What other guy? Did you get hit up twice about this?" Hillary interrupted.

"No, just that guy who was going around with you. He drove a blue car, an Intrepid, I think. I thought maybe it was your dad."

"Jonathon, I visited you by myself. There was no one with me."

"That's strange. I could've sworn the guy by the car was with you."

Hillary and Melinda glanced at each other. "Mel, do you think…?"

Melinda grabbed Hillary's hand. "Maybe. It just might be."

"What's going on?" Jonathon asked.

All three smiled at him.

"We'll tell you later," John answered. "Too many weird topics for one night. Call me tomorrow, okay?" He shook hands with Jonathon again.

"Sure."

"Hillary, you need a ride home?" Melinda asked.

"Yeah, can I catch one with you? That'd be great." She turned to Jonathon. "It's been great to get to know you, Jonathon. Thanks for coming tonight."

"Thanks for inviting me. Uh, I could give you a ride home, if you want."

"No," she hesitated. "That's all right. The Camelsons live down the street from me. See you around."

He watched the three of them leave. Hillary looked back, gave a memorable smile and quickly turned away.

He found his own way out the front doors. The chilly night felt great.

*****

"Where ya been?" The interrogation began before the screen door slammed closed.

"Hi, Mom. How was your night?"

"Just worryin' 'bout you. That's all." His mom sat on the davenport in her housecoat, doing crossword puzzles.

"Don't be worrying about me, Mom. You'll be glad to know I was out with a new friend."

"Oh? Guy or doll?"

"I guess you'd call this one a doll, Mom. Really though, just friends, okay?"

"Sure, hon. I know just what 'cha mean."

"Anything happen around here?"

She returned to her crosswords. "You had a phone call. It was Noelle."

"You're kidding."

"Nope. She said something 'bout wanting to talk to you about an i-mail you sent."

"C'mon, Mom. Don't tease me. Noelle really called?"

"Yup. If you'd been home with your mom, you would have got to talk at her."

"Well, what'd she say?" He sat down on the davenport and took the crossword book away from her. "Talk to me."

She sighed, crossing her arms. "She didn't say much. I tried to talk at her—'bout school, you know. She didn't offer much. Said things were fine. Said to tell you to check your i-mail."

"It's e-mail, Mom."

"Doesn't matter."

He could hardly wait until morning.

Chapter 8

*T*he Harmon County Library opened at nine o'clock. Jonathon was there at 9:02. He would have been earlier except for the grilling his mother gave him that morning. When she heard where he'd been last night, she lit into him.

"What's wrong with our church?" She gave no evidence of holding her composure.

"Mom, it was just a concert."

"Yeah, that's how they getcha. First you're there for a pretty girly, then they suck you on in."

He turned his back to her so she couldn't see him roll his eyes.

"Don't go twisting your eyeballs, Jonathon Edward Thompson."

"How do you do that?"

"It's a gift, I s'pose. Don't change the subject."

"Mom, I'm not leaving First Congregational."

"Promise?"

He turned to face her. "Promise. Now look, I gotta go. Can we do this later?"

"Whatever, honey. You be workin' tonight?"

"Yup, I'll be home before midnight." He pinned his name tag on his shirt pocket, knowing what she wanted. "I'll be up to go to church with you in the morning."

"That's my sugar. You go tell Noelle hi for me."

*****

He flipped on the switch behind the computer and logged on. The library was quiet; he had all three terminals to himself.

After selecting the e-mail connection, instead of the usual sound of dial tones and whistles, he got a message box: "No dial tone. Make sure the modem

59

is correctly connected to the computer and phone line." He clicked "connect" again and got the same message.

"Oh, c'mon."

He popped the power to another computer beside him, and while it booted up he wiggled phone lines and wires. The second computer gave him the same message...five times. He went to the third computer. Same message.

He walked over to the library counter. A television was blaring in the office just behind the desk.

"Excuse me?" he said louder than he was used to speaking in the library.

A boy looking about twelve, bearing lots of freckles and a mop of red tangles across his head, came out of the office.

"Hi. I'm trying to get online and the computers won't connect over there. Can you get someone to help me?"

"Whaddayamean?"

Isn't there anyone else here? He reminded himself this was Windwood.

"The computers won't work. Can you get someone to help me?"

"Whadya try?"

"I'm trying to get online. Look, I use these every week—I know what I'm doing. Something's wrong with the connection. Can you help me?"

"I'm not s'posed to mess widdem."

"Is there someone else who can help?"

"I'm the only one here. You know, it's Saturday."

Like that's a reason the library can be staffed with delinquents. "Listen, the computers don't work. I think you'd better call someone to fix them."

"I could do that, I s'pose."

"Yeah, do that. I'd appreciate it."

Jonathon walked back to the computers and wiggled more wires, finding the phone line jack. Pulling the line out, he solidly inserted it again into the modem box.

Confidently clicking on "connection," he found it did no good. The same error message scoffed at him. He pulled the line out again and licked the end of it with his tongue. He'd seen his father do that a long time ago to get a light bulb to work. He'd even tried it himself when he was seven, on an extension cord that was plugged in. He'd never do that again.

But it still didn't work.

"C'mon, someone's got to be able to help," he said under his breath.

He thought again about his dad. Times like these made him wish he was around. The guy was a walking toolbox, handy with construction, electrical, plumbing, you name it. Computers weren't available back when his dad lived at home, but if they were, he would have built one from scratch.

"They said they'd be down." The boy shouted from across the library study area. Nobody in the building seemed to care.

"Did they say when?"

"Uh, sometime close to noon."

"Noon?"

The boy was already gone, back to his television.

*****

Noelle checked her screen often that morning, keeping watch on her Instant Message box. If he connected, she'd know.

She'd played it out in her mind all last night after her phone call to Windwood. In retrospect, that was a mistake. She was relieved when he wasn't home. *Stay cool, distant. Just offer a couple electronic lines of hello, then pick up on the NanoMed thing.*

She sat at her terminal from 9:00 to 9:30, reading junk forwards from her brother and waiting for the IM bell to ring.

Nothing.

She drummed her fingers along the edge of the keyboard. His mother had said he didn't have to work until later. She said he was free all morning.

Pulling open her English Composition text file, she tried to concentrate on an assignment. "Where are you, Jonathon?" she mumbled to herself.

She opened her "sent" mail and reread her message to him. No big dance. She had phrased it carefully. "Everything fine at SLU, thanks for the earlier notes, always nice to hear from Windwood, and btw, I know a bit about NanoMed. Big research firm, nanotechnology stuff. I'll find out more. Gotta go, lots happening in the big city."

Okay, it wasn't much of a tease, but it didn't take much. At least, it didn't used to.

So, where are you, Jonathon?

She ran to the kitchen an hour later, grabbed a Diet Coke and sat down again at the screen. It remained the same. She wrote a note to her mom, then

61

did a web search on nanotechnology. Finding a couple of interesting pages, she printed them.

The noise of the printer made a stark contrast to the silence of her apartment. She fingered the pages. Folded them. Folded them again. She was diligent in seeing just how many times she could fold them, down to the size of a small jewelry box.

Where are you, Jon!

*****

Jonathon wandered the downtown stretch, comprised of a short line of boutiques and home-grown stores across two blocks. It was a sunny morning, soothing his frustration over the computer at the library. The air was wintry cool, his ears burning the longer he walked. The only stores open were the Coffee Corner and Pritchett's Drug Store. A line of about twenty folks were huddling near Darla's Dress Barn. It was Crazy Dayz. During this annual occasion, on the first hour of business everything was twenty percent off. While it wasn't much of a sale, patrons who came in pajamas got another ten percent. That was a sale in Windwood.

Ladies of all shapes and sizes, giggling with their steaming mugs and Styrofoam cups, crowded the sidewalk. Three or four moms brought their kids, also decked out in PJs. Slippers were the biggest eyesore, a menagerie of shoebox-sized fuzzy animals, cartoon characters, or pastel mohair. Extending from the slippers were various widths of legs surrounded by either furry or flowery robes, bodies huddled together outside the door of Darla's, waiting for ten o'clock when the store would open.

He dodged into Pritchett's to avoid the mob.

Browsing the narrow aisles of cough syrups lined beside ceramic miniatures, he asked God why he couldn't use the library computer: *It's not fair. Today's the first day I really needed it, God.*

Seeking just a little alone time, he saw a body move down the same aisle. Without glancing up, Jonathon moved around the corner to the next aisle of plastic flowers and aspirin.

Please, God, send someone to fix that computer. May it be only a small glitch. You know how much I've been wanting to hear from her.

Jonathon glanced down the aisle and saw the same person, a man a few years older than himself wearing an olive green trench coat, invading his aisle again. Meeting eyes, the man smiled slightly at Jonathon. His high cheekbones and styled bronze hair set him apart from the usual Windwood fare. With a sheepish smile Jonathon turned away, moving two aisles down to the hand lotions and candy.

Before he had time to pray again, he found the man turn the corner of the aisle.

"What's going on?" Jonathon muttered under his breath, a little peeved.

"I know you don't know me, Jonathon." The man's strong face contrasted with his gentle voice. "I just wanted to ask you to go check on Samantha Harris outside. She's over at Darla's. They think she might be sick. Could you run over there?"

"Me? I guess I could. I don't know if I'd be much help."

Must be a patient. He had learned that when people know you work at the hospital they think you know everything.

"Guess I could look."

"I know they'd appreciate it."

He was so gentlemanly that it made Jonathon restless. He moved for the front door and was glad to see the man didn't follow him.

Outside, Jonathon eyed the gaggle of ladies seeking who would belong to a Samantha Harris. It didn't appear that anyone was too concerned. A wild cackle sounded from a lady in a leopard robe and the whole group laughed with her. Jonathon turned back to look for the man in the trench coat when a shriek sounded toward the front of the line of ladies. "Oh my God, Sammy!"

Every robe suddenly crowded toward the still screaming woman. A voice shouted from the bodies, "She's blue. She can't breathe!"

Two women glanced up from the circle that had formed at the locked front door of Darla's. Their eyes were wide with alarm, looking every direction before one of them saw Jonathon.

"Help us!"

A woman he didn't recognize because of her facial mask pulled him in by the arm. "Here, Jonathon's a nurse. Let him through."

Still, he had to fight his way to the center of the crowd. Reaching the mom, he found her cradling a four-year-old girl with little eyes already rolled back and thin lips that were dark purple. Though she was breathing, he only heard a gaspy wheeze.

"She's got asthma. Help her, you've got to help her!" The white-masked lady yelled.

He mother, near hysterics, cried out, "I've given her an inhaler. It's not working!"

"Get an ambulance. Call 9-1-1!" someone shouted from the back.

Two women were banging on the doors of Darla's, but there was no response. The store was not to open for fifteen minutes. The racket would be considered normal for Crazy Dayz.

Someone suggested running to the Coffee Corner and calling, but Jonathon knew there was no time. This girl was suffocating. Her mom was sobbing deeply, hyperventilating, and out of control. She now held her daughter loosely, her little head and arms falling back limply in a deathly release of life.

Jonathon knelt down and reached for the young girl's ashen wrist, feeling a thready, rapid pulse. Her breathing was barely audible, if present at all. Someone yelled to do CPR, and he looked around for help when it hit him.

A tingle in his back.

He reflexively grabbed the shoulders of the girl and held her close, away from the mother.

"Not my baby!" she screamed, fighting to hold onto her daughter.

It took only a moment. He closed his eyes, feeling the warm burning in his chest. Whispering words in obedience to his heavenly Father, he released his grasp of the girl and her mother immediately scooped her up in her arms again.

He fell back on his haunches. Cries and yelling continued around him by the panicked ladies in their bathrobes. It was Samantha's mom who first noticed.

"She's breathing. Look at her, she's pink again!"

The little eyes opened, pupils big as grapes. She looked up and yelled, "Mommy!" giving her mom a huge hug with her spindly arms.

"She's okay." The mom blubbered, convincing herself. "She's okay."

A calm fell upon the group, everyone pausing to catch their own breath. The hesitation gave time for the realization of what happened.

"Jonathon, how'd you do that?" the woman with the white cheeks asked.

"What was it you did? I've never seen anything turn that fast," another lady in curlers said.

"Uh, all I did was pray, really." He said. "I just asked God to not let her die."

"Son, if that was a prayer, then I'd say you...healed her!" an older woman exclaimed.

"Did you see how fast she got better? That was a miracle!"

He stood up and started to back out of the crowd encircling him.

"It was Jesus, really. Not me." He stuttered and turned to the mom. "I better go, but you ought to take her to the hospital. Just to be sure." He took a step away as the women in robes parted for him. Feeling a bit more confident to finish the work he'd begun, he said, "But she's going to be fine. Just thank God for her life."

He walked away. Turning once to look back, he saw all of them still staring. Two women called him to come back.

The relief he felt turned into a smile, and he shook his head and held his hands open as he shrugged his shoulders, communicating, "I don't get it either," without saying a word.

The gaze of every woman still followed him, like hunters stumbling upon a six-point buck.

He broke into a run back to the library.

Out of breath when he entered the building, he feared someone would be coming on his heels. He saw the red-haired boy at the book counter and pointed to the terminals.

"They work now," the boy responded.

No one followed him, so Jonathon sat down and checked his e-mail, still puffing. It was nearly noon.

There it was, a message from Noelle. He opened it full and read the six-line note. He printed the page and shut down his e-mail. Ripping the hard copy off the printer, he banged through the library doors to his car and drove home to await the nightmare he'd only dreamed of.

*****

"So what'd Noelle have to say that was so almighty important?" His mom questioned him as soon as he opened the front door.

"Mom, I healed somebody. Right downtown. Right in front of everybody."

The phone rang, interrupting them. Mother and son stared at each other; neither moved.

Three rings.

"Don't answer it," Jonathon almost whispered. "I'm not ready yet."

Four, five rings.

"We're going to have to deal with it," Elaine whispered back, smoothing down her apron.

Six, seven rings…it stopped.

"Okay, sit yerself down. I'll make coffee. Tell your mom what ya sparkled this time."

He relayed the story of the girl with the asthma attack. His mom wanted details, trying to figure out who was who. It all happened so fast, Jonathon was of little help.

Five minutes through his story, the phone rang again. This time she picked it up.

"He can't come to the phone—Yeah, I knows what happened. Well maybe you just better take that up with the lady and her kid. No, I don't know." Reaching behind her back, she jerked the ties to her apron. "You should go to your Bible for that question. No. He's not Jesus Christ, for pity's sake—Don't be ridiculous!" She slammed the phone onto its cradle. "There, that wasn't so bad."

He frowned. She forced a smile back at him.

"We knew it would happen 'ventually. God's timing is perfect, Jonathon. Remember that." She folded the apron in half and fingered the crease.

"Should I go to work, Mom?"

"I think so. We gotta keep life normal."

The phone rang again.

The door bell rang.

They didn't answer either one.

Chapter 9

*I*t had to be Nurse Chandler who saw Jonathon first.

"Hey, what's this I hear about you?" she bellowed from down the hall as he approached the nurses' station.

"Nothing." Grabbing a clipboard of the daily admissions, he went into the nurses' report room.

"Nothing?" She followed after him. "They're all saying you healed somebody downtown. Is that so?"

He focused on the clipboard but his thoughts were swimming. "It wasn't me." He looked up at Martha Chandler and in a quiet voice said, "It was God. I didn't do anything."

The large framed woman held her tongue and placed a hand on his shoulder. "I don't know what happened, Jonathon. But I'm sure glad it did. That mom was bragging about you all over the emergency room."

"Was the girl okay?"

"Fit as a fiddle. They didn't find a thing wrong with her."

"Let's leave it then. I don't want it to become an issue around here."

"You might be a bit late for that. But I won't say another word." Nurse Chandler squeezed his shoulder hard and left the room, yelling for a nurse to explain why the IV had run out in 138.

The hospital was more full today. Jonathon was working the south hall with ten patients; he only recognized a couple of names. Three were marked for probable dismissal tomorrow. He hung up the clipboard and stepped back to the nurses' station.

"Jonathon, we want to hear all about it." Mary, the med nurse caught him first. "Let me finish passing my three o'clocks and then tell us." She raced past him, and he was called from behind.

"Hey, there he is! You've got the magic touch, is that right?" It was Carmen, the ward clerk.

Jonathon looked down the hall and saw Nurse Chandler staring at him, arms stiffly folded across her prominent bosom. He raised his hands to say "what do I do?"

She stepped forward and announced in her revelry voice, "Folks, here's the plan. Let's get meds passed and patients cared for. But in twenty minutes, at report, Jonathon here will sit down and tell us what happened today. For right now, you all do your jobs. Got it?"

Everyone turned on dimes and got busy. Jonathon mouthed a "thank you" to Chandler. She returned a rare smile.

At report, after Nurse Chandler and the day nurses had gone through each patient's record, all ears turned to Jonathon as he briefly told how Samantha Harris had an asthma attack, and how he prayed for her and she suddenly got better. Thinking he was done, he looked at Chandler, expecting her to order everyone back to work. Instead, she asked him a question.

"So you really think you healed her?"

"No, I don't. I think God healed her. I just offered a prayer in a crisis."

Before he could add more, Carmen asked, "Have you ever done that before?"

"I pray a lot, don't you guys?" He started to get up out of his chair. "Sure, I've prayed for people to get better."

"But," Charlene, another aide, spoke up, "Has it worked for you before? Do people get better when you pray?"

"Only if it's God's will." He eyed Nurse Chandler again. "I guess we should get to the patients. It looks like I've got quite a list tonight." He headed for the door. As he walked out, he heard Mary whisper to someone, "Don't believe a word of it."

Heading down the hall to his first patient, he heard Nurse Chandler bark his name.

"Jonathon, not so fast." He stopped as she approached him.

"I'm not sure about all you said in there. Is this something you do regularly?"

"C'mon, Martha. I pray for folks. I pray for you sometimes. Is that wrong?"

She softened slightly. "No, of course not. I was wondering about a few of your patients of late. Like Wittenburg and Smitherton. Are you messing with them?"

"I prayed for them, if that's what you mean."

She was cornered. "Okay then. If that's all you're doing."
He turned to get away.
She called again. "Jonathon?"
He stopped and turned.
"Thanks for uh...for praying for me."
"No problem."

*****

His first patient was Royce Horton in 117. He'd had a TURP, a transurethral prostatectomy. His prostate had been enlarged for years, but regular ultrasound reports had not revealed any evidence of tumor. Surgery had been advised to reduce the size of the swollen organ. The operation was done three days ago and his recovery was uneventful, until today. His pathology report had just returned, showing surprising evidence of an aggressive cancer.

Horton was the mayor of Windwood, had been for two terms. He was a kind man, but his wife was a worrier. At report, everyone was subtly reminded to treat him with the best of care, "as we do for all patients." Most importantly, his treatment would be all over the local news and street gossip. If he did well, the hospital would look great. If he faired poorly, more people would go down the road to Rollings for health care.

"Good afternoon, Mayor Horton." Jonathon pulled out his cheeriest greeting.

Mayor Horton looked anything but mayorly in his starched white hospital gown and attached IV line. Undoubtedly, that was Mrs. Horton with the gray hair, sitting in the recliner. She immediately leaned her thin frame forward when Jonathon came in.

"Did you hear my husband has cancer?" Mrs. Horton's weak voice shook like her hands.

"Yes, Mrs. Horton. We're very sorry to hear that." He turned quickly to the mayor. "So how can I help you right now?"

Mayor Horton gave a smile. "I'm okay, I guess."

"Can you tell us why you couldn't have found the cancer any sooner?" Mrs. Horton warbled.

"No, Mrs. Horton. I'm an aide. I'm not fully aware of your husband's course, so you should ask your doctor those questions. I'll do everything I can to help you both today."

Mayor Horton asked genuinely, "Does that mean you'd...pray for my healing?"

"You've heard too." Jonathon's voice sank.

"Is it true?" Mrs. Horton worked hard to stand and moved to her husband's bedside. "Can you heal him?"

"No, it's not like that." Jonathon fought against a teasing anger. "We can't test God like this."

"I believe in God," Mayor Horton offered.

"We're both faithful to Parkview Methodist. Been there for years." Mrs. Horton reached for Jonathon's hand. "Won't you please help my husband?"

The thin, wrinkled flesh in his hand was warm and fragile. Holding her hand, he looked over his shoulder out the door to see if anyone was watching. A strong odor of something like Avon overcame him as he felt her other hand join his.

"Please help him."

"I want to, Mrs. Horton. Let me pray about it—think it through. Maybe I can give you an answer tomorrow. We've got to be careful. I'm going to see my other patients, but I'll be back."

The mayor smiled again, embarrassed.

Mrs. Horton wiped her eyes.

He put his hand on the door. "I promise I'll let you know tomorrow."

*****

Hillary picked up the phone to call John and Melinda. They needed to know. More than that, she herself needed some advice.

"Hello, John?"

"Yes. Hi, Hillary. I bet I know why you've called."

"You heard about Jonathon?"

"It's quite a story. What do you think?"

"I'm surprised, I guess. He didn't strike me as someone who could...well, he just didn't seem that spiritual." Hillary started playing with the phone cord.

"Why do you say that?"

"He was really uncomfortable in our worship service. I could tell, when we were praying at the end, he wanted out of there."

"And that means God can't give him a spiritual gift?" John's voice was kind but pointed.

"No, but most people I've seen who are healers, they're pretty into it. Like charismatic folks, right?"

"I don't know any healers, Hillary. Just what I see when I'm surfing the TV. I'm not sure they set the standard for God."

"I guess you're right."

"Anyway, we're not truly sure he healed the Harris girl."

"Okay. I don't want to jump ahead. It's just that we've been praying through all this Mark Chapter 16 stuff. We gotta believe He's doing something here. Responding to our prayer."

"I'm with you. But I also believe the enemy would love to get us all mixed up. But the timing is great—he's supposed to call me so we can get together. That'll be a great chance to talk with him more."

"Good, John. One more thing."

"What's that?"

"He doesn't believe in angels."

"He told you that?"

"Well, he didn't actually say it. But I'm pretty sure that's what he was thinking."

"That's God's turf, Hillary. Let Him take care of that. I didn't believe in them either, until my mission trip to Russia."

"Just thought you should know."

"Okay. I'll call you after I visit with him."

"Thanks. Tell Melinda hi."

*****

Mr. Smitherton sat in a soft, black leather sofa that squeaked each time he moved. The black and white tile flooring made him just a little dizzy, so he kept his gaze on the arboretum of green plants sweeping across the back white wall of the spacious office. Recorded classical music was playing somewhere among the plants; he thought it was Tchaikovsky. The natural lighting from the expanse of glass on the north side tempted him to get up to enjoy the view.

But he was told to sit. So he did.

He waited fifteen minutes this time. That wasn't bad.

"Ah, Mr. Smitherton." In shuffled a short man with a round, bald head, meticulously dressed in a black suit and open-collared matching, black shirt. Henry knew him only as Dr. Troy.

He came straight to Mr. Smitherton and reached out a hand. "Please, don't get up. I know once I sit in that couch, I need two people to pull me up." A wave of expensive cologne rolled past.

Behind him entered Dr. Feddersen, shaking hands with Mr. Smitherton in turn. "Great to see you doing so much better, Henry."

"I'm doing fine, thank you." Henry spoke in his strongest voice, which cracked on the last word.

"Dr. Feddersen tells me you've completely recovered. It's truly amazing, Mr. Smitherton. You made medical history again. No one has yet survived DIC."

"Is that what it was?"

"Disseminated intravascular coagulation," Dr. Feddersen explained. "Your blood cells entered a crisis, preventing the natural clotting mechanisms. It often leads to individuals bleeding to death."

"I see."

"But you beat it, Mr. Smitherton. History, I tell you," Dr. Troy piped.

"So is this the last one for a while? I think I need to rest up."

"Of course. You rest as long as you need to. One more week? That should be no problem."

"Actually, I was wondering about waiting until after Christmas."

"Oh, my. That would not be possible, Mr. Smitherton. The research cannot be held off that long or the study results would be jeopardized. You understand."

"So I'll have to come back here in a week?"

"Dr. Feddersen can set the time for you. Let's say a week for your next injection." He fingered one of three gold bands on his left hand. "That will free you up for Thanksgiving, yes? Enjoy your family, then we'll see you the next week. The hospitalization should be short." Dr. Troy wandered over to the green plants and gently petted a six foot tall Thai plant.

"Do you garden, Mr. Smitherton?"

Henry was still processing the next injection date. "I dabble with it."

Dr. Troy surveyed his greenhouse. "It's a wonderful hobby. Relaxing. I marvel at the strength of an organism that thrives on sunlight and water alone. Such a peaceful existence."

"I suppose so."

"Life gets very complicated, Mr. Smitherton. We need these plants. They remind us to keep it simple." Dr. Troy turned back. "It's very easy, really. Sun and water, a bit of food. We don't need to make it so hard."

Henry didn't know how to respond. He watched Dr. Feddersen for a cue. Instead, there was silence. It didn't matter to Dr. Troy.

"We will see you then, after your next injection and repair. Here's what we owe you." He reached into his breast pocket and handed Henry an unmarked white envelope. "It's a pleasure working with you, Mr. Smitherton." As abruptly as he entered, he left the room.

"One more thing, Henry," Dr. Feddersen added. "Have you been asked any unusual questions about your treatment?"

"Of course not." Henry fingered his envelope.

"You remember our policy on this. The research would be compromised if we spoke of it to anyone, correct?"

"Yes, I remember."

"How is your daughter—Denise, is it?"

"She's fine." Henry's mouth was suddenly dry.

"And naturally, you're not speaking to our nursing staff about this?"

Henry cleared his throat to find his voice. Shifting in his seat, the leather rubbed against him loudly, almost muffling his word, "No."

"It seems Jonathon Thompson has taken an interest in you. He's a fine young man. But his attention wouldn't include this?" Dr. Feddersen pointed a finger at the envelope.

The envelope slipped from Henry's grasp and fell to the tiles. He wiped his palms on his legs and picked it up. Getting up from the sofa was difficult. "There's no problem. Please. Let's set the date for the next shot."

"No problem at all, Henry. Just wanted to be sure." Dr. Feddersen put a hand on his shoulder. "A week from today?"

Chapter 10

*N*oelle was still in the oversized T-shirt she had slept in, a can of Mountain Dew at her side. She sat on the floor, leaning against the wall beside her pile of chemistry texts, notes, manuals, and a calculator. The algebra was unbearable. Crushing a sheet of notebook paper, she tossed it into a pile of five others.

The phone rang. *C'mon, be him; be him.*

"Hello?"

"Noelle?"

"Jonathon. You must have finally gotten my e-mail." She spoke softly, tired.

"Yesterday was a zoo, Noelle. I didn't get to the library until around noon and was only on for a minute. But yes, I got it. How are you?"

She kicked away the paper wads and stretched out on the floor. "It's tough. I've got a chem test tomorrow morning and English Comp in the afternoon. Bio's on Tuesday and I haven't even started. There's just so much."

"You can do it, Noelle."

She started to respond, but had to stop. Her eyes filled.

"Noelle?"

"Yeah?" It was a weak yes, but it was all she could muster. Tears overflowed.

"I thought maybe we'd gotten cut off."

"I'm here." Her voice cracked. *Now he would know.*

"That stuff you sent me on nanotechnology was pretty incredible. I hadn't heard of it."

She couldn't speak.

"I can't believe they're able to do that. I mean, create microscopic robots all over the place. It sounds like it's really taking off."

"Uh-huh," she mumbled.

That *Wired* magazine article by Bill Joy was amazing. He compares nanotechnology to the development of the atomic bomb. It's scary where this could be heading.

"I'm going to look into it around here, see if that is what this NanoMed place is into. They've got something going at the hospital. Thanks for the info." He paused and she was silent.

She knew she needed to pull it together. Noelle held the phone away from her mouth to hide the next torrent.

"The Wildcats won this past weekend," he continued. "We played Marksville. First win of the season, you know? Kind of reminds me that nothing changes."

Weeping silently, she cradled the phone to her ear but kept the mouthpiece up.

"Hey, Noelle…it's okay."

What does that mean?

"Really, it's okay. You're having a hard time. I can't imagine what it's like for you, all alone, cramming every hour. You probably haven't had a break for weeks, if I know you."

There was a pause, but it didn't seem to faze him.

"So I'll ramble a bit and let you pull yourself together. When you're ready we can talk. Is that okay with you?"

She brought the cradle down to her lips. "Yes," her voice sounded a little more controlled.

"I'm getting ready to head to church in an hour or so. I went to Windwood Community Church last week. It was different, Noelle. You definitely would have hated it. But something about it—I don't know—I want to check into it. I mean, they do all the hand-raising stuff, people crying out, you know. But it seemed more real than I figured it would. There was this lady in a wheelchair, singing a solo. She had an amazing voice, and when she sang, it was weird how all of a sudden the whole church was glued to her. I was too. Mom always told me to stay away from it, but I think I might try it again." He paused. "How are you doing?"

"I'm okay." But she knew she was not very convincing.

"Good. Tell me if I say something I shouldn't."

"Keep it light, Jonathon." She cleared her throat. "So really, you're thinking of going to a new church?"

"I don't know, Noelle. Something was happening there. I want to see what it is. How about you? Are you going to any church?"

"I've looked at some, but haven't found one I want to try yet," she lied.

"You should ask around. See if you could go with someone."

"Maybe. I'll see what I can find. Anyway, glad the nanotech stuff is helpful. What's going on with that?"

"I don't know, Noelle. I think our hospital is working that NanoMed company. No one talks about it, but I saw one of our lab techs giving a patient a shot of medicine labeled with that name. Sad thing, the lab guy wound up dying in a hit-and-run the day after. Kind of shook up the hospital. But still, no one talks about NanoMed."

"Sounds pretty high-tech for our hometown."

"That's why I need to understand it more. Maybe no one's supposed to know. I may be crazy, but it's like I may have stumbled onto something."

"You're dreaming, Jonathon. Wake up."

He made a snoring sound in the phone, and she giggled back.

"So what's the latest in your life?" he asked.

"Nothing much. Today I'm cramming algebra formulas into my head. They're not fitting."

"I'm so glad I'm not there. I hated math. Never did get it. I made it only because of you." He sounded like he meant it.

"I don't believe you."

"I've been praying for you, Noelle. I hope you can see God's working all around you." Jonathon sounded different, serious.

"Sometimes it's hard," she said softly. "I need those…prayers."

"I'm sure." He was silent.

She couldn't speak.

"Well, I guess I better go."

"Thanks," was all that leaked out without a gush of tears.

"I'll call you later. Really, Noelle, it's okay."

There was a long silence before she heard the phone disconnect.

Then the dam burst.

*****

Jonathon laid the phone in the cradle and sat back in his chair. The morning sun beamed across the living room, toasting his legs despite the chilly day outside. His eyes closed. He prayed for her.

Ten minutes later he was interrupted by his mother. "'Bout ready to go?"

"Sure, Mom."

"How's Noelle doin'?"

"How'd you know I called her? I still can't figure out how you do that. Anyway, she's fine, I guess. School sounds tough. She hadn't heard about what happened yesterday. I'm sure glad for that."

"She's pretty hard on you with your sparklin', eh?"

"She doesn't like it, that's for sure. Doesn't believe in it."

They both headed out to the car and drove to church.

"Mom, someone at the hospital asked me to heal them. It's the mayor."

"Has God told you to do it?"

"I don't know. I'm not sure I'm hearing Him so well."

"Better not sparkle on anybody unless He's told ya. That part seems perty clear."

Church was the usual routine. The Wittenburgs still sat on the other side, but they waved hello. That seemed to help Elaine.

Jonathon's mind was elsewhere. Everyone, everything, was so mechanical. The hymns were dry, effortless. The scripture recitation, this week read by Marvel Woodruff, was rote and without feeling. Bullet crawled over the pew and, despite Jonathon trying to catch him, banged his head loudly. The cries that followed made Marvel race to the end of the passage. She slammed the pulpit Bible and stepped down, grabbing Bullet and comforting him gently while the whole congregation watched. Happened every time she was the reader.

At the Country Inn after church, Jonathon asked his mother, "How was church for you?"

"Fine." She rhythmically chewed her steak.

"I was surprised no one asked me about the Harris girl. Do you think they know?"

"Oh, they know alright. They all knew about Wittenburg's healin'. This falls right in line."

He put his fork down. "They'll never talk to us about it, will they?"

"Nope," she chewed on.

"They don't believe in it."

77

"Yup."

"The hospital gang all talks to me about it. More than I wish. What's the difference?"

"It's personal at church. Too personal."

"Mom, it's not right. You and I both need some support here. Is this God's work or not?"

"Sure is, Jonathon. Don't ever think otherwise."

"So why can't our church be there for us?"

"It's not the church you need. You'll be fine."

He picked up his fork and tried to eat a few bites in silence. Then he asked, "What'd you think of the sermon?"

"Good today."

"What do you think it was about?"

"God's love." She stuck a spoonful of peas in her mouth.

"I thought so too. Isn't that what last week's was on?"

She looked up and winked at Jonathon. "Sure was. Now you got it."

"But, Mom, he can't keep preaching the same thing each week."

"He'll preach it if we're needin' to hear it." She went back to slicing her chicken-fried steak.

"But it's the same thing each week. Don't you want to hear something fresh?"

"What's fresher than God's love?" She took a sip of coffee and stared at her son.

"You know, Mom, I just want to hear something new, challenging." She stared at him even longer. Then she went back to her steak, mumbling, "It's that other church. They got to ya."

He stopped there. This wasn't going anywhere.

*****

That afternoon when he entered the hospital nurses' lounge for his shift, he found an envelope stuck to his locker. It was hospital stationery with his name hand written across it.

Inside he found a short note from Dr. Martin Feddersen himself. It asked him to come directly to his office.

Again.

It was Sunday. Dr. Feddersen didn't work Sundays.

78

Jonathon wandered through the darkened administrative cubicles to Dr. Feddersen's office, the door being just ajar. Knocking on the door opened it farther, and he was immediately greeted.

"Jonathon, good to see you again," Dr. Feddersen's voice hung in the air with anticipation. His usual smile was there, and the handshake was warm and firm. He grabbed Jonathon's shoulder kindly, welcoming him into the plush office again.

"You're the local hero, Jonathon, and I wanted to personally thank you. I heard about how you helped the young girl downtown yesterday, and frankly it was amazing. You must be very excited."

"Uh, yeah, but it wasn't that big of a deal."

"Oh, but that's not true, Jonathon. You healed someone. By prayer. I just want you to know, I believe you did it."

"You do?"

"Definitely. I find it fascinating. Tell me more, Jonathon. Do you heal people often?" He motioned for Jonathon to sit and moved around the desk to his own chair.

Jonathon sighed. "I don't do the healing, Dr. Feddersen. I just pray when God leads. He's the one who heals."

"But of course. It's God's work. But He's chosen you, Jonathon, to be his tool. How long have you known about this—gift?"

Trying to make sense of the conversation, Jonathon answered reluctantly. "Since I was young. Do you know much about healing, I mean miraculous healing?"

"As a matter of fact, I do. That's why I'm so interested in you. I do some consulting with a research firm. They're perfecting technology to allow us to heal and prevent disease. Maybe you've heard of it—NanoMed."

"I know the name. I don't know much about it though."

"Let me give you a short lesson. We actually have much in common, Jonathon." He stood and came around his desk, sitting on its edge, directly in front of him.

"Nanotechnology is the concept of building things from the smallest of particles, the atom. A nanometer is one billionth of a meter. That's one thousand million times smaller than a meter, about three to four atoms wide." Dr. Feddersen held up his pinched thumb and finger, leaving no space in between. "We can now engineer microscopic tools that work at this level. We can actually build molecules from atoms. It's free and the resources—atoms—

are always available, mostly from the palm of our hand. You see, we can virtually build anything from scratch." Dr. Feddersen stood and walked to a bookcase.

"So NanoMed is building computerized robots," Dr. Feddersen continued. "Robots so small they fit on the point of a pin. These robots can be placed in a person's body, and they can be programmed to search out any infection, diseased organ, or cancer. The robots, at a molecular level, can fix the organ, kill the bacteria, or eliminate cancer cells. It's healing."

"Have you seen it done?" Jonathon asked.

"I have. It's amazing. And it is here, Jonathon."

"That's great, Dr. Feddersen. But what's it got to do with me?"

"You see, Jonathon, we're both healers. You do it one way, and NanoMed does it another. We'd like to learn from you," he turned from his books and eyed Jonathon directly. "Perhaps there is a relationship between our forms of healing. You're able to cause the body to use this same technology in a natural way, by your own means of healing. You have much to teach us."

"Thanks, really. But I don't think there could be anything in what I do that you—"

"Not true, Jonathon. We've already seen it. In Henry Smitherton. You prayed for him, am I correct?"

"I pray for a lot of people—all the time." Jonathon felt sweat forming under his arms.

"Mr. Smitherton, you see, is in our study. We saw physical evidence of your prayer working. We measured it."

"I don't understand."

"It's simple really, but it's part of an incredibly complex system. We were monitoring Mr. Smitherton, observing the potential of nanotechnology to work in his body. NanoMed watches its clients very closely. We can relate the time you prayed for Mr. Smitherton specifically to when his body demonstrated molecular changes in his blood cells that corrected themselves—and he was healed. You knew you healed him, didn't you?"

"Well, I wondered. But it didn't seem like it was me."

"You see, it wasn't. You merely activated his own body's natural healing properties. You call it God's work, and it certainly is. It happens all the time, we're sure of that. But we are actually able to document it. Truly, we're on the brink of a major landmark in medicine. The cure for cancer, healing any disease. No birth defects. The prevention of aging. And you're the key, Jonathon. You're the key."

Jonathon felt himself melting into the leather around him. "I still don't know about this. What are you wanting from me? Where is this heading?"

"We want you to heal Mayor Horton."

Chapter 11

"*W*hat?" Jonathon leaned up in his chair, pulling his glasses from his face.

"Mayor Horton has asked you to pray for his healing. We'd like you to do so. Confidentially, of course. We're not here to make a scene, Jonathon. We're here to learn. You can be our teacher."

"I can't believe this." He rubbed his glass lenses against his white smock.

"Here's what I suggest, Jonathon. We have monitored Mayor Horton's condition carefully. You just do your prayer. We don't even need to be present. No one needs to know. But afterward, we will trace his healing, document every molecular change. It's the first case of its kind. And it will happen right here in Windwood."

Standing, Jonathon replaced his glasses and walked away from Feddersen to a second bookcase on the opposite wall. His eyes glanced at titles, including telephone book-sized medical texts, multiple-volume clinical studies, and in the midst of them, a smaller book with the spine reading, "Holy Bible."

"So you think we can prove a healing?"

"Undoubtedly." Dr. Feddersen stood back at his desk and crossed his arms. "I know it's not important to you, Jonathon, but you should realize if this is successful, it could be life-changing. You would be highly sought after, a celebrity of sorts. I just want you to count the costs carefully."

"But we would prove that God's healing is true." The con was obvious, but something was pinching Jonathon's confidence.

Could this prove God is a healer? Could this bring Him glory on a huge scale? And Noelle—she'd finally have to believe me.

"I'm not in this for fame, Dr. Feddersen. But I'll pray for Mayor Horton if God leads me. That's the best I can do."

"You just think about it, Jonathon. It doesn't matter when you do it. We'll keep NanoMed out of it, completely confidential. There's no reason to mention them until they have something to offer."

*****

Jonathon walked down the hospital hall to room 117. Starting to enter the room, Nurse Chandler's bark sounded behind him. "Jonathon!"

"Yes, Martha?"

"What's going on? Why were you so late? You missed report."

"I had a meeting, sorry. I'll get caught up, don't worry. I promised the Hortons I would see them first thing today. As soon as I'm done here, I'll go over the rest of my patients."

"Socializing comes after work, Jonathon. This doesn't have anything to do with our talk yesterday, does it? I heard the Hortons asked you about healings."

"Yes, they asked me. I'm going in right now to settle it so it doesn't interfere with the rest of the day. Don't worry, I won't be long."

"Are you going to pray?"

"Always, Martha, always. I just promised I'd talk to them first thing today. I feel like I have to keep my promise. Please just give me a couple of minutes."

"Okay." She was reticent, but she had no argument. "Just get to work as quickly as you can, we've got a houseful today." She moved on down the hall, checking off details on her clipboard.

He knocked twice and entered the room.

"Good afternoon, Mr. Horton, Mrs. Horton."

Royce Horton was reclined, the Sunday newspaper scattered across his bed. Mrs. Horton sat at his side, nicely preened in a dark blue dress with a silver broach shaped like a small dove over her chest. Her eyes betrayed her fatigue.

"We're so glad to see you again," she replied.

"How are you feeling today, Mayor?"

"I guess I'm still getting better, except for the..." He hesitated, unable to say the word.

"It's hard, isn't it? You want to feel better, but all you can think of is your diagnosis," Jonathon responded.

"So will you help us, Jonathon? Will you pray for my husband's healing?"

"Willa, now let's not pressure the boy," Mayor Horton piped in. "It's completely up to him. We're just ready and willing."

"Good news for you both. I do wish to pray for your healing, Mayor Horton. If it's still acceptable with you, I believe God is leading. Let's just be sure He receives the glory."

"Thank you so much!" Willa grabbed Jonathon's hand, massaging more than shaking it. "This is such a special moment. We've prayed for you all night long."

"Let's bow, shall we? I'll just place my hand on your shoulder, Mr. Horton." He reached out to rest a hand while Mrs. Horton came around to the other side of the bed and gingerly followed suit.

"Lord, we bring Your servant here to seek Your touch in his life. You know his cancer, Lord, and I ask that You heal him now, in the name of Jesus Christ. That all the cancer may be cleared and you receive the highest praise."

Jonathon waited for the tingling to begin.

"May You move in Your perfect way, Lord, that Mayor Horton may know that his body has been cleansed by You. Cancer takes life, but You're the Life-giver, and we trust You to be able to heal."

No burning, no shivers. Jonathon didn't feel anything—except suddenly a little sheepish. Grasping the mayor's shoulder more tightly he continued. Willa grabbed the opposite shoulder just as firmly.

"Please answer our prayer, Lord. We desire to only be Your faithful servants, and we know that You promise to be in our midst when even two or three gather in Your name. Lord, Your love knows no boundaries, so we ask that Your loving, healing touch save Mayor Horton. And we pledge to be sure You receive the glory."

Still nothing. Jonathon cleared his throat and fumbled for words. "We ask this in Your holy name. Amen."

Willa sighed, "Amen," and reached immediately for a tissue. Mayor Horton's eyes were also full.

"Thank you so much," the mayor whispered in a tearful voice.

"It's fine. Remember, it's the Lord who heals." Jonathon looked at his palms and rubbed them together. No tingling. He wanted out of the room.

The mayor hesitated. "I guess now we wait?"

"Yes, just keep up with your doctor. He'll be ordering some tests, I'm sure. That should show something."

"Yes, of course. Thank you, Jonathon. You don't know how much this means."

Willa gained her composure. "Do you think—I don't know how to ask this but do you think it worked?"

"Let's just trust God, Mrs. Horton." He sniffed the air, only smelling stale Avon and bathroom deodorizer. "His timing is always perfect, right? But I gotta go."

A thud sounded behind them and the door burst open. A dozen people rushed in with Carmen, the ward clerk, at the lead. Before John could say a word, a photographer snapped two pictures.

"You did it, didn't you, Jonathon? You healed the mayor!" Carmen shouted.

"What's going on?" Jonathon exclaimed. He eyed Nurse Chandler in the hall, peering in. "Listen, I've got to go to work," he fumed. "You all talk to the mayor if you want. I can't believe this is happening!" He forced his way through the nurses, aides, and lab people. Once in the hall, he saw Dr. Feddersen with a lab technologist at his side and went straight to them.

"Did you do this?" Jonathon rattled.

"Absolutely not. I guess word got around. I'm not surprised. Everyone's expecting big things from you, Jonathon. Don't worry about it. Were you able to pray?"

"Yes. But it's God. It's not me. Let's keep that clear."

"Of course." Dr. Feddersen nodded to the lab tech. "Okay, Ted. Draw two red top tubes and send them in immediately." He turned to Jonathon. "We'll be drawing blood samples hourly, checking for a drop in the antigen released by the prostate cancer. Let's see if we can place a miracle in the history books." As Ted walked to Mayor Horton's room, Dr. Feddersen whispered to Jonathon, "Just remember, let's keep NanoMed out of this for now. The press could make a mess if they thought it was the work of man. Let's keep it in God's hands."

"Just what kind of secret are we keeping?" Jonathon walked down the hall before Dr. Feddersen could respond.

Throughout the rest of the shift, Jonathon had to put up with back slaps and winks as the whole hospital knew the mayor was going to be healed. A couple of people approached him about praying for a relative. He responded the first of several times saying he would only do what God wanted, and that he would pray about it. Nurse Chandler approached him later, and after he assured her he was caught up in his work, she asked him not to plan any further healings on work time. Then she smiled.

He was thankful; it gave him an excuse for other patients. It was a running joke. The guy in room 108 asked him to put a hand on his abdomen. He'd just had his gall bladder removed, but wanted to be sure it was done right. The obstetrics patient in 125 asked him to pray for their new baby, that he would sleep through the nights. Jonathon smirked to both of them, "Sorry, can't do it on work time."

When he entered Mayor Horton's room later in the day, the Hortons smiled at him as if they were long-lost friends. After chatting about family, they offered to fix Jonathon up with their niece in Rollings. At each visit later in the day they were overly gracious in thanking him. He reminded them again and again who the Healer was.

Seeking Dr. Feddersen later in the day, he found his office closed and dark.

Toward the end of his shift, Jonathon was in with Mrs. Knudson, a docile but incoherent elderly patient with Alzheimer's disease, changing her adult diaper. The local evening news out of Rollings played on the television in the background and was easily ignored, until Jonathon heard, "Next up, a young man in Windwood saves the life of a little girl. It's a miracle, but he says it happens all the time. Stay tuned."

During the commercial break he hurriedly finished cleaning her. "Watch this, Mrs. Knudson, you won't believe it. I don't believe it." She stared blankly over his head. After pulling her sheets up around her, he stepped away to close the door and returned to sit on the edge of her bed.

The news program began with a shot of Samantha Harris and her mom in front of the Dress Barn. Mrs. Harris told the story, complete with tears and a big hug for Sammy. Next flashed a high school graduation shot of Jonathon; he'd forgotten how gauche he appeared then. A picture of their small, white ranch house in town followed.

"Jonathon and his mother, Mrs. Elaine Thompson, live a simple life in Windwood. Mrs. Thompson told us that Jonathon was not available for comment, and refused to go on camera herself." Next was a shot of their church and a brief word of how the pastor was also unavailable.

"But we did speak with Mr. Thompson's work supervisor, Martha Chandler, Department Head of Nursing at Windwood Community Hospital."

Nurse Chandler's head filled the screen, and she spoke with authority. "Jonathon has always been a faithful employee. He's a humble man, shy. But he told me he prays like this all the time."

Jonathon responded to the TV, "Hey, thanks, Martha. You really do like me."

Mrs. Knudson sighed blindly.

The show returned to the two anchors who smiled politely and with raised eyebrows made light comments about how the Windwood hospital may soon be expecting more patients. Without dropping a beat, they moved on to recap the weather for the upcoming Thanksgiving week.

"So what do you think, Mrs. Knudson? Am I a healer?"

Another heavy sigh came from her drug-induced sleep.

"Am I a healer?" he asked God quietly. "Did I heal Mayor Horton? God, I'm not sure." He reached out and wrapped his fingers around Mrs. Knudson's warm, limp hand. "Should I heal this woman, Lord?"

No burning, no tingle.

"Okay. I won't."

He left her room, feeling the same as after he had prayed for Mayor Horton. No spine shivers, no warmth in his chest, no smell of lilacs. "Did I do the right thing, God?" he prayed. "This could all backfire on both of us."

Entering the hall, Carmen and two nurses down the hall applauded. "Did you see it?" she asked.

He smiled obligingly. "Yes."

Nurse Chandler spoke from the other side of the hall. "You owe me, Thompson."

"Don't I always?" He quickly went into the linens room.

Chapter 12

*W*hen Jonathon sneaked through the door of his home it was almost one o'clock in the morning. The lights were off, and her dark form slowly rocked in the living room chair.

"Did you see the news, Mom?"

"Sure."

"Hope they didn't hassle you too much." He walked over and patted her hand before sitting on the floor beside her.

She kept rocking. "They were decent folks. It's the newspaper I got mad at."

"What do you mean?"

"They kept calling, only wanting you. Snooty folks. I finally laid into them."

"Oh no, Mom."

"They got no bizwax treatin' me like that." She rocked faster.

"You're right. Maybe they'll just drop the whole story. There's got to be other news."

"Some guy called you. Wants you to call him back. His number's on the fridge. Name was Camelson." Her chair moved even faster. "He said he was from that church."

"Thanks, Mom." He reached for her hand again. "It's nothing for you to worry about."

"They're sinking teeth into you, son. And you're lettin' 'em chew."

"No, Mom. I'm just talking to somebody who goes to a different church than us. Don't go reading a lot into this."

"I can't read much, but this one isn't hard to figure. They gotcha, Jonathon. Either back away, or they'll suck ya right in. I seen it before."

"Okay, Mom. I'll be careful." He squeezed her hand and stretched out on the floor on his back, hands behind his head.

"Are ya gonna call him?" The rocker started to slow a bit.

"Maybe." He dodged her. "I've got to tell you something else."

"You sparkled tonight?"

"Yeah. The mayor. It just seemed right."

She stopped rocking. "Did ya know for sure?"

"That's been harder lately, Mom." He sat up and crossed his knees. "I think I may be growing out of the feelings I get in my back. Maybe God wants me to use my own common sense. Kind of like He's testing my faith."

"Seems like He'd still make ya tingle if He wanted to."

"Maybe. Anyway, this one might get some news too." He tried to soften what he knew would be an inevitable storm.

They both sat in the darkness. She started rocking slowly again.

"Are we ready for this, Mom?"

"You can handle it. Your Aunt Emma knew ya could." The quiet surrounded them. "I just wish your father was here."

"You miss him?"

"You're like him, Jonathon. More'n ya know."

They had come this far before. He'd always wanted to ask. "Do you ever think of looking for him, Mom?"

"Never." She stopped rocking. "Better go to bed."

"You or me? I've got tomorrow off."

"Okay, me then. I open the store in the morning. Gotta go in early."

"Night, Mom. You're the best."

"That's right, son."

*****

The next morning Jonathon was up at the library first thing. The sky was overcast, a hint of snow in the air. Brown construction paper handprints with colored fingers adorned the library windows, making a line of Thanksgiving turkeys from the local grade school. He popped on the e-mail and sent Noelle a note of congrats for making it through her biology and English tests. Worried about what she would do when she heard of the healings, he wrestled whether to tell her. He started several sentences but kept deleting them.

"How's my favorite bidder?" Mrs. Davis came up behind him.

"Hi, Mrs. Davis. Did you get your teacup yet?"

"Should be in the mail today, hopefully. Jonathon, why don't you call me Grandma Davis. That 'Mrs.' sounds so stuffy."

"I'll do that. I need a grandma, anyway."

Grandma Davis rested a hand on his shoulder. "I heard about you helping someone downtown, is that so?"

"Uh, yes. I think so. You mean the Harris girl?" He turned his head to look at her.

"So, you're a praying boy?" Her voice warbled, but her blue eyes were bolted to his.

"As much as I can. It's God who answers though. We just need to be asking."

"Well said, well said." She rubbed his shoulder kindly. "But we've got to be careful…when we have powerful gifts."

Grandma Davis released her hand and suddenly Jonathon felt a chill.

"There's much required of those who have been given much. If I can dabble in being a grandmother to you, I just want to warn you, help you."

Shivering with his first word, Jonathon mumbled, "What are you saying?"

Her eyes were steel blue marbles that locked onto his like magnets. "You're facing trouble, Jonathon. You need the Word in your heart. Get back to the Word."

"Okay. Thanks." He couldn't move away from her. Then she shifted her gaze and glanced at his e-mail. Her hand was back on his shoulder, and warmth fell across his back again. He didn't want her to leave.

"So you must have a pretty good friend there," she remarked.

He felt dazed. "Yeah, she's had a hard weekend. I just thought I'd encourage her a bit." Despite the awkwardness, he had to ask. "Grandma Davis, do you ever feel something inside, like when you know you need to do something?"

"All the time. That's how I know it's right. With me it's my knees. Doctor says it's arthritis. But they tingle." Her voice softened as if she was saying it to herself. "Like they did just now talking to you."

"Tingle?"

"You've got to be sure—right, Jonathon? It's not a guessing game. Anyway, great to see you again. I've got to put these books back." She walked away in a spry step. Wanting to call her back, he found nothing more to say. She glanced over her shoulder at him once, her sapphire eyes twinkling with a smile before she disappeared down a row of shelves.

Sitting back, he stared at his computer screen. Words wouldn't come. He left the message as it was, added a quick goodbye, and signed off.

He stood and scanned the room. There was only one other gentleman in the library that he could see. The man stood from his seat near the front door and donned an olive green trench coat. It was the mysterious man from Pritchett's Drug Store. The man looked across the room and nodded to Jonathon with a smile, then moved quickly to the exit.

"Hey, wait!" Jonathon called out, but the man was already pushing open the door.

Jonathon grabbed his coat and raced between tables to the library exit. Outside, the cold air turned to miniature white clouds at his lips as he exhaled. He looked up the street toward the Dress Barn. Nobody. In the opposite direction, there the man was, just turning the corner of the next block. Jonathon called again, but the man was out of view behind the real estate office building.

Breaking into a jog, Jonathon chased him along the empty sidewalk. Downtown was quiet this early on a Monday morning; he could catch him in less than a minute. Sprinting, he approached the corner and slowed to make the turn, then stopped. Both sides of the street were empty. He ran down past the real estate office to the next business, Friendly Dentistry. Poking his head in the front door, the smell of strong antiseptic greeted him. The small waiting room seated three ladies, but not his friend. The next office was the Windwood National Bank, not open until ten o'clock. Panting in the chilly air, he peered down an alley at the far side of the bank, but there was no way the guy could have gotten that far. Across the street was Jones' Barber Shop, always closed on Mondays, and beside it stood a vacant storefront of an old JC Penney's store.

No one was in sight.

He walked back to the real estate office, although he was sure he would have seen someone enter. Cracking the door, he found a receptionist at a desk talking with a man in a tan short jacket. His hair was black, not bronze.

Jonathon interrupted in his own frustration. "Excuse me, by any chance did a guy in a green trench coat step in here?"

The man at the desk turned around, and Jonathon recognized John Camelson.

"Hello, Jonathon." He smiled and looked around. "No, haven't seen anyone here."

"Okay, thanks." Jonathon stepped back out and waited at the corner, catching his breath and thinking through his confusion.

Where'd the guy go?

Mr. Camelson came out right behind him. "Did you lose somebody?"
"I guess so. I could have sworn he walked right down this street."
"Who was it—a friend?" John asked kindly.
"I don't know him really, but he was the one who led me to that girl, Samantha Harris. I suppose you heard about that."
John nodded his head. "Hasn't everyone?" He grinned warmly. "I tried to call you yesterday, just to see how it was going. Did your mom tell you?"
"She did. I was going to call you today. Things have been a little busy, you know."
He laughed. "I'm sure. Anyway, have you got time to visit now?"
"I don't know. Maybe I should try to find that guy, but he's probably long gone by now. So, yeah, why not? Where do you want to go?"
"How about the Coffee Corner? Can I buy you a cup?"
"Sure."

*****

Noelle stewed over her final midterm exam in English Comprehension. *Who cares about predicate nominatives and nonessential appositives? I thought I was done with this stuff in high school.*

She corrected the sentence structure in her last three problems and assembled the test and answer sheet together. Inside, she wanted to scream for joy.

Leaving the test room, she raced for the door of the Humanities Building. Outside, breathing in the brisk sunny air, she smelled the frosted decaying leaves welcoming her first sense of freedom. For the next whole week, she had no classes or assignments. She was done. And she did scream.

It felt good.

She ran down the steps of the archaic university building to get back to her apartment two blocks away. A quick pack of dirty laundry into a duffle and she would be on I-70, back toward home. She flicked on her computer to send a quick e-mail to her folks. They wanted to know what time she was leaving. She could see her bedroom at home now and was ready to jump into fresh sheets, bundling up with her grandmother's lavender patchwork quilt. Poppyseed bread would be freshly baked and sliced, laying out in the kitchen. Her mom and dad would wrap her in their arms and listen carefully through every story she had to tell.

It felt good.

A knock sounded at her door. She put her eye to the peephole and saw Dave.

Placing the chain lock, she allowed the door to open two inches.

"Yes?"

"Noelle, I wanted to see you before you left."

"Look, Dave. I'm in a big hurry—"

"No, really. We gotta talk this out. Can I come in?"

"I don't think that'd be a good idea. I got to go." She closed the door.

"Noelle, c'mon. I'm just going to say it—I'm sorry. Sorry for what I've done. It was all my fault."

Noelle stood with her back to the door. All she wanted was to go home.

"I think you're special, Noelle. I want to see if we can make it work. Just tell me. Can we try?"

She took a deep breath and let it go. "We're too different, Dave. I think you'd best go." *Too different. That's what I'd always say about Jonathon.*

"Is there somebody else? Is that it?"

"No."

"Then what, Noelle? I think about you all the time. Can't you give us a chance?"

His voice was muffled by her thoughts. She walked away from the door, the computer beckoning her. Clicking "send" on her computer, her e-mail to her parents left the screen. In its place a bold line showed she had a message.

From Jonathon.

It was just a short note encouraging her in her tests. He was praying for her.

She heard pounding at her door again.

"Noelle, answer me!" Dave shouted. "Don't let me down like this. If there's no else, let's see about us. What have you got to lose?"

She walked back to the door and cracked it open.

"Dave, there's someone else." She closed the door.

There was no sound outside. She peeked through the hole and saw him standing there, head down.

"I'm going home to see him, Dave. It just won't work."

She watched him meander away, down the hall to the stairs.

There, that wasn't so bad.

She went back to her duffle and stuffed it full. Turning off her computer, she grabbed her keys and headed for the door.

It felt good.

Yes, there is someone else.

Chapter 13

"**I**'ve been looking forward to the chance to talk with you," John Camelson began after they sat down in one of the vinyl red booths of the Coffee Corner. Ten or so men with seed corn caps were seated around the center table of the restaurant, mostly retirees who started their day here. Jonathon felt out of place with the age of everyone else in the room, but John put him at ease.

"They're going to stare at you for a while. They're not used to such young bucks like us." John broke out a smile.

Jonathon grinned back. "I was wondering if they were staring at me because of what happened to the Harris girl." He took a bite of a cherry turnover.

"I suppose that may be a part of it too. It's certainly something we're not used to in Windwood."

"Isn't that the truth."

"Jonathon, that's one of the things I wanted to talk about with you. Do you mind if I ask you a couple questions about the healing?"

"Join the crowd."

"Do you have the spiritual gift of healing?"

He set his turnover down and held his mug filled with hot chocolate. "Nobody's quite asked it that way before." He avoided John's eyes. "Yes, I believe I do."

Leaning forward, John lightly grasped Jonathon's forearm. "I believe you, Jonathon."

Jonathon raised his eyes, finding acceptance and understanding. "So you believe in healing?"

"Without a doubt. There's a lot of things I believe now that I used to question. Healing's one of them. You know, it's all over the Bible. Unless God changed the rules, I think we have to believe in healing."

"Do you have the gift?"

John laughed. "Healing? Oh no, not me. That I know for sure. I can tell you that I do have the gift of mercy, though. And I wonder if I might have the gift of prophecy."

"Whoa. What's that all about?"

"The spiritual gifts, you know, out of Ephesians and Corinthians. I've been studying them. Actually, our whole church is learning about them together. We've been praying, Jonathon. Praying that God will show us that His gifts are for today. We've seen Him answer us in wonderful ways. Many people in our church are discovering gifts that they never knew they had. Like teaching, hospitality, giving, wisdom. But quite honestly, we've been stuck on that one gift—the gift of healing. We've seen evidence of every other one, plus some others that the Bible doesn't mention. But healing, that's been a tough one for us. So we've been praying—the whole church—that God would teach us about the gift of healing.

"And now I show up."

"Exactly."

John took a swallow of coffee. Jonathon took a bite of turnover and looked over at the center table. Immediately, three heads who had been staring at him quickly turned away.

"Haven't they ever seen a guy eat a turnover before?"

"It's the price of fame, Jonathon."

That made Jonathon choke on his turnover. He grabbed a swig of hot chocolate and asked another question. "So, you think you might be a prophet?"

"I can't say that quite yet. You'd have to define what you mean by 'prophet.' I can tell you about a dream I had that came true. And when I lead worship, I think sometimes the Lord fills me with a sense of what we should sing, or what should be said. Is that a prophet? I'm not sure."

"Do you always know what God wants you to do?"

"Far from it. That's why it's hard. Many people think you've got to be one hundred percent right on prophesying or it can't be from God. Well then, I fail that test miserably. But there are times when I know without a doubt what God is doing."

Jonathon glanced over as the door to the restaurant opened. Henry Smitherton walked in and stood at the seed corn table, greeting his fellow retirees. As he reached for a chair from a nearby table, Jonathon caught his eye, offering him a nod. Mr. Smitherton's face turned to surprise, and he gave

Jonathon an awkward nod back. He let go of the chair behind him and said a few words to his buddies before leaving again.

"That's weird." Jonathon murmured.

"What?"

"That guy who just came in. I know him from the hospital. Actually, I prayed for him about a week ago, and he was healed. Pretty sick guy. Anyway, he saw me here and took off."

"Are you sure?"

"I think so."

John sat back in his booth. "People have a hard time with these gifts."

Jonathon nodded, finishing his hot chocolate. "I've got to tell you something. When I was at your church, I was really impressed with your wife and her singing."

"Thanks. We wonder how to classify that as a spiritual gift. God is really using her."

"But more than that. I think God may have been wanting me to pray for her. To heal her."

John slowly brought his coffee cup down to the table. Jonathon maintained a lock on his eyes, then looked away at the group in the middle. "'People have a hard time with these gifts.'"

"Jonathon, are you serious? Do you think God has told you to pray for my wife's healing?"

"I think so. How sure do you need me to be? I'm like you, I don't always know."

John fingered his cup. "Let me talk to her. We need to get together with her. But, if you're serious, Jonathon, we'll want to consider it with you."

"Great. Just let me know."

"By the way, what church do you go to?"

"First Congregational. It's my mom's church."

"Do they support your healing gift?"

"Not exactly. It's not where they're at, you know what I mean?"

"Yeah. What's your mom think? Does she know?"

"She's great. She's taught me all I know about healing. She's pretty careful about it, but she keeps me in line." He grinned at John and received back a knowing smile.

"I gotta go, Jonathon, but it's been great to visit with you. How about I'll call you after I've talked with Melinda. We'll get together again."

"Sure. Thanks for the hot chocolate; it's great to talk about this stuff with somebody who understands."

They stood to leave, and both of them felt the eyes of the center table follow them out the door.

*****

Dr. Jack Mittlestedt was enraged. "What's going on at this hospital? We struggle enough to keep up with current medical technology, but now we offer alternative healings?" He banged his stack of charts on the nurses' desk. "Does Feddersen know about this?"

Martha Chandler spoke with her own authority, indifferent to another doctor tantrum. "Dr. Feddersen was here when Thompson prayed for Mayor Horton. That's all that happened. We didn't know it was against hospital policy to pray for your patients, Dr. Mittlestedt."

"It's more than that, Chandler. You know what I mean." Starting down the hall to make morning rounds, he checked himself and doubled back, exclaiming to anyone who'd listen, or even if they wouldn't. "What am I suppose to do now? Just sit on his cancer and wait for him to be healed? C'mon people, you know better than that."

Grabbing his charts again, he headed to room 117. Upon entering the room, he changed his demeanor, albeit only slightly. Drawing the short straw, Martha followed him in.

"Good morning, Mayor. I heard you had a little extra help in here yesterday."

Mayor Horton was just finishing breakfast. "Uh, yes. I guess you heard. I hope that was okay with you."

"Not exactly, Royce." He sat down at the foot of the hospital bed. "It makes it a little difficult for me to know what you want me to do." Opening the chart, he feigned looking over some lab work while trying to control his anger. "As we had already discussed, I was planning to have you see the oncologist, and we had you down for an orchiectomy next week. I'm wondering what you wanted me to do about all that?" Only after he finished his words did he look up at the mayor.

"Well, I don't know. Isn't there something you can do to check to see how I am? I mean, Jonathon said you'd do some test to check on the cancer."

"Oh, I see." Dr. Mittlestedt slammed the chart closed, fiercely passing it to Nurse Chandler. "So the aide is telling you how I should treat my patients?"

Standing, he moved to the head of the bed, brandishing his stethoscope and briefly placing it over two spots on the mayor's chest before ripping the ear pieces off his head and throwing the tubing over his neck.

Both Mayor Horton and Nurse Chandler were speechless.

"Let's order a PSA for today and schedule him for a second cystoscopy." He spoke harshly but controlled. "I doubt if your insurance will pay for these extra tests, Royce. The hospital will have you sign a form that you're willing to pay for this on your own. Agreed?"

Royce nodded quickly. "Of course. Whatever you say."

"Keep your appointment with the oncologist. You need his counsel here. I'm not going to tell him about this prayer thing. You tell him about it."

"That sounds good, Dr. Mittlestedt. Really, I appreciate all that you're doing."

Dr. Mittlestedt ignored the compliment. Snatching the chart from Nurse Chandler again, he murmured through his teeth, "I'm going straight to Feddersen about this."

Martha followed him out of the room after offering a weak smile to the mayor. As soon as they were in the hall, she unloaded.

"I don't care who you think you are, Dr. Mittlestedt. You cannot treat patients like that."

Dr. Mittlestedt turned, his face florid. "How dare you!"

She moved beside him against the wall and lowered her voice for only him to hear. "No, how dare you, Jack. How dare you talk to me or Mayor Horton as if the world revolves around your little pill bottles. I don't care what your religious preference may be, you've got to allow someone to believe they could be healed. Do you think you're so almighty that God can't make someone better without your permission?"

He started to move down the hall. Martha stepped forward to follow him and he spun around, scowling. "Don't. I don't need anymore from you." He bustled down the hall.

She stood alone, standing firm but shaking like a leaf.

*****

The Windwood *Herald Press* came out by mid-afternoon each weekday. As a twenty-page newspaper, it was mostly filled with national headlines copied from *USA Today* and high school sports from around the area. The Letters to the Editor section was widely read, as was the senior citizens' column. The middle pages covered weddings, anniversary receptions, obituaries, Elks, Optimists and Rotary meetings, and school lunch announcements. The back page was reserved for the legal report, usually listing nuisance police calls and divorce announcements.

But today the newspaper had a new cover story, following the headlines: "Mayor Horton Receives Healer's Touch." The front page photo showed Jonathon Thompson with his mouth wide open and his hands reaching out. Behind him was an obviously tearful Mayor Horton hugged by his equally weepy wife.

"Windwood Mayor Royce Horton received a prayer for healing yesterday at Windwood Community Hospital by Jonathon Thompson, a nurse's aide. Immediately following the prayer, Mayor Horton remarked, 'I think it worked.' Thompson was recently credited with the miraculous healing of Samantha Harris, daughter of Dorothy and the late Ben Harris, from a life-threatening asthma attack.

"Mayor Horton was admitted to the hospital last Monday for a biopsy after tests revealed an abnormal mass on his prostate gland. The pathology results returned with a diagnosis of a deadly form of cancer. That's when the mayor decided to ask Jonathon Thompson for healing."

*****

Jonathon spent the rest of the day at the library. He began a computer search of nanotechnology and time escaped as he delved deep into the plethora of sites, both real and contrived. Beside him at a separate computer was the young teen, Joey, who was working last weekend when he couldn't get online. Jonathon showed him a few lead articles on the topic, and Joey took the challenge to help him find more.

"Here's one on K. Eric Drexler," Joey offered.

"That's the guy, bro. Some call him the father of nanogeeks. Print it."

"Here's a site at nano-dot-gov. It's called the 'National Nanotechnology Initiative.'" Joey whistled and Jonathon leaned over to look at his screen. "The government is funding nanotech research at the Department of Defense and through the National Science Foundation. Money's also going to the Department of Energy, NASA, and the National Institutes of Health. This is all over the place, Jonathon."

"And no one seems to know anything about it. Right."

"Says here the president's budget includes a $225 million increase in the federal government's investment in nanotechnology research and development. Says it doubles what was spent last year."

"Good find, Joey. Print it all."

Jonathon left about eight o'clock in the evening after Joey helped him load a pile of print-outs into the back of his car.

When he got home, his mother immediately showed him the Herald Press article. It was actually a fair piece. Jonathon just wished he would know if it were true. Was Mayor Horton healed?

Over chicken and noodles, Jonathon tried to visit with his mom about her day at the store, but often they both fell silent. She didn't ask, and he was thankful to not have to explain anything about Horton or his day. She'd flip if he told her about meeting with Mr. Camelson, and she would just plain not understand nanotechnology. He wasn't sure how much of it was sinking in with him. The phone rang three times that evening, but each time Elaine shouted for him to just let it ring.

It was ten o'clock when the doorbell rang. Elaine was in her nightgown and insisted Jonathon ignore it. After missing whatever phone calls had come, he couldn't help but check. Turning the outside light on, he looked out the window beside the door.

"Noelle!"

He threw open the door, surprised by her smiling face. She was dressed simply in jeans and a white T-shirt, but looked gorgeous nevertheless. His heart said to offer a hug. He ignored it and extended his hand cautiously. She gave a wonderful laugh, took his hand, and reached around his waist with her other hand for a short but welcome embrace.

"Happy Turkey Day, Jonathon."

When she stepped back again, he saw in her hand a copy of the *Herald Press*.

Chapter 14

"**W**hen did you get in?" He stepped out on the porch with her. "Just a few hours ago. Is this too late?" Noelle eyed Jonathon carefully.

"Nah, but my mom's going to bed." He slipped his hands into his jean pockets and shivered.

"You're cold."

"It's okay. Are you?"

"I'm fine. I like it this way." She took a breath and sighed. "I smell your pine trees."

"Mom says they grew a foot this year."

"How's she doing?"

"Still working hard, but she's fine."

"That's good."

Jonathon hesitated. "How are your folks? I bet they really missed you."

"They're great. They had a big welcome home sign out for me. I missed them too."

Jonathon slapped his head. "Oh, man, Noelle. I'm not being much of a host. Do you want to go out somewhere, go get a Coke or something?"

"No, that's okay. I just wanted to let you know I was back in town." She was hoping he'd ask again, and then she'd say yes.

"Well, okay. I'm sure glad you stopped by. What are your plans this week?"

Her heart sunk. "I'll be around until Sunday." She weighed her words and then added, "Why?"

"That's a good break from school. I'm glad you get that much time off." He might as well have thrown a brick at her.

"Well, maybe I better get back home. My parents didn't know I'd left." But she didn't turn away.

"It's really great to see you again, Noelle."

"You too." She hesitated to leave.

"I guess…I thought you might be kind of mad at me." His gaze looked off into the distance for the first time.

"Mad? What about?"

He pointed to the newspaper in her hand. "The mayor. Didn't you read about it?"

She handed the newspaper to him. "Oh, yes. I wanted to give it to you. Thought your mom might like an extra copy."

"Wait a minute." He didn't take the paper she offered. "Doesn't that bug you?"

Stepping away, she rolled the paper and turned to look out across the small Thompson yard. "Not really, Jonathon."

He didn't respond, but she could feel his eyes on her.

"You've got to do what you feel strongly about. I don't want to get in your way." She turned around to face him. "Jonathon, our friendship is too important for that."

"Come here," he took her hand. "I want to show you something."

They stepped off the porch and she followed him around the outside of the house. Brushing past two big pine trees, they entered the backyard. He dropped her hand and ran to the swings.

"Over here. Sit down and swing with me."

"What are you doing, Jonathon?" She walked to the swing beside his.

"Nothing. Just swingin'." He began sailing back and forth.

Starting a slight swing, she tried to get lost in whatever mood he was setting.

"Just swing, Noelle," he yelled to her.

Her nose and ears were biting cold as she adjusted her seat and started pumping her legs. She gained on the height he had already achieved.

"Aren't you freezing?" she shouted.

His slender arms were tight as he grabbed the chains and pushed himself higher, his T-shirt flapping in the breeze. "C'mon!"

Taking his challenge, she began swinging with all her might, pulling her body forward against the seat, then flattening herself out as she flew back through the arc.

Finally, it hit her. They used to do this as kids, competing for the highest swings, right here in his backyard. She hadn't been in these swings for ten years, but she used to always beat him, swinging higher.

"Get up here," he shouted.

"I'm coming!" She was nearly at his height, pointing her toes straight up in the air as she pulled forward.

Suddenly the whole swing set lurched forward and fell back.

"Whoa!" he yelled and immediately dropped his feet to scrape the ground.

She was just at the top of her back swing when the frame did the same thing, this time lurching backward. Jonathon leaped out of his swing and grabbed the side bars to steady it.

Letting her feet stop the swing, she stepped out and burst into laughter.

"Guess we're not eight years old anymore!" He laughed and sat back down in his swing.

She fell in the grass, still giggling. "Oh this feels good," she gasped before she bent over, holding her sides.

"You haven't laughed for a while." He smiled, beginning a slow swing. "This thing never rocked like that for me."

"I got higher than you."

"Did not."

"You still can't swing as high as me," she teased.

"You weren't even close. And then you had to go and break the whole swing."

"Did not," she mimicked him, reaching over to grab his foot and pull him out of his seat. "Get out of there before it falls over on you."

When he plopped on the ground, she fell in the grass again, laughing uncontrollably. He stared at her as she kept up her enjoyable fit.

It was good to see his gorgeous smile pointing her way. Her laughter faded as she returned his gaze.

"Where are your glasses? Don't tell me you finally got contacts."

"No, I just left them inside. Didn't think I'd have a reason to need them—until now."

She felt her skin blush. "You're not missing much."

"You don't know. It's really good to see you again, Noelle. It's been a long couple of months. Sounds like it's been tough on you too."

"It's hard. Harder than I thought it would be." She sat up with her arms wrapped around her bent knees. "It meant a lot to get your e-mails."

"Yeah, I appreciated all yours too."

She grabbed a handful of grass and threw it at him. "I was busy; it's not like I had all the time in the world."

"Like me?" he responded sarcastically. "Like I had all the time in the world to write e-mails to you?"

She laughed. "Oh, that's right. You've been up at the hospital, busy healing folks."

He pulled out two clumps of grass and tossed them, brown slivers catching in her hair. She screamed playfully.

"Just remember, you're the one who brought it up."

"Okay, so I did. Now seriously, do you really think you healed the mayor?"

"It seems like everyone else thinks so."

"That's not what I asked. What do you think?"

Standing from his swing, he walked to the faded picket fence beside the garden.

He stayed there, so Noelle got up and went over to him. She touched his arm. "You are freezing," she whispered.

He turned to her, the moonlight hitting his face. Tears moistened his cheeks.

"What's wrong?" she asked.

"I don't think I healed him, Noelle."

She reached her hand to his shoulder and he bowed his head. Moving closer, his arms wrapped around her waist, his tears continuing in the silence. Noelle felt the warmth of his body next to hers and suddenly stiffened. Images of an ugly night not that long ago flashed through her mind. Indelibly scarred sensations of an unwanted intimacy crowded her fledgling compassion for Jonathon.

He released his arms. "What's wrong?"

She looked away. "I'm sorry. I've got to go."

"No, wait. What did I do?"

"Nothing, Jonathon. It's late. I've got to get home." She walked back around the house.

He followed her. "Noelle, I'm sorry. I didn't mean—"

"Don't, Jonathon." Her voice sobbed and she ran to her car.

*****

The next morning when Dr. Mittlestedt arrived at the hospital, he bypassed the coffee in the doctors' lounge and headed straight for the nurses' desk thirty minutes earlier than usual. Though the nurses weren't done writing on Mayor Horton's chart, they gave it to the doctor. He popped it open, flipped up the tab marked "lab," and made a squiggle of a signature as he strode down the hall to room 117.

"Good morning, Mayor."

"Morning, Dr. Mittlestedt. Do you have any news yet?"

"Yes, we do." Mittlestedt sat on the edge of Horton's bed. "Your PSA is back. That's the prostatic-specific antigen. It goes up in the presence of prostate cancer. Today's report is 42.1, Royce. Normal is under four. The last one we have on you is 27.2. You're ten times the normal limit."

"So that means—?"

"That means the cancer's still there, Royce. It's getting worse rather than better.

"But maybe it takes a little longer for the blood tests to show."

"Maybe. How long do you want to wait?" Mittlestedt slapped the chart loudly on the bedside stand and rose from the bed. "Your cystoscope is this morning. If they still see tumor, you've got to get on this. I don't want to insult your faith, but we can treat this cancer if you'll let us."

"I might call the Thompson boy and see what he says."

"Royce, we're not playing games here. That kid is a nut—he certainly doesn't know anything about medicine. You've got to choose: am I taking care of you, or is he?"

Royce fiddled with his bed sheets, smoothing out the creases.

"Who is it, Royce?" he demanded.

Mayor Horton answered softly. "I want you, Jack."

"Then stick with me. Don't be chasing fake healers."

Royce found a few more wrinkles to work on, avoiding his doctor's glare.

"We may beat this thing yet. I'll call the oncologist and be sure you can still get in today after your scope."

Mayor Horton still spoke quietly. "Thanks."

"You're doing the right thing, Royce."

"I hope my wife agrees. She's become quite religious."

"Hey, I might not be the pope," Dr. Mittlestedt smiled for the first time, "but sometimes I think God wants us to use our common sense. He's given us brains, right?"

106

Mayor Horton nodded his head and looked up.

"I'm gonna do all I can for you, Royce." He left the room, scribbling on his chart.

*****

"He thinks maybe he can heal you, Mel." John Camelson sat with his wife at the kitchen table for lunch. "He said he had a feeling come over him when he heard you sing last Friday."

Melinda placed her hands on her side wheels and pushed herself away from the table. "I thought we went through this already." Looking up, she shook her head, her brown locks catching glints of sunshine from the bay window. "Do you think he's for real?"

"He's sincere—but maybe impulsive too. His heart's in the right place, Melinda. He's got nothing to gain from this."

"What church does he go to?"

"First Congregational."

"What? You think spiritual gifts would show up in that church?"

"Honey, you don't know what God's plan is." John got up out of his chair and walked around behind her. "Let's get away from these dishes." He rolled her chair into the living room, sitting down in a recliner beside her.

"I told him I'd call him after I talked to you."

"We've got to pray about this, John. I'm not ready to go through it again."

He reached over for her hand.

"I thought we both clearly felt God had told us to be content. I haven't prayed for my legs for years. I've accepted it. Do you really think He wants to heal me after all that?"

"We can stop right here, Mel. Say no, and I'll tell him we're just not ready. If you don't think it's right, I'd rather follow you."

She sighed and squeezed his hand. "Let's pray about it. See what happens with the mayor. I guess it wouldn't hurt to talk with Jonathon. He seems like a kind young man."

"He's pretty confused lately with all that's happening around him, but I think you'd like him. You two are a lot alike, actually."

"What's Hillary think of him?" she asked.

"She doesn't know what to make of him. She told me she was going to invite him to church Sunday."

Michael J. Huckabee

"Already?"

"What's there to lose? Especially if he's the answer to our prayers. What a great miracle, Mel—all the gifts of the Holy Spirit evidenced at one time in our church."

"I just hope she's keeping her head on straight."

"She's a solid gal. I think she's doing alright. Let's pray."

He turned out of his recliner so his knees hit the carpet. Keeping his wife's hand in his, he kneeled as she sat, and they entered holy ground.

*****

"Nurse Chandler, line three. Nurse Chandler, line three." The ward clerk's voice paged across the hospital corridors.

Martha picked up the yellow nurses' phone at her desk. "Chandler here."

"Martha, I just heard back from Horton's cysto." It was Dr. Mittlestedt. "He's still got the tumor. I told him we'd let him know as soon as we heard."

"You want me to tell him he's still got cancer?" She hated dump jobs.

"I warned him this morning that it was still there. Just tell him Dr. Blodgett will stop by around five o'clock to visit with him about surgery."

"You're enjoying this, aren't you, Jack?"

"Actually, not at all. I'm calling Feddersen. I'm afraid you're going to be losing an aide."

"Thompson's young, Jack. Idealistic. That's not all bad."

He ignored her. "I'll be up for rounds close to seven."

The phone was dead, but she kept talking into the mouthpiece. "Always nice to talk with you too Dr. Mittlestedt."

108

Chapter 15

*T*he wind whipped a mixture of dried cornstalks, weeds, and trash along the chain-link fence surrounding the NanoMed offices, though very few people noticed. A century-old farmhouse sat deep within acres of cornfields, forty-five minutes by dirt road from Highway 6. Since summer, the structures were hidden from view by tall corn; only now that harvest was completed could the buildings be seen again. The occasionally lost UPS driver would stumble upon what appeared as a simple family farm home, except for the six-foot fence wrapped around the spacious yard of the property. A cracked and unlevel concrete sidewalk, only wide enough for single file intruders, led to a weathered front door that no one ever answered. A rusty mailbox hanging cock-eyed from a single nail on the doorframe served as the anchor for cobwebs that fluttered across the width of the entry.

Jeraldo Troy left no name on the mailbox. Nor were there any signs on the two metal buildings set squarely behind the house.

He maintained a discrete existence, despite holding MD and PhD degrees, both from the International University of Jamaica. After six years of applying to various medical residency programs across the United States, he tired of selling himself to American university medical centers as a legitimately educated physician.

As rejection notices piled up, he worked as a research assistant in the laboratory of Helen McCain, international expert in biotechnology at the University of California at Berkeley. Among the first to offer warning cries that technology was expanding beyond ethical boundaries, McCain was easily shouted down by the rise of capital supporters. Seeing the trend of research becoming increasingly driven by investors, she left the limelight as her career ebbed, purposely shelving research that combined biotechnology with robotics, all before the term "nanotechnology" was widespread.

As a faithful employee, Troy quickly became a personal companion to the elder McCain. When she died in a tragic car accident, no one was surprised to learn that her accumulations were bequeathed to Jeraldo. Only a handful knew that his gain was in the millions from her miserly investing in pharmaceuticals and technology stocks. No one but he knew of McCain's research files.

One of the benefits of nanotechnology is that it does not require multiple personnel or meticulous research laboratories. The process primarily unfolds in a computer, and the products are made from wires and chemicals available at any Wal-Mart.

All Dr. Troy required was experimental models, a medium for disease, and a cure, all to be combined and observed. Enter Dr. Feddersen.

Troy met Feddersen during an interview at the University of Nebraska Medical Center. They both applied for family practice residencies and found themselves in the same hotel lobby bar in Omaha over drinks late one night after the grueling interview panel. The idealistic Feddersen was captivated by Troy's research tales and his predictions of miraculous cures. When Feddersen was accepted to the residency and Troy was rejected, they stayed in touch. Later Troy convinced Feddersen to team up with him on NanoMed.

Now, eight years later, Troy was on the verge of releasing a landmark study. The unrecognized, foreign-trained physician would become a household name across scientific communities worldwide.

A lone green Concorde drove down the dirt road, triggering digital cameras hidden behind field posts advertising seed corn brands. With less than a mile yet to go, the road took a sharp ninety-degree turn, forcing the Concorde to slow and allowing photographs of the license plate. With the car thus identified, Martin Feddersen was approved to enter the complex. After driving through an electronic gate in the fence, he parked inside the first out-building, the two-story garage door shutting tightly behind him.

Feddersen stepped over to silver elevator doors and bent slightly to peer into an iris scanner. The doors opened and he entered. Without pushing a button, the doors closed and he was transported two floors below ground level.

"Good afternoon, Dr. Feddersen." He was greeted by his partner with overdone professionalism as the doors opened.

"To you also, Dr. Troy," he returned the feigned formality. "What can you tell from the data on Smitherton?"

"Dr. Feddersen, please. You must slow down—smell the roses." Troy gently caressed a long-stemmed ruby rose, contrasted against his white suit and red, open-collared shirt.

"Don't be trite, Jerry. It's me, you don't have to put on a show. What have you got on Smitherton?" Feddersen walked into Troy's office and sat down in a burgundy leather sofa, leaving his old friend still at the oak-lined elevator doorway.

"Truly, Marty—when will you relax? Everything is going incredibly well."

"I'll relax when you get a grip on reality. Everything is not going that well."

"Look, we've got excellent data on Smitherton. We've pulled him back from a myocardial infarction, bilateral *Staph* pneumonia, and now DIC. I'd go to the press now if it wasn't for you." He walked to a computer screen and entered his password on the keyboard with one hand.

"And you'd have egg all over your face," Feddersen said. "It's credibility we need—valid and verifiable results. We don't want this in *Family Circle*. We need this in *JAMA* or *The New England Journal of Medicine*. Let's do it right, Jerry."

"And that's why I wait—with you. So what don't you think is going well?"

"Let me see your data." Feddersen stood and moved to a second computer screen across the room.

"Here's what I have on the last one, serial measurements of coagulation factors, platelet counts, and some great photos. When we gave him the NL3819, it was amazing how fast he improved clinically. If the lab values aren't enough, the color photos tell the whole story."

"How much NL3819?"

"Six ccs."

Feddersen whipped around to face Troy. "What?" he barked. "You increased the dose again?"

"We had to, Marty."

"You can't keep changing the methods. It distorts our stats." He marched across the room and used the keyboard himself, calling up data files.

Calmly stepping back, Troy fingered the thorns on his rose. He peered into three nearby hanging baskets of exotic flowers, each lit by a small ultraviolet bulb above each plant.

"But it worked," he said. "We saved his life."

"I need it quiet. I've got to study this data." His fingers banged the keyboard.

"I'll leave. Just don't worry so much. It's working, Marty."

"I need a couple of hours."

Troy walked to the elevator and placed his eye next to the iris scanner. "By the way, what about the kid?"

"The healer? He's as a good as gone—labeled the town fool by tonight."

Troy had stepped into the elevator. "Much more convenient than what transpired with the lab tech, Crenshaw."

"Come back in a couple of hours. We've got to go over Smitherton."

*****

When Noelle left last night, Jonathon was confused. Not able to sleep and unwilling to face his mother, he took a midnight walk. Replaying the evening over and over, he could not detect where he had slipped. She was so different at first; she cared about him. He thought she'd be undone by the news story on his healing work, but she seemed almost accepting. What had she said? "Our friendship is too important for that." He smiled, recalling the swing set almost toppling over and her simple laughter. It'd had been a year since he'd enjoyed those happiest of sounds.

He shouldn't have embraced her. That was it. He was vulnerable, worrying about himself, when he reached around her. She was soft, comforting. He didn't mean anything more than companionship, he figured she would know that.

She didn't understand; she was scared. Afraid to get too close. He could deal with that. He planned to call her tomorrow.

He circled the block and went home to bed, emotionally exhausted. But he still couldn't sleep.

Lord, we've got to deal with this healing. I know You're tired of this, but I've got to know. Do I still have Your gift? How do I know if You're out there, Lord?

He paused to wait for a response, but heard none.

I confess, Lord. I haven't been walking like you may have wanted me to. But I don't understand—would you really take a gift away from me? God, I am sorry. I am sorry that I haven't been the kind of guy you may have wanted to be able to heal through. If you don't want me to do it anymore, that's fine with me. But I just need to know, Lord. How can I know?

The prayer was repeated as he laid in bed, kicking covers off and pulling them back on. While he wasn't expecting a lightning bolt, he did hope something would happen. Maybe a tingle in his spine, just so he'd know God heard. He smelled the air hopefully for lilacs, but the only odor was the faint draft of dirty socks.

In the presence of fatigue and the absence of answers, desperation took root. *How can I call myself a Christian if I can't even find You? I guess no one really knows for sure.*

His head pounded the pillow as the digital clock beside his bed glowed three in the morning. He threw the sheets off one more time and curled up on his side, his conscious finally fatigued from the single question that formed behind all the others: *What am I going to do now?* In the stark absence of answers, Jonathon fell asleep.

The next time he saw on his clock was two minutes after noon. Groaning, he hit the pillow with his face. The memory of her voice echoed in his head, "Our friendship is too important." In his half-awake stupor the words gradually became more shrill, almost noisy. When he lifted his pillow to smother his head beneath it, he recognized the phone ringing outside his room.

Leaping out the door, he caught it, surely after ten rings. "Hello?"

"Hello, Jonathon? This is Hillary."

He put a hand over the mouth piece to clear his throat. "Hillary? Hey, how are you doing?"

"Great. Sorry to bother you, you must have been busy with something."

"Nah, just couldn't get to the phone. What's up?" He made his voice sound perky.

"Thought I might see you at church last Sunday."

"Oh yeah, well, I had to go to my own church. With my mom, you know?"

"That's so sweet. Your mom must be a great lady. You take such good care of her."

"It's the other way around, actually. But she is great. You've got to meet her."

"Sure. Anyway, the reason I called was to invite you to go swimming with our youth group at church. No big deal, but we're going down to the Community Center tomorrow night and I thought you might like it. Lots of the guys you met at the worship concert will be there. You can invite a friend if you want. What do you think?"

"Sounds good. I'm off work and haven't got anything planned."

"And Jonathon, I know it may seem weird for me to call you about this, but you know, this is just friends, right?"

"That's cool. That's where I'm at, Hillary. Just friends. Speaking of which, would it be okay if I invited Noelle Lewis? Do you know her?"

"She's the one you said is like me, right? Sure she's welcome to come. Just bring your swimsuits and three bucks. They'll have pizza there for us. Starts at six, okay?"

"Six. I'm not sure about Noelle, but I'll be there either way. Thanks, Hillary."

As soon as he put the phone down, it rang again.

"Hello?"

"Hello, Jonathon? Martha Chandler."

"Hey, Martha. Need me for that double shift again?"

"Not this time. I need you to come early. It's about the mayor, Jonathon. Can you come at one-thirty instead of two? Just come straight to my office, I'll wait for you."

"What's wrong, Martha? It doesn't sound good."

"It isn't. Let's not talk about it until you get here." She paused. "And Jonathon—I'd avoid everyone up here if I were you. You know what I'm saying?"

He hesitated, not wanting to know. "Yeah, I think I do."

"See you in an hour."

"Right."

Chapter 16

Jonathon entered the nurses' lounge just before one-thirty to report for work. The custodian, Wilbur, placed his broom against a locker and hastily left the room without saying a word.

Passing the nurses' desk, he glanced at the roster of patients. Mayor Horton's name had a line crossed through it. Neither the ward clerk nor the nurse charting at the counter looked his way. He made his way down the hall to Nurse Chandler's office.

"Thanks for coming in early, Jonathon." Martha didn't look up from her desk, piled high with old charts and quality control documents. He closed the door himself before saying a word.

"What's going on, Martha? Where's Mayor Horton?"

"He was transferred. Went to Rollings for surgery tomorrow with his urologist. We tried to convince him to stay here; we do prostatectomies all the time. Didn't help."

Jonathon leaned back against the door. "His tests?"

"Still cancer. They scoped him today, and the tumor was even bigger. His PSA was up." She spoke abruptly, just the facts.

He stammered. "Sometimes I'm not as sure as I'd like to be, Martha."

"Yeah, I know. Here's what else I know." She grabbed a manila envelope and put it on the corner of the desk for him. Her eyes focused on the corner of the ceiling. "It's over, Jonathon. I've been asked to let you go."

"What?"

"It's Dr. Feddersen's decision, but it's my job to tell you. I don't like any of this, Jonathon, but it's done." She looked at him for the first time, her eyes cool and hard. "He didn't even want you to stay tonight, but I begged him. We're short staffed, and we need you."

"No way, Martha. Don't fire me. I love this job." He felt tears rising. "I can't lose this. Not now."

"I did what I could, but how do you argue with what's happened?" She got up out of her chair and came around the desk. "This whole thing is going to hurt. If the mayor won't stay here, you can imagine what that's going to say to everyone else in Windwood."

His head drooped and Martha came closer to rest a hand on his shoulder. "Maybe Dr. Feddersen will change his mind." Her voice softened. "Lord knows we need to keep good ones like you."

Jonathon turned to the door. "I know you tried, Martha."

Walking back to the nurses' station, he picked up his assigned patients before heading into nurses' report. Sounds of laughter immediately stopped when he entered, and the group of ward clerks and nurses stiffened as he took a chair. The starched silence pressed hard against him.

"All right, everyone," he blurted out. "So the mayor didn't get healed. No one said it was a promise."

"It's okay with me, Jonathon. You're a praying man, that's what's important," Carmen said.

Nurse Chandler entered and interrupted. "Time for report, gang. Let's go down the list."

Jonathon overheard Mary whisper to Charlene across the room, "I told you it wouldn't work." Jonathon looked away and would have walked out if he hadn't known Martha would make him come back. Instead he endured the report and left the minute it was over. The others could finish their gossiping. He wouldn't have to tolerate their stares after tonight.

The headline story in the *Herald Press* ran with Olympic coverage: "Mayor's Cancer Turns Worse: Immediate Surgery Required." The story dealt mostly with the details of Mayor Horton's transfer to Rollings for "a higher level of care." Only one paragraph referred to the healing. It was reported as "a desperate escapade that stole valuable time." Dr. Feddersen was quoted saying that Mr. Thompson would be relieved of his duties and the state nursing board had been notified. "His behavior was certainly beyond the scope of practice expected of our nurses at Windwood Community Hospital."

*****

"Room 142. Room 142."

The public address system called the room that Jonathon recognized as the elderly, incoherent Mrs. Knudson.

Probably another diaper change.

At least he was busy, without even time to read the newspaper. The blazing headline was enough to tell it all. He was a medicine show scam without a horse to ride out of town. Entering Mrs. Knudson's room, he was surprised to see she had a visitor.

"Grandma Davis?"

"Why, hello, Jonathon. Are you taking care of my dear friend?" She sat relaxed in a rocker beside Mrs. Knudson's bed, her lap holding an opened Bible.

"I didn't know you were friends," he muttered, distracted with his own problems.

"From a long time ago. We committed ourselves to growing old together." She patted Mrs. Knudson's arm. "But you're beating me to it, Ruth. Don't go so fast." She beamed a smile at Jonathon, and he tossed his head back and looked away.

"Hey, that's not much of a smile for your business partner."

"Yeah, well, business isn't so good for me these days." He bumped past the rocker and turned Mrs. Knudson to change her pad.

"You're part owner of a blue-and-white teacup; life can't be that bad." She leaned over to the deaf ear of Mrs. Knudson. "He's the cute one I was telling you about, Ruth. He gave me ten dollars to raise the bid. Saved this damsel in distress, I'm telling you."

Jonathon ignored the remarks and bent over the bed to roll his patient to the opposite side. Grabbing the bed sheets, he pulled them forward and bumped a water pitcher with his elbow. Ice water splashed across the sheets before the container hit the floor.

Expletives passed through his mind, but he thought better of it with Grandma Davis there.

"Drat it," she offered in his place. "I'm probably hanging too close to let you do your work, son. Let me get a towel."

"It's fine; fits my day. Just sorry poor Mrs. Knudson has to put up with me." He pulled the bed sheets back again to change them.

"Don't you worry about Ruth, this is the highlight of her day. You haven't had so much fun in a long time, right dear?" She patted her friend's hand and gripped it tight. "So, Jonathon, tell me about your gift of healing."

"Ah, I don't think you've heard the latest. Better read today's paper."

"I don't read it. Rather hear from real people, wouldn't you?"

117

"I gotta do my job here, Grandma Davis." He stopped himself. "What's left of it."

"What's that, son? You having troubles here?"

He reached around Mrs. Knudson again to move her onto the new sheets. "They're letting me go. I thought I could heal the mayor, Grandma Davis. I didn't, and they said I'm outta here."

She was suddenly quiet. "Oh, my."

"Yeah. One day I'm the hero, and the next I'm fired." His voice raised in anger and he grabbed Mrs. Knudson more roughly to roll her once more to her side.

She coughed and choked, her breathing suddenly turning raspy.

"Oh, God!" He adjusted her head, cocking her chin down and forward. "C'mon, don't go out on me now." Her back began to arch, her thin neck muscles tightening to reach more air.

Grandma Davis began whispering, praying. She reached for her friend's shoulder.

Reflexively, Jonathon reached a finger into her mouth and found her tongue shoved back in her throat. He pulled it forward and her breathing suddenly became quiet. She sighed and her spine relaxed.

"Should I call for help?" Grandma Davis offered.

He reached for Mrs. Knudson's wrist to feel her pulse. It was strong and regular.

"Wait a minute. I think she's okay now." His voice shook and he kneeled to the floor, keeping his fingers on the pulse. The color drained from his face.

"Jonathon, are you okay?" Grandma Davis reached out to his shoulder. "You did it. You saved her."

"No, no, I almost killed her." He leaned his head against the bed.

"Here, sit in this chair." She brought the rocker to him and he rose off the floor to sit, keeping a check on his patient. Wiping tears from his cheeks with his spare hand, he held back the flood of failed efforts flowing inside of him.

Lord, why? What are You doing to me?

Grandma Davis stroked the back of his hair. He didn't even notice it at first, but as his tears dried, he heard her whispering again, words in prayer. He did not take his eyes off Mrs. Knudson, needing every assurance that she would remain stable, but after several minutes, he glanced up to Grandma Davis. Her blue eyes twinkled warmly.

"It's okay, Jonathon."

He sighed. "How could that be? There's not much 'okay' going on today. Don't you see? I'm labeled a liar, I've lost my job, and I almost killed a helpless patient right in front of you. What's okay about that?"

"There's bound to come some trouble to your life. What I can't figure out is why you're surprised." Her smile remained unchanged. "You think God has abandoned you, right?"

He nodded his head twice.

"I know what it's like. I've been there before. It's nothing to be afraid of."

He ran his fingers through his hair and wiped his eyes, leaning back in the rocker.

"You haven't heard what I've been saying to you lately," she continued. "You keep thinking maybe it'll get better, that maybe all this will go away. But maybe is not enough to go by, is it? You need something to hold onto. Don't hold onto *maybe*, Jonathon. If you've got a gift—and a wonderful gift it is—there's going to be trouble. There's no reason to fear it." She sat at Mrs. Knudson's bedside and gently stroked her cheek. "Here's what you do: reach out to Jesus. Hold on tight. He's been there before and He is here. He knows what it's like."

She stood and walked to the door.

"I'm going to leave you with Ruth. She's closer to Jesus right now than any of us. You care for her, and talk with Him."

"But Grandma Davis—"

"No arguing, Jonathon. Do it now, settle this. You're a mess and you've got to get yourself straightened out—with God." She left, closing the door tight behind her.

She's right about that, I'm a mess. He looked at the frail form before him, lifeless save for the silent rise and fall of her chest.

"Mrs. Knudson, I, uh, I'm sorry for what happened here." He brushed the thin, gray hair out of her eyes. "Let me finish getting your bed made." He moved to the corners to tuck the sheets in. Bending over, he found Grandma Davis' Bible open on the floor. He started to lay it on the table when blue ink underlining a few lines caught his eyes.

But we have this treasure in jars of clay to show that this all-surpassing power is from God and not from us. We are hard pressed on every side, but not crushed; perplexed, but not in despair; persecuted, but not abandoned; struck down, but not destroyed.

He sat down on the bed beside his patient and read the next verse.

We always carry around in our body the death of Jesus, so that the life of Jesus may also be revealed in our body."

"That's you, Mrs. Knudson, isn't it? You're carrying the death of Jesus. Help me. Help me see the life of Jesus."
He returned to the scripture.

For we who are alive are always being given over to death for Jesus' sake, so that his life may be revealed in our mortal body. So then, death is at work in us, but life is at work in you."

"So I'm carrying the death of Jesus, too?" he said to the unresponsive woman. "I don't understand. I can see it in you, Mrs. Knudson, but do I have the death of Jesus in me? Is His life revealed in me?"

Staring at the motionless, frail body, he waited for her answer. Nothing came. How could it? She was so near death. That's all he could see in her body. There was less life in her than death.

Something moved. Almost imperceptibly, something happened. She looked different, at her face, her mouth. It wasn't that way a moment ago. The ends of her ruby lips were curled upward gently, smoothly.

A smile?

Her whole face changed; she was in peace, in joy.

I'm seeing the life of Jesus, revealed, Jonathon thought.

He knelt at the bedside and talked—and listened more—to Mrs. Knudson's Friend.

*****

The odor of curry and chicken filled the Lewis home. Noelle had been in her room most of the day. When her mom asked if she could help, Noelle just said she was cleaning her closets, going through old memories. Mom knew better than to pry, instead she went to the kitchen to draw out her daughter with her favorite meal.

Sitting in the middle of her room, Noelle surrounded herself with mementos of her last four years: school newspapers, yearbooks, a shoe box of notes from Jonathon, her art class oil paintings, two Windwood High purple and gold sweatshirts, and a pre-calculus math trophy. In her hands was a framed photo of herself with Dr. Mittlestedt standing in front of his lemon yellow Viper.

After staring at the photo for several minutes, she tossed it, still in the frame, under her bed and gathered up the newspapers and books, loading everything into a large cardboard box. The curry aroma began circulating in her room; the time for her favorite meal was approaching.

A knock came at the door. "Noelle, honey, it's almost time to eat."

"I've been dying over that smell, Mom. You're killing me."

"Let me open the door; you won't be able to resist."

"Sure, come on in."

The door cracked. "Can you handle it?"

Noelle took a deep breath through her nose. "I'm in heaven, Mom. It's so good to be home."

"It's great to have you, but you've been a stranger today already. What's been taking up your time?"

"I just wanted to go through these things." Grabbing a sweatshirt, she threw it across her chest. "Windwood High, it was a great time."

"Did you see Jonathon last night? How is he?"

"He's doing fine. Yeah, it was good to see him again, I guess."

"What do you make of this healing stuff, Noelle? How'd he get caught up in that?"

"It's no big deal, Mom. The press is blowing it out of proportion. He's a kind guy and likes to pray for people. That's all."

"The *Herald Press* strikes again, making a big deal out of nothing."

"I bet he's taking it kind of hard, though." Noelle responded, placing the lid back on the box of his letters as if she was securing priceless jewels.

"You still like him, don't you?"

"I thought I was over him. I just don't know if we'd ever really make it."

"You've got to go by your feelings, Noelle, and then work at it if you want to follow those feelings. You'll know if it's right, but you won't find out if you don't allow yourself to try. Now come on down for dinner."

The phone rang and Noelle picked up her extension beside her bed. "Hello?"

"It's me, Noelle," Jonathon's voice sounded apologetic. "How are you doing?"

She grinned at her mother and wiggled a finger. Her mother smiled back and left the room mouthing again that it was time to eat.

Noelle answered nonchalantly, "I'm all right. Uh, sorry about last night."

"That's okay. I hope I didn't do something wrong."

"No, no. It's just me. Don't worry about it." She caught her image in the bedroom mirror and brushed her hair behind her ears.

"I'm at work now so I can't talk long. It's been a bad day, Noelle. You wouldn't believe it. I'm hoping you'll be my bright spot. Tomorrow night there's a swim party down at the Community Center. Can you go? There'll be a bunch of other people."

"Who will be there?" She stood sideways to examine her slender waist in profile.

"It's a gang I'm just getting to know myself. Hillary Wells is the one who put it together, but there'll be a bunch of others. She's a lot like you, Noelle. You'd like her."

She sat down on her bed, insecure and wanting a friend.

"I'm not sure. I need to spend time with my family."

"C'mon, it won't be all night, just a couple hours. I want to tell you about what just happened to me here at work. It's kind of strange...I was just with this lady who's comatose. She can't talk or anything. But what I felt...well, I can't talk now, but will you try to come?"

"I'll think about it, Jonathon. Let me ask my parents. Manny's coming over tomorrow and I need to spend some time with him." She opened a dresser drawer and pulled out a swimsuit she hadn't worn in six months, faded from chlorine and sun.

"How is your bro doing? I haven't seen him for years."

"He's fine. I haven't seen him either since last Christmas. But he's doing great." She held the suit against her and stood in front of the mirror.

"Well, bring him swimming with you. We'd have a great time, Noelle. Like old times."

"I'll see. I gotta go." She pulled the Spandex material, and it snapped back into form.

"Me too. Really try to make it, Noelle. I'll be looking for you. Six o'clock."

Chapter 17

*T*he alarm sounded the next morning at 6:30. Jonathon stirred, slapping the clock before throwing the pillow over his head.

Ten minutes later it sounded again and he moaned. Sliding out of bed, he went across the hall to the bathroom and splashed cold water on his face. Back in the hall, light beamed from the living room, creating a shadow of a woman kneeling on the floor beside her rocker. Long accustomed to her ritual, he typically vacillated between wonderment at her consistency and questioning the value of it all. When he was nine, she had made him get up and kneel with her, walking through a prayer for his father, for school, for church, and for his gift. At fourteen he convinced her it wasn't necessary for him; he could pray on his own.

She rarely missed a day. He could never say the same.

Today would be different. His time with Mrs. Knudson convinced him that a change was needed. Returning to his room, he looked through a bookcase in the corner, moving piles of school papers and dated junior high comics in search of a single volume.

Not finding it, he moved to the desk drawers, rustling through old notebooks, soccer magazines, a stash of ten-year-old baseball cards, and rock hard Halloween candy from last year, or the year before.

It wasn't there.

At the closet he tossed out a wad of pants that were too short and winter sweaters that were too ugly. Reaching beyond a couple of large plastic garbage bags of garage sale clothes from his childhood, all he found were a couple of old CDs that he had borrowed from a friend last summer. He'd have to give those back.

What he was hunting for was still missing.

He lifted up the sheets to peer under his bed, revealing a roach's haven. Used paper plates, a half-empty package of Oreos, torn potato chip bags, and crushed Mountain Dew cans flew out as he took one arm and swept across the floor. Taking another look under the bed, he smiled.

There it was: a light blue imitation leather King James Bible. He pulled it out as a precious antique, moving his finger gently across his own gold scripted name along the bottom of the cover. Just inside he read his Aunt Emma's signature alongside a reference, "First Corinthians 12:1-11." He let the book fall open on his lap, naturally going to this page, marked by a slim white silk marker attached to the binding. He recalled the stubby pencil he used to underline the verses the first time his aunt had pointed them out to him. "But the manifestation of the Spirit is given to every man to profit withal. For to one is given by the Spirit the word of wisdom; to another the word of knowledge by the same Spirit; to another faith by the same Spirit; and to another the gifts of healing by the same Spirit."

He read the words again, including the surrounding verses. Going on into chapter thirteen, he landed on another underlined passage, "Charity never faileth."

Okay, God, I'm back with You. This is my starting point, our common ground. You took me from here years ago and have led me all the way. I'm sorry I walked away, Lord Jesus. I didn't want to stay with You, and thought I could go at it on my own. I know You are guiding me now. I praise You.

He held the open Bible tight to his bare chest, as if to move the scripture close to his heart. *I'm yours, Lord. I'm sorry I attempted to heal apart from You, and I will wait for Your call. I see Your perfect design in all You have done in the past, so please make me usable for the future. I'm giving it to You, Lord. Here's my hospital job that I screwed up, here's the mayor, here's Noelle, here's Hillary, here's my mom. Take my thoughts and make them Yours, Lord, that I may know only You.*

He rested on his knees, his head bowed low.

Lord, I mean it. I don't want to play anymore games with You. Help me, for I don't know what to do. The tenderness of the moment was not missed. Jonathon sensed a reconnection, a devotion returning that he had not known for some time.

He got up, threw on a T-shirt and moved to the living room, quietly kneeling at the couch beside his mom's rocker. Through the frost on the window, the early morning sun streamed across his back. Elaine remained in prayer on her woven, red kneeling blanket. There were worn spots where the carpeting showed through the small mat, a testimony of years of spiritual labor. She didn't look up, but he heard a small gasp from her when he hit the floor.

The silence in the room was suddenly claustrophobic; his muscles tightened, sweat beading under his arms. He tried to focus on prayer, but glancing toward his mom, he found her frame trembling. His eyes wouldn't leave her, and after another minute, a gush of weeping erupted from her. He wiped his own eyes with his arms and laid a hand on her shoulder.

She turned, her eyes wet and red, her mouth wide and grinning. With a massive and prolonged hug she nearly took his breath away.

"Oh, Jonathon. Praise God!" She sobbed deeply and Jonathon wrapped his arms around her, squeezing her in the same embrace.

She snickered. "Land sakes, son. You're gonna mash the juice right out of me."

"Just giving you back a little of the same love you're giving, Mom."

Another bear hug made them both laugh at each other.

"'Nuff of that now, my ribs are bruisin'," she said.

"You're the best, Mom. I couldn't make it without you."

"Not true, not true. What you need is the Lord. That's what'll get you through."

"And He's there for me, Mom. I know He's there."

Her eyes glistened again, and she could hardly get out the words. "I can tell He is. I see Him. In your eyes."

He grabbed her hand. "They fired me at the hospital. Mayor Horton didn't get healed." He turned his head away.

"So?" She hadn't known, but she gave no hint of being surprised or disappointed. "Ya don't need them. There's loads of work you'll be fine at. Tell 'em 'so long'."

She got up from her knees. "I'm gonna make ya some breakfast. How 'bout cakes and bacon? Sound good?"

"I don't get it, Mom. Why aren't you upset?"

"Nothing to get upset over. Besides, some guy told me you were gonna be just fine. He knew I been worried over ya. Said that you're okay."

"What's that about? Who said that?"

"I dunno. Nice enough guy. He was all dressed up in a trench coat, classy guy. I thought you musta known him."

"Do you remember the color of his coat? Was it greenish?"

"Yup, like pea soup; that's the guy. Who is he, anyway?"

"I have no idea, Mom. He's the guy who told me about Samantha Harris when she was sick, and I saw him the other day downtown."

"Well he knows you, Jonathon. I'd keep him as a friend. He mentioned Mr. Smitherton, asked me if you was gonna try and find him."

"Mr. Smitherton? Why him?" His voice raised.

"Don't holler at me, I dunno why. I guess that's the price of being a celeb. People know ya better'n ya know them."

When she left for the kitchen, he rolled over on his back, positioning himself so the sunshine warmed his head and chest. Closing his eyes, he took his thoughts to his Lord.

Father, I also give you Mr. Smitherton and this man in the trench coat. It's all Yours, Lord. I can't understand it. I just want to be Yours too. Lead me, that I may follow You.

*****

Over a scrumptious breakfast, Jonathon asked his mom all she knew of the man she talked to about Mr. Smitherton.

"I just bumped into him at the grocery store yesterday, in the turkey aisle. They were twenty-seven cents a pound. Got a twelve-pounder for tomorrow. Anyway, he was greetin' me like he knew me. I figured he was a buddy of yours and didn't give it another thought."

She began to clear the breakfast dishes before she added, "Wonderful man. Wished I was 'bout twenty years younger, and I'd be winkin' at him."

Jonathon laughed out loud, and his mom threw a wash rag at him, adding, "You jus' keep laughing, an' I'll bean you with a green potater."

The phone interrupted them and Jonathon answered it, finding it to be John Camelson. He called to invite Jonathon over to meet with him and Melinda.

Jonathon planned to be at their house at noon, which would give him the rest of the morning to track down Mr. Smitherton.

*****

The phone listed the only Smitherton in Windwood at 201 Winchester Avenue. Jonathon decided not to call ahead but just show up, curious about the element of surprise occurring at the Coffee Corner two days ago.

126

A small immaculate lawn bordered a towering oak tree that still held half its leaves, directly in front of the small sky blue bungalow with bright gold numbers of two, zero, and one over the front door. Jonathon parked his Chevette at the curb and walked along a sidewalk lined by four-foot, tightly trimmed evergreens. He rang the doorbell twice before knocking on the metal screen door. No answer.

Returning along the same walkway, he paused around the side of the house to see a detached single car garage painted in the same light blue just behind the residence. The sound of an iron tool hitting a concrete floor came from within.

A small doorway stood wide open on the back side. Inside, he could see the back of Mr. Smitherton, hunched over a red, six-drawer tool chest. Garden tools, green hoses, and sprinkler heads hung neatly from pegboard behind him.

"Mr. Smitherton?"

A crowbar dropped from the old man's hand as he spun around. "What?"

His startled eyes were not unlike the expression Jonathon faced at the Coffee Corner.

"Excuse me, Mr. Smitherton. I rang the doorbell at the house and then heard you back here. Didn't mean to sneak up—"

"Of course not. I just wasn't expecting company." He was shaken, but he tried to play cordial. "You're the young aide from the hospital. Jonathon, right?"

"Yes. Sorry to barge in on you, but I wondered if we could visit for just a minute."

Henry picked up the crowbar and held it in both hands, not in a threatening manner, but protective.

"Of course." His eyes darted around as if looking for a reason to leave. "I was just sorting my tools. They say winter may come quickly."

"You're quite a gardener; I'll bet you watch the seasons carefully."

"My favorite time of year is right now. Weeds are gone, the trees have colored well, and no more mowing the lawn. I enjoy putting the garden to rest." He laid the crowbar in the tool chest.

"And it probably does wonders for your health to work outside. It's great that we haven't seen you at the hospital lately."

"A spell of good fortune, my health. Doc Mittlestedt says I'm paying now for my years of Winstons." He reached into his pocket for a pack. "It's hard to say goodbye to a friend of forty years."

Jonathon thought better than to discourage his smoke. "I wanted to ask you about Nanotech."

Henry fingered a wooden match and struck it against an iron vise at his side. The flame quivered as he lit his cigarette.

"Nanotech? Never heard of it. Why?" He turned his back on Jonathon and rummaged a hand in the toolbox.

"Listen, Mr. Smitherton. I don't mean to pry, but there's something that you and I both know isn't right. You were scared to death when you fell out of bed a month ago, and you were sure someone was trying to kill you. You weren't crazy. Then you were back in with that bruising and you almost died. You told me again that someone was killing you, maybe the doctor. But the next day you were virtually healed, and denied you had said anything earlier." Jonathon walked to Henry's side. "You're not crazy. In fact, I think you are very wise. I want to help you."

Mr. Smitherton's tanned, wrinkled hand came out of the tools and rested on the chest frame, the opposite hand bringing his cigarette up for another long drag. He looked at the open rafters and blew out smoke with a sigh.

"It's almost over." His eyes were sunken and weary.

"It doesn't have to be, Mr. Smitherton." Jonathon murmured.

"No, it's best. This is the last time." Henry eyed Jonathon. "It's nothing you need to worry about, but I appreciate your concern. You needn't look any further though…please."

Jonathon kept his voice low. "It's more than just about you, Mr. Smitherton. I lost my job at the hospital over these miracle healings. If you know something, you could help me as much as I could help you."

Moving to a side workbench filled with herbicides and bug sprays, Henry kept his back to Jonathon. "Your prayers didn't work, did they?"

"I didn't know how much you knew about me."

"I read the papers."

"I was praying for you, Mr. Smitherton."

Henry turned around, angry. "And you think you healed me? Is that why you came here?"

Jonathon hesitated as the truth set in clearly. He dropped his head. "No. I didn't heal you."

"Then that's all you need to know." Henry returned to sorting his chemicals, loudly banging the canisters into a box.

Jonathon stumbled for words, but not finding any, he walked to the door. Taking one step outside, he stopped. "So what did heal you, Mr. Smitherton?"

Henry lifted the box, glared once at Jonathon, and walked to the back of the garage, out of sight.

*****

John Camelson greeted Jonathon with a smile and a comforting handshake.

"It's great to see you again, Jonathon. Please come in."

Melinda was in the living room and yelled out, "Hi, Jonathon!" Her beauty remained striking, though she was dressed in a simple yellow blouse and jeans, her long, brown hair falling loosely over her shoulders. She was barefoot and Jonathon couldn't help but stare at her tiny feet, contorted from years of contractures.

"Please, sit down," Melinda gestured, and he sat in a cushioned side chair across the room. John laid a tray with three cups of hot tea on the center coffee table before sitting on the couch beside Melinda.

"You have a nice house." Jonathon offered.

"Thanks," John responded. "It's all Melinda's doing. What she touches turns beautiful before your eyes."

"So what happened to you?" Melinda grinned and grabbed her husband's ruddy chin to wiggle it.

He replied, "You should have seen me before I met you. I was much uglier than I am now."

Jonathon joined their laughter, immediately at ease. They talked of the beautiful fall weather, the pleasure of lying in piles of crunchy leaves, and the mess of combing leaf shreds out of Melinda's hair. They laughed again and together sipped their tea.

"So, Jonathon, my husband tells me you have the gift of healing." She smiled warmly. "We want you to know we believe in such a gift. In fact, we've been praying in our church to have this gift revealed. You have dramatically caught our attention in these past few days."

"Mel and I have prayed for you a lot lately, Jonathon," John added. "I'm sure it's been challenging to have so many people looking for you to perform."

Jonathon relaxed in his chair. "You have no idea."

Mel continued. "You're exactly right. We don't have any idea what it has been like for you. But we'd love to hear about it. Please tell us, how did you learn of your gift?"

"It might be a long story," Jonathon sighed.

"Take a sip of tea and let's hear it," John warmly smiled.

It was a story Jonathon had never told outside of his family, but it seemed natural to share it with these two people. Somehow the couple he barely knew days ago now seemed closer than family, caring and unselfish. He told of his prayer at the age of four, and Aunt Emma's finger injury. He related the sensations he experienced in healings, sharing all he knew. He teared as he spoke of his aunt's death, and how much he wished to have healed her; Mr. Smitherton's rare diseases and the interactions they had together; Samantha Harris' healing downtown; and the man in the trench coat all came out. He ended with the mayor's request for prayer and Dr. Feddersen's encouragement, which led to him being fired.

The Camelsons listened intently. John refilled the tea twice before Jonathon finished.

"Now I'm not sure what God wants me to do," Jonathon said. "I still believe I have a gift of healing. He wouldn't take it away, would He?"

"No," John answered. "We've seen the work of the Holy Spirit sometimes expressed fully for a season, and then perhaps not evidenced as dramatically for a time. I believe true gifts are not taken away, otherwise they would not be gifts. Still, we're responsible to be sure they're not abused."

"That's where I'm guilty. I shouldn't have listened to Dr. Feddersen. I knew God wasn't calling me to heal the mayor." Jonathon paused. "But the other side is also true. We shouldn't abuse a gift from God, but we must use it as God leads. That's why I've been wanting to meet with you."

Melinda spoke softly as she looked closely at Jonathon's eyes. "You think God wants you to heal...me?"

"The first time I saw you, when you were singing at church, I sensed God directing me here." Jonathon glanced at John and back to Melinda. "I'd like to pray for you to walk again. Are you ready?"

Chapter 18

A year before, in the microcosm of molecules, the enemy materialized. In the split second of an ordinary day, ever so subtly, one fragment of protein was exchanged for another in a quartet of puzzle pieces. Spontaneously, without man's intention, a completely new strand of DNA was formed. The trade was magically performed, an extraordinary pickpocket, but the result was a deadly poison. Without drawing any attention to the surrounding protein structures, the new DNA created a single virulent copy of itself. In minutes, the wicked partners silently fathered additional chains, granting each mature offspring the power to spawn more.

In hours a molecular army emerged, dividing in networks of melanocytes as they marched throughout the skin. Millions of foreboding cells, each an exact replica of another, choked and smothered unsuspecting nuclei. By two weeks, the devastation erupted to the surface of the epidermis, declaring its presence to the world in the form of a black blemish the diameter of a pin; its secret mission proceeding exactly as planned, catching everyone unaware.

"Mom, I can't wear this. Gross." Noelle positioned herself sideways in front of a mirror, hoping a different angle would make an improvement.

"It looks fine. Why are you in such a fret?" Her mother stepped into the bathroom.

"I must have gained some weight. I don't remember ever looking like this." Noelle craned her neck around to see her back. "Look at all my moles; they're so ugly. If I only had a little tan."

"They're not that noticeable. Besides, you'll be in the water the whole time."

"We've gotta go shopping, Mom. Please. The party's not until six."

"And where are you going to find a swimsuit in Windwood in November?"

Noelle didn't answer but just stared at her mom.

"I'm not driving to Rollings."

"C'mon, Mom. We have to—we've got five hours. Some great mother-daughter time." Flashing a pleading smile, she shinnied up to her mom.

"Don't smooth talk me. I can't just drop everything for your swimming party. Manny should be here anytime; I've got to finish baking."

"Please, Mom. I'll be fast. I can't wear that old thing." Mom was weakening. Noelle laid down the killer words. "I need you."

Moving to the door, her mother paused. "I suppose I could put something on time-bake."

"You're the best, Mom. I'll be ready in five minutes." The door closed as she yelled. "Let me help you with the baking."

Looking at herself one more time, she scowled as she turned her back to the mirror.

*****

John filled Melinda's tea cup again. Jonathon looked at both of them for a response, anxious over the brief but intentional delay. Neither one of the Camelsons seemed to want to respond.

Melinda finally spoke. "When I was fifteen I was horseback riding with my father. I loved horses; they were my life. This one was named Flavio, an appaloosa stallion, grayish white with a brown spotted rump. I'd ridden him for two years, knew him as my best friend. Father and I were riding across a field a mile or so away from our home." She smiled and glanced away. "It was a gorgeous day, springtime. I remember wild white daisies dotting the path." She looked back at Jonathon. "Nobody's sure what happened, maybe he got stung by a wasp, or maybe I pulled something the wrong way, but all of a sudden, Flavio drew his ears back, snorted, and reared. I flew off like a rag doll, landing on my back. Father was beside me in seconds, cradling my head. I never lost consciousness, and I still remember his first words: 'Jesus, protect my baby.'

"I said, 'I'm okay,' and put my hands behind me to lift myself up. As I tried to rise, it felt like someone had tied salt blocks to my waist, dragging me down. I couldn't move, couldn't feel, couldn't even wiggle.

"Over the next weeks, my father had trouble handling my injury. The doctors identified a completely severed spinal cord and gave no hope of my ever walking, but Father knew better. 'Jesus is going to heal you,' he'd tell me. 'I'm praying for you every night.'

"A week after I came home from the rehab center, he woke me early one Sunday morning." She bit her lower lip before continuing. "He was so sure. He whispered in my ear, 'Today's the day, Sugar.' I had no reason not to believe.

"He moved my wheelchair out of my room and said, 'Let's go for a walk.' I knew it was going to work. Father was all smiles, so confident. I smiled back, and he moved me to the side of my bed. I sat on the edge with my hands supporting my weight. Must have looked like Humpty Dumpty tottering on the wall.

"Father stepped away and said, 'Just trust Jesus.' He was so sure."

Melinda clenched the side arms of her chair, her knuckles white. She leaned forward as if to stand even now. Her arms started shaking as they held her whole weight from tumbling from the chair. Grimacing, her eyes tightly closed, she finally fell back in her chair with a sigh. A tear trickled down her cheek.

"I fell so hard that morning that I had a bloody nose and a black eye. The rest of the family went to church. I stayed home in bed.

"Something happened to Father after that. A year later he died. It was the middle of the night. I heard the gunshot in the basement. Eric, my older brother, got to him right afterward. He knew CPR, but I guess there was nothing left that he could breathe into. All I could do was lay in my room, listening." She shook her head to avoid the memory, "In the darkness…voices…screams…cries."

Jonathon pained over the sorrow Melinda expressed. He felt a strange mix of sadness and awe.

Beside her, John offered a couple of tissues, and she wiped her eyes before looking back at him. Through tears, her lips curled slightly as if to say, "I'm okay." He leaned back with a hand on her shoulder and remained silent.

"After that, I stopped thinking about being healed. I stopped thinking about God at all. What kind of a god would hand me that? It was ten long years of loneliness and self-pity before God was able break my hard heart. I began to understand slowly, but surely, that His love for me never changed after my accident."

When she paused, Jonathon asked, "What made the difference? What brought you back?"

Melinda smirked and eyed her husband.

"That'd be me," John said. "This gorgeous girl came into the lumber and hardware store where I was working, asking for some advice on building a bookshelf. She had measurements on this little drawing and was planning to build it herself. I was amazed at her tenacity right from the start. I found myself ignoring her wheelchair as her independence overshadowed her disability."

Melinda jumped in. "To make a long story short, he asked me out. That first night, he talked to me about Jesus; he was so comfortable in mentioning His name. I thought I knew about God, but I hadn't understood Him at all. John spoke of Jesus in such a personal way, like he knew Him as a friend. Behind his words he lived it—through his kindness, how few things upset him. It was easy to see that his relationship with Jesus had changed his life. He even prayed with me. I'd never met a man like him."

"It was a God thing," John added. "She was so open to Christ; so ready to see Him change her life. She had a good foundation from her family, and it was God's perfect timing when I got to pray with her to commit her life to Christ."

"I had no idea I had buried such anger in my heart up to that point," Melinda continued. "I simply broke and asked God to forgive me for not trusting Him. With John's help, I asked Jesus to be Lord of my life. It was a real challenge for me to do that. I had to tell Him that I would accept myself just the way I was. Then I had to convince myself that I was okay—this way." She slapped her shrunken legs and frowned, then broke out with a giggle. "And He did! I sensed His love for me, right then as I prayed that first time."

"It was a huge transformation for Mel," John said. "She suddenly had joy in her heart, because she knew Christ loved her, whether she could walk or not. I'll never forget that day."

"You see, Jonathon, He desired my heart—not my legs. Ever since then I've stopped looking for a healing of my back. I believe if it hadn't been for my injury, I would have never understood Christ's love for me. I thank God for my accident, for it brought me to Jesus."

Her eyes glistened, shining bright as she sipped her tea. The silence gave a quiet utterance of respect and wonderment. As neither man could respond, Melinda added her final sentiment.

"That's why I can't ask you to pray for my healing."

*****

Dr. Feddersen's voice was tense as he stood with a stack of computer reports in his hands. "This one's got to be by the protocol, Jerry."

Dr. Troy stood with his back to his partner in the lower level greenhouse, relishing a row of hybrid Dutch hyacinths with astounding, blended colors. Artificial ultraviolet lighting came from individual spotlights above each plant, casting a luminous glow around their master in the otherwise darkened room.

"Not a problem, Marty."

"I'm serious. No more sloppy research. So far we can't go to print with anything we've got. It's got to be clean."

"I'll see to it." He caressed a mixed orange and pink blossom with his fingers.

"No changes in dosages, no conflicting treatments, no errors."

When Troy didn't respond, Feddersen threw the pack of reports down with a smack on a mahogany end table and began furiously typing on a nearby keyboard. He scanned through multiple screens of additional data, fuming.

"It's not here. What's going on, Jerry?"

Troy moved to the next plant in line without a word, facing a thick spike of mixed dark blue and lime green blossoms.

"There's nothing in here about Smitherton's next inoculation. He's on for Monday, right?"

"Yes, Monday. It's scheduled." Troy's voice was calm and bored.

"But there's nothing recorded yet. Jerry, this is what I'm talking about. What's the plan?" Feddersen collapsed in the couch in exasperation.

"Adenocarcinoma."

"You're joking, right?"

"Pancreatic adenocarcinoma."

"How? You can't spring an oncogene and expect it to show up in a few hours. Cancer, even with accelerated growth, takes weeks to months. We can't monitor Smitherton for that long without someone catching on."

Troy turned and faced Feddersen. "What if he's had it for months?" The words came out as if he was reading a children's story. "What if all we do on Monday is trigger a programed mutation. The DNA has been present and reproducing for eighty-nine days, counting today. Monday we'll give him a little nano-juice that switches the incubating DNA to a virulent pathogen."

"You inoculated him with pancreatic cancer three months ago?" Feddersen stood with fire in his eyes. "Jerry, you can't run the research this way. It's unacceptable. Do you think this is just a game? We're sitting on prime technology; no one else is even close. And you're playing Solitaire."

Troy returned to his hyacinths, this one with yellow and black blooms. "It will clearly demonstrate the power we have. There'll be no mistakes. We will cure cancer."

"But we're causing cancer. How do you expect any ethics board to accept that? This is crazy."

"What's the difference?" He squeezed his fingers into the pot's soil. "We've blocked his coronary arteries and shot him with *Staph*. It's just part of the magic, isn't it? We make him better—we heal, Marty. That's what everyone wants to see."

Feddersen walked over to the line of bizarre flowers and spoke quietly. "This has got to be it, Jerry. If we do it well, it can stand alone. A man comes to us with cancer of the pancreas. We fix him. If it works, we'll change medical history. We can't write up the other experiments; the methodologies are too scrambled. Let's do this one right."

"Of course."

Grabbing the stack of papers, Feddersen rambled. "What would be nice is to find someone with a tumor. Rather than iatrogenically creating disease, we could heal a truly spontaneous cancer. That'll be the next step. A large clinical trial with hundreds of individuals around the country, perhaps the world, all coming to be healed of their disease. You'll be the lead consultant on the greatest of medical therapies." He looked at Troy's back but found no audience.

"Keep me in the loop, Jerry. Don't block me out. We need each other, right?"

Troy turned, his fingers muddied with the rich, dark potting soil. A closer look revealed the black and yellow flower petals pulled apart in his hands. The rest of the plant was uprooted, lying on top of the potted soil. His lips curved into a smile, bearing his teeth in a hyena's grin.

Feddersen's voice whispered. "What's going on, Jerry? Are you okay?"

"I'm excellent." The blooms sifted between Troy's fingers, falling to the floor. "How about you?" His eyes narrowed as the smile broadened even further.

Feddersen backed away. "You haven't been outside of this place for a while. Maybe it's time for a break." His voice trembled, and he cleared his throat in hopes of hiding it. "I'll come see you tomorrow. It's Thanksgiving, you know. You want to go out for dinner?"

The smile faded and Troy turned away. "Don't bother. I've got work to do."

"I'm coming out, Jerry. I'll bring something for us to share. It's Thanksgiving."

"No turkey."

"Right. Maybe some veggie lasagna. See you tomorrow."

Chapter 19

I *still look fat.*
　　Pulling at every edge of her new swimsuit, Noelle tried to cover more. It was a one-piece job, purple with light blue vertical strips. The back was not as revealing as most, covering a multitude of her moles. As she lined herself up with the mirror above the row of sinks, she still questioned if the new suit really made any difference.

　　The repercussion of the indoor diving board sounded in the dressing room, shouts and screams echoing through the tiled walls. She was an hour late; the trip to Rollings ate up more time than she had expected. When she got home, Manny surprised her by agreeing to come, so she couldn't back out, though she was completely ready to by then.

　　"C'mon, Noelle!"

　　Her brother's voice rang out across the walls as he yelled from the pool-side door.

　　"I'm coming. You go on in." She yelled back, buying only minutes before the inevitable.

　　She grabbed her beach towel and laid it across her shoulders, letting the ends drop to her waist. She turned to the right, then left, eyeing herself in the mirror one final time, still not satisfied that it covered enough.

　　Walking into the showers, she turned off two nozzles that were spraying against empty walls before going to a third cubicle. She put her towel on a hook and stepped in to carefully let the tepid water hit against her front and back without wetting her hair. Long enough to be misted, she then replaced her towel over her shoulders and practiced her confident smile as she approached the doorway to the pool.

　　As she stepped out, the bright lights made her feel she was being showcased, but a quick look around revealed she wasn't even noticed. The pool was full of forty or so guys and girls, all in a variety of dunkings, dives, or volleyball slams. The high-dive offered a cannonball splash every minute from individuals of all sizes. As she glanced across the room, she realized she wasn't as bad off as she thought in her new suit.

"Noelle!" Manny waved to her from the deep end, just before plunging off the board. She couldn't help but notice that he looked great, a muscled body that compared with the best, even if he was two to four years older than the rest of the room. As he pulled himself out of the pool, his left calf showed the massive gouge where the surgeons had removed his melanoma years ago. The leg was markedly thinned and he still walked with a negligible limp, but he was alive. That was something they didn't expect when it was diagnosed seven years ago. It was great to see him alive.

She moved to the edge of the pool, across the room from where he dived, before she realized she didn't know anyone else there. She wondered where Jonathon was. After all, he was the reason she was standing there hiding behind her towel.

A look around the room found Jonathon in the whirlpool. Her count was efficient: there were five other girls with him, no guys. His back was to her, and it was easy to see he was keeping his audience's attention. Directly across from him, a blonde splashed water in Jonathon's face, followed by the other girls in the tub shooting waves at him.

Must have been one of his bad jokes.

She hesitated to interrupt the fun, but knew nowhere else to turn unless she did high-dives with her brother. She clutched her towel at her shoulders and gingerly walked to the whirlpool. The blonde nodded and smiled at her, bringing Jonathon's attention around.

"Noelle, you made it!" He stood and introduced her to the other girls. She knew a couple vaguely from high school, and met Hillary as the blonde who had just smiled at her.

"C'mon in, Noelle. It's harmless here compared to the war zone over there." Hillary nodded at the pool volleyball game.

"I agree." She looked away, distracted by the spikers and still holding her towel tightly. It was either spanking a ball around or whirlpooling here. She brought her towel to her waist for one last stroke of security, then dropped it and quickly sank into the bubbles, stopping just short of getting her hair wet.

"So you're at St. Louis University?" Hillary asked.

She nodded. "Doing pre-med…at least trying," she responded.

"She's a brain, don't let her fool you," Jonathon piped in. "She got me through more than one class at Windwood High."

139

"My dad's a doctor," Hillary offered. "Not sure I'd wish that on anyone." She smiled, but Noelle saw sincerity behind her words. This girl wasn't afraid to be friendly—or vulnerable. It made Noelle want to know her more.

"Who's your dad?"

"Dr. Wells, over at Family Health Specialties."

"I've heard of him. I know Dr. Mittlestedt over there pretty well."

"He's a great guy. That's who I go to when Dad decides I'm too much for him."

"Like, all the time," Jonathon smirked.

Hillary splashed him again.

"Why do you want to be a doctor, Noelle?" she asked.

"Hey! What's going on?" Suddenly two giant hands came under each of Jonathon's arms, and he was elevated out of the whirlpool, half-carried, half-dragged away as the girls all started laughing.

"Manny! It's gotta be you. Just how big are you now?"

"Big enough to dunk ya," a husky voice responded. Someone grabbed Jonathon's feet, and he was flung into the air before belly-flopping into the water.

He surfaced to smiling stares from the crowd around him.

"Good to see you, too, Manny," he feigned calmness.

"You're as fun as ever, Jonathon." Manny cannonballed in right beside him.

Immediately some of the other guys in the pool offered hands to Jonathon and Manny to slap, followed by introductions. Neither of them had ever enjoyed such friendliness in a group of peers. The gang invited them to join the volleyball game, and both swam over to swap in for other players.

A half-hour later, the game ended in a rousing overtime, Manny spiking the ball into a hole on the other team to finish the game. Most of the players took a break from the water and went to a room off to the side of the pool to get some drinks and snacks.

Jonathon collapsed in a chair with a plate piled with barbecue chips topped with squeeze cheese. Beside him, Manny dropped into a chair with a handful of pretzels.

"What a game, Manny. Where'd you learn to play like that?"

"I used to come to this pool all the time before college. I did a lot of my rehab here after my surgery, way back when."

"It sure paid off. I couldn't come close to keeping up with you."

"Just making up for lost time. I couldn't keep up with anyone last time I saw you."

"It's all behind you now?"

"Definitely. That was quite a trip. Scared everybody. I remember it was especially hard on Noelle. I never knew what to say to her." He sighed. "Glad you were there for her." Leaning back, he placed his thick arms behind his head and spoke in a hushed tone. "I still remember when you prayed for me."

Jonathon looked down, playing with his chips. "That was an amazing time, wasn't it?"

"Like, incredible. You did something then, Jonathon. Have you ever thought about it?" The words were slow and quiet. "That maybe your prayer...I mean, really...cured me?"

"You must not have read the paper lately, Manny," he mumbled.

"Huh?"

"Never mind. Yeah, I've thought about it. I have some ideas, but I wonder more what you think."

He dropped his arms and slapped Jonathon's thigh hard enough to sting. "Lilacs. That was it. I smelled lilacs after you prayed. It was the dead of winter."

Rubbing his hip, he almost lost his plate of chips. "You really think it made a difference?"

"Difference? I'm alive. That's a difference." Manny laughed out loud.

"But I mean, in your life otherwise. Like, did it make you think about God?"

"It did a little bit, back then."

"I'm gonna level with you." Jonathon set his chips down on the floor and sat up. "I think God used me to heal you, Manny. It wasn't me, don't get me wrong. But I think He was shaking your tree. God decided to spare your life because of that prayer. Don't you think it's possible? Considering how bleak the doctor's report was on you."

"I know. That was the weird part. They were so shocked themselves when my tests came back clear."

"So why do you think maybe God wanted to heal you?"

"Clueless, Jonathon." He tapped a long finger on his own chest. "There's little here that God would want out of me."

"Not true, Manny. He loves you. He's after you. Passionate about you. He died for you so He could save you. And now He's healed you." Jonathon held his tongue, fearing his boldness was too much.

141

"Hadn't thought about it that way," Manny mused.

"You gotta get plugged in. Have you heard about how Christ wants to be Lord of your life?"

"Sure, in Sunday School as a kid. You really think there's something to it, don't you?"

"I'm sure of it, Manny. You need to be too. Would you want to pray about it?"

"Whoa now, not so fast," he chuckled and stood.

"That's cool. When you're ready, you'll know."

"My little sister's friend, the preacher now, eh?"

But he didn't leave.

"I'm no preacher, that's for sure. But since you brought it up, you ever think about going to church?"

"Not since I left for college. Bugs my mom that I don't go, but you know, it's pretty dull."

"Do this, Manny." He pointed out to the pool. "Try the church these guys go to. It's Windwood Community Church. They've got a great service. I bet you'd like it."

"Are you going there?"

"Thinking about it, but I still go to First Congo with my mom."

"Well, call me if you're ever going. Maybe I'll go with you."

"Like this weekend?" Jonathon felt confident as he pushed on.

Manny paused and looked into the air. "Sure. Sunday morning. Call me with the time. Let's try it out. If what you're saying is true, maybe I should check this God stuff out a little better."

Manny left the room to swim. Alone with his pile of chips, Jonathon wasn't hungry. He had more than food filling his soul.

*****

"So anyway, you were going to tell me why you want to be a doctor, Noelle." Hillary was back in the whirlpool after seeing Manny and Jonathon get into the volleyball game.

The chlorine steam slightly burned inside Noelle's nose, but the churning jets against her back gave a delightful massage. "It just seemed like the thing to do, I guess. I talked with Dr. Mittlestedt some, and he really encouraged me."

"Just don't let it do to you what it did to my dad."

"What's that?"

Hillary sunk deep, leaving her chin just above the water. "He got so busy, he buried himself in it. I think he figured if he couldn't solve his problems at home, he'd just cover them up by his work."

"It's been pretty rough?"

"My parents split a year ago. They just couldn't get over a bunch of issues."

"I'm sorry, Hillary."

"Nah, it's okay. God's really taken care of me through it. I wish it wasn't so hard on Dad. It just seemed he'd rather be a doctor than face real life. You know what I mean?"

Noelle knew too well. She didn't answer, didn't want to think that hard. Instead, she stretched her legs flat against the side wall, letting the jets fire away along her whole body.

"What's St. Louis like?" Hillary asked.

"It's okay for a big city."

"Lots of great guys to choose from?"

Noelle closed her eyes and frowned. "Not really."

"Ah, c'mon. St. Louis has got to have some studs."

"Not the ones I saw." Noelle slumped deeper in the water, glancing at her shoulders to be sure her hair was dry. "Some are real jerks if you ask me. Windwood does just as well—like right here."

Hillary giggled and popped up. She moved herself up to the whirlpool ledge, dangling her feet while she looked over the pool crowd.

"Your brother sure is cute." She paused and asked sincerely, "How'd he hurt his leg?"

"He had a bad bout with cancer. Actually, it almost killed him. They did surgery and got it all, just in time. He's very lucky."

"Wow, that must have been scary."

"I was around twelve then, and it was a big deal. I guess they really thought he wouldn't do this well."

"Must have been God."

"Sure, and a good surgeon."

Hillary panned the pool again. "Are you and Jonathon seeing each other?"

"No, not really. We've been friends for a long time. Used to go out some, but nothing serious."

"He seems like a great guy, Noelle."

"Yeah, he is." She raised an arm out of the water and watched the iridescent purples in the foam fade along her wrist and hand. "Who knows what the future will bring?"

"Do you ever think God has just the right person for you?"

Noelle was caught by Hillary's ease of talking about God. The steaming bubbles surrounding her lulled her into a deep honesty. It seemed easy to be transparent.

"I've thought some about that. I think He'd let us choose. Not just one right person; we need to shop around some."

"So how will you know? When will you know if it's right?"

Noelle moved back to sit, bringing her shoulders out of the water. She met eyes with Hillary, surprising herself with the harshness of her own voice: "All I know is, I'll know when it's not right. That's for sure." She dropped her head.

Hillary was still staring, and Noelle wished she could take back the words.

"You've been hurt, Noelle." Her voice dropped to a whisper. "Was it Jonathon?"

"No, no. He'd never hurt anyone." This was too honest. "I'm okay, really." She moved up to the ledge. "I'm going to go swim."

"Noelle, wait." Hillary reached Noelle's shoulder. "Can we talk a bit more?"

Noelle turned back and leaned against the tub wall, wondering why Hillary showed such interest.

"I've had a struggle in my life, and it hurts," Hillary spoke softly. "I know it too well. I got really down on myself before my folks split up. I knew it was my fault. Took me to a pretty low point, like...like suicide. I tried twice, Noelle." The words came out firmly; she was forcing herself to say it. "The second time they had to shock my heart back to life."

A shiver rode down Noelle's spine, dulling the sensation of warm bubbles around her ankles.

"All that made me sensitive now when I see pain in other people. Pain like mine. I don't want you to go where I was, Noelle. You don't have to talk it out now. I'm just telling you, you gotta go to somebody. It was a complete stranger that put me back on track. You need somebody too."

Noelle hesitated between bewilderment and anger, then stood. "You've been kind, thanks. I think I'll go swim." Stepping out of the whirlpool, she looked back at Hillary and tried to offer a smile but felt a tear at her eye instead.

Quickly turning away, she dove into the pool, no longer caring about her hair getting wet.

*****

Jonathon left the snack room and entered the water for the chicken wrestling, girls on guys' shoulders, the winner being the last pair standing. Noelle and Manny were unbeatable until the group insisted all partners trade. Manny's new partner was a taller basketball star named Carol, and they became a tipsy mark that evened the field. Jonathon held his own with a couple of different girls he'd never met before, and though they usually went down among the middle of the contests, the fun easily outlasted the competition. He only saw Noelle when she would tumble by him into the water, but she was enthusiastic in yanking, jerking, and screaming with the rest.

After the pool shut down, he waited outside with Manny. Some of the guys asked them to go out for a movie, and Manny jumped on it.

"You want to go, Jonathon?"

"I'm beat, Manny. You go ahead."

"Would you take Noelle home? We rode together."

"No problem. She'll be out in an hour, I suppose."

"Give her two. I could just stop by for her after the movie," he laughed and jumped into a van with his new friends.

Ten minutes later, she came out.

"You're early, Noelle." Jonathon grinned.

"Funny. Where's Manny?"

"He went off with some of the guys to a movie. I told him I'd take you home, 'kay?"

"That's fine. I better hurry, though. I promised Mom I'd help with some pies for tomorrow."

"Sure thing. Hop in." He cracked the door for her to step into his Chevette, then jumped in the driver's seat and drove toward her home.

"I'm sure glad you made it work tonight. What'd you think of the group here?"

"It was fun, Jonathon. I'm glad I came."

"You got to visit with Hillary some. She's the one who put it all together."

"Yeah." She didn't offer more.

"So when do you head back for SLU?"

145

"I'm going on Saturday. I need to get a few things done for a lab I have to turn in on Monday."

"Figures. I was hoping maybe you could go to church with Manny and I. He's gonna try these guys' church with me."

"You're kidding. Manny's going to church?"

"No big deal. He wants to check it out. I told him I'd go too."

"What's your mom gonna say?"

"It won't be pretty."

"If it helps, I bet my folks will be thrilled about Manny. Take it easy on him, Jonathon."

"Yes, yes. I remember."

He pulled up to her driveway and got out with her.

"We need some time of our own, Noelle." He walked her to the door. "Maybe Friday?"

"I'd like to, but I need to check and see what my folks have planned."

"I'll call you. Have a great Thanksgiving." He placed his hand on her arm and gave it a gentle squeeze. Her eyes met his and she sighed, curving her lips upward.

That was enough. No need to repeat the scene of the other night. He tugged her arm once more and went back to his car. In his rearview mirror he saw her standing at the door as he drove away.

She stood there, staring his direction, for as long as he could see her in the distance.

The enemy moves strategically, spreading its plague in a macabre madness that still transcends technology. Now more than molecules, the reproduction grows to an ever-multiplying epidemic. Thousands at a time, healthy cells are hindered, halted, layer by layer, replaced by the unseen reaper. Like the tip of an iceberg, it grows across an innocent millimeter of epidermis, while underneath it intuitively invades deeper structures two hundred times its own size. Without raising suspicion, the thriving disease ravages the normal tissue.

Chapter 20

*F*eddersen went overboard for a holiday meal. His partner needed a break, a respite. Thanksgiving seemed to offer the moment. He wasn't much of a chef, but between frozen lasagna, a cornucopia filled with fruit, and a bottle of the most expensive wine available at the grocery counter, he felt he'd done well. The foil tray of pasta had baked in his oven for an hour, and now he was on the dry and dusty cornfield road at eleven that morning. They'd drink, eat, and remember old and better times. He'd even look with interest at the flowers; anything to get Jerry to relax and be himself again. Maybe a drive to Rollings, just to escape for a few hours.

With arms loaded, he rode the elevator to the basement level two floors down. Stepping out, he yelled for his partner.

No response.

He entered Troy's office, tidy as always. The only signs of life were the three hanging baskets of exotic purple and gold blooms under artificial light. He left the food there and stepped across the short hall to the garden room.

"Jerry? You here?"

A bank of ultraviolet lights lined the back wall over the pots that had held the Dutch hyacinths. Only now each pot was closely cropped with a short, thick green stem just above the soil line. A clean cut of each stem prepared Martin for finding a beautiful but eccentric bouquet of colors somewhere else. He left the room to hunt further.

At this level there was only one other area, the lab where Troy prepared his nano-concoctions. The room was dark, and Marty flicked the overhead light just to be sure everything was in its place. A long table held small vials in two plastic racks, appearing something like a child's chemistry set. Everything was meticulously clean and orderly. Troy's computer sat on a bench behind the table, glowing with a screensaver of a tropical plant with a large central orange blossom. Two Nanomed syringes laid next to the terminal on a folded green surgical cloth, both exactly parallel with each other.

He wasn't here.

Martin questioned lugging the lasagna around on his search, fearing it would be cold soon. The only oven was in the adjoining house where Troy greeted select consultants and a rare patient.

Putting his eye to the iris scanner, he entered the elevator and returned to the ground level. Exiting the metal outbuilding, he glanced at the clouds portending rain before entering a wooden screen door to the back of the farmhouse. The external appearance of dilapidation quickly departed as he entered the spacious lobby flooded with hazy light from the north wall of glass and skylights.

Stark white walls and black and white checkerboard tile flooring gave the room a feeling of depth and business, despite it being empty. Large-leaved green plants splashed the only color in the room as Tchaikovsky played softly in the background.

Troy had to be here.

The hair on the back of Feddersen's neck rose. Rather then yell for his partner, he walked the length of the room, keeping his feet noiseless as he made his way to a side hall leading to the small galley kitchen and dining area.

The lights were already on as he passed through the kitchen. He placed the lasagna pan beside a crystal wine glass that still contained a fresh drop of ruby liquid. Around the corner in the dining room was the floral spray of Dutch hyacinths he was expecting, squarely placed in the center of the dining table. Place settings were set for two, complete with double spoons and forks. The moment his heel hit the floor of the dining room, he flinched, hearing a voice.

"Dr. Feddersen, happy Thanksgiving."

Troy stood in the corner of the room, leaning against the wall beside a column window. He was dressed in a brilliant blue blazer with matching open-collared shirt and black slacks. His hand swirled wine in a crystal stemmed glass.

"I began to wonder if you would come." Troy's voice was dancing, playful.

"I've been hunting for you. Didn't expect to find you here." Martin tried to hide his frustration; there was no reason to belabor his past quarter hour of searching.

"You think I work too hard, my friend," the singsong phrases were condescending. "But I know when diversions are needed. Your offer of a meal was timely."

"I brought lasagna, but we'll need to warm it up."

"Perfect." His inflections lingered on the word. "Let's have a drink, a toast."

Returning to the kitchen, Feddersen set the oven temperature and slipped in the lasagna. Troy opened the refrigerator and pulled out a crystal goblet already filled with wine.

"The glass is chilled?" Feddersen asked when it was handed to him. Troy nodded and grinned, lifting his own glass to the air.

"To you and I, Marty. To NanoMed."

"Agreed." They clinked glasses and Feddersen smiled. Troy was relaxed, cheerful. Quite a switch from yesterday. The wine tasted delightful, a nice surprise compared to what he'd brought from the grocers. Leaning back on the kitchen counter, he asked, "So you feel good about Smitherton's next treatment?"

"It will be fine." Troy smiled broadly. "But enough about work, let's talk about life." His words sounded slightly slurred.

"Yes, life." That's just where Feddersen wanted the conversation to head. "Some of our best days…" a quick wave of nausea interrupted him, forcing a deep breath followed by another sip of wine.

"We've had some great times together, Marty." Troy's speech was definitely slurred; it also echoed as if he was speaking in a tunnel.

Feddersen added, "Like when we first met in Omahoggle." He caught himself. "No, that's not right. It was Omilia. No waysh…Shomaga."

He looked at Troy who continued to smile and stepped closer. Feddersen's chilled glass of wine was taken out of his hand. It was difficult to hear, but it distantly sounded as if Troy said, "Have a good nap, Marty."

Blurring to gray, a cloud swept through his vision and mind. As he collapsed, Feddersen was unconscious before he could feel the impact of his own body against the floor.

*****

The phone rang early but Jonathon was already up. On his knees in his room, he heard his mom answer. His Bible was open to the story of Gideon, and he continued in prayer. "Lord, I feel just like this guy; I'm the weakest link You've got. I just don't know if I'm hearing You anymore—but I desire to honor You. If You don't want me to heal any more, that's fine, but I want to still hear You, know You. If I was wrong about healing Mr. Smitherton and the mayor, and now wrong about healing Melinda, then perhaps I shouldn't be the one for this gift. I just want to know You, Lord. Help me."

A knock on the door interrupted him. "Phone's for you, son." Rising, he grabbed the phone in the hall.

"Hello?"

"Jonathon? This is Chandler. Happy Thanksgiving." Except her voice didn't sound happy.

"You too. Do you call all your ex-employees on holidays?"

"Just the ones I need. We're in a pinch. I talked to Dr. Feddersen; there was little he could say. We've got three aides sick and two out of town. It's a full house here and there's no one but you. Are you available?"

"I suppose so. Are you sure it's cleared? I don't want to mess with Dr. Feddersen again."

"It's fine, guaranteed. Only—"

"No healing. You don't need to say it, Martha. I wouldn't think of it."

"Dr. Feddersen was explicit on that. I'll use his words: 'No healing, no talk of healing, no wiggling your nose or waving your hands.' I've instructed the staff not to even wink at you about it."

"I get the point. When do you need me?"

"Two hours ago. Can you come up immediately?"

"I can be there in ten minutes."

"Then what are you talking to me for?" She hung up.

When he set the phone down his mother appeared from around the corner. "They can't live without ya, can they?"

"I guess they're really busy, Mom. They've asked me to come to work right away. Do you mind postponing our Thanksgiving dinner?"

"Course not. You go show 'em your stuff. I knew they'd come around."

"So what'll you do?"

"Right now I'm gonna go finish telling the Lord thanks for getting yer job back. You be careful about sparklin' on anyone now." She turned to go back to the living room.

"Can't. They've told me I can't even think about it."

Elaine whipped her head around. "Not use your gift? But what if God tells ya to?"

"Mom, I can't. They made it clear. Even God knows that."

"Don't be so sure. You obey Him first, Son. Don't let the world break what God has given ya."

"I dunno, Mom. I wonder if maybe I don't have the gift anymore."
Her face flushed red. "That's foolishness; don't be talkin' that way. God don't give a gift and then take it back, does He? No, sir. What He gives ya is yours. Use it His way."
Jonathon shook his head slightly before catching himself.
"What's gotten into ya, Jonathon? Remember Aunt Emma's words? 'You been chosen.' Now act like it." She slapped her hand on his chest and turned, going to the bedroom rather than back out to her kneeling blanket in the living room.
She's mad. Too mad to keep praying. That's trouble.

*****

Feddersen's eyelids weighed ten pounds. He tried to lift them but was unsuccessful. The only familiar sense was the sound of Tchaikovsky music nearby. Cool leather rubbed against his arms as he fingered his eyes to make them crack. With this help, he squinted at the bright light, finding himself stretched out on a black sofa, surrounded by white walls and the checkerboard floor. Attempting to call for Troy, his parched lips only allowed a grunt.
Pain stabbed straight through his brain when he raised up, forcing him to flatten his head to the cushion. An odor of Italian spices wafted past him, and he heard footsteps approach on the tile. It was much easier to keep his eyes closed.
"Ready to eat?" Troy's voice was right in front of him. "We have so much to be thankful for."
He reached for his eyes again, this time feeling a pull on his skin near his left elbow. He touched the spot and found a cotton ball taped to the inside of his arm. A needle mark dotted his arm under the cotton. "What—?" his voice was a coarse whisper. "What did you do?"
"Not to worry. We need more subjects, more data. You said it yourself. We've just doubled our test population. Why, ninety days from now, we'll save your life, Marty."
Feddersen's eyes could not yet open on their own. "You're crazy," he croaked.
"Surely not. After we save Smitherton, we'll do it all over again with you. You both will have identical cases of pancreatic cancer, cured. Who can argue with that?" The footsteps began to walk away.
"Great lasagna, by the way. I'll be sure to save you some."

151

*****

At the hospital, the nursing staff seemed glad to have Jonathon back. They definitely needed the help, as he had twice the number of patients to care for. With very little free time, he found the day pass by quickly. Everyone had been coached well; no one, including patients, mentioned anything about healing gifts. It was almost pleasant to return to anonymity as just an average nursing aide.

He was spooning ice cream into a two-year-old's mouth to soothe the sore throat of a tonsillectomy when the call sounded throughout the hospital.

"Code Blue, 142. Code Blue, 142."

Feet bustled outside his door.

"That's Mrs. Knudson," Jonathon said to himself. "Can't believe they're doing a code on her."

He put another spoonful in the boy. He had sent his mother out to the lobby for a break fifteen minutes ago. Hospital moms worried far too much, got little if any sleep, and then were worthless when it was time to dismiss their own tykes to their care at home. He made a point to get moms out of the room so they could gain a little time for themselves.

I should go, but I can't leave Justin. Anyway, poor Mrs. Knudson, she shouldn't have to go through all this mess; not in her condition. Why would anyone want to have her coded?

"I'm doing you a favor, feeding you, Justin. Do you hear all the ruckus in the hall? But I'm gonna stay right here with you until your mom comes back."

In response, Justin gurgled and melted ice cream oozed from his lips.

"Yeah, you need me more than old Mrs. Knudson."

Jonathon reasoned to himself that the hospital needed to do a better job with these advanced directives. Mrs. Knudson needs a plan for this kind of thing. No way should they try to save her life, not the way she was living.

He heard someone yell, and through a crack in the door he could see a red cart zoom down the hall.

Why are they pulling out all the stops? Why race to save someone who's already comatose? She has no chance of waking. It can't be a full code; they know she's ready to die. It's the only way she'll ever get out of this place.

The door opened and Justin's mom entered. "I heard all the commotion and thought I should come back. Do you need to go?"

"I suppose I should, although I don't think it's too serious. Here's the last couple bites of ice cream. Justin's doing great with swallowing this stuff." He mussed the boy's hair and handed Justin's mother the spoon. "I'll be back in a minute to clean up."

Often they wanted Jonathon in on codes if he was the only male on the shift, in case a back-breaking lift was required, or lengthy CPR. Neither should be the case with Mrs. Knudson. Rounding the corner to room 142, he passed the nurses station. Nodding at Carmen, the clerk at the desk, he asked, "That's Mrs. Knudson's room right? I'm surprised we're working so hard at it."

"That's Knudson's room, but the code is for someone else in there. A visitor she had collapsed."

Breaking into a run, Jonathon dashed down the hall and opened the door to find six people all clammering around a body on the floor. Mrs. Knudson, lying serenely on her bed, was pushed to the side to make more room.

Nurse Chandler was over the top of the body on the floor, loudly calling the numbers as she gave carefully timed chest compressions in sets of five.

"One—and—two—and—three—and—four—and—five—and—"

Jonathon nudged into the group, but so many hands were in the way that he couldn't see the face of the victim. The respiratory technician squeezed a large, black bag after every five chest thrusts, sending air into the endotracheal tube already placed in the person's throat.

"Who is it?" he asked.

A nurse putting an intravenous needle in an arm turned. "I think her name is Davis. She's almost always here with Mrs. Knudson. When Nurse Chandler came in, she found her unconscious on the floor. No one's sure how long it's been."

Jonathon stretched his neck forward and whispered what he hoped wasn't true. "Grandma Davis."

"You know her?" the nurse asked.

He could see her now. The silver hair in perfect form seemed a mismatch with the gaunt face. He'd never noticed how thin and wrinkled her skin was as it sagged across her cheeks.

Nurse Chandler shouted breathlessly in her continued cadence. "One—and—two—and—Jonathon—give me a—break."

Stepping over Grandma Davis's legs, he eyed their mottled, blue color, a telltale sign that she had been there a while. As he kneeled alongside Nurse

Chandler, he moved a couple of electrode wires snaking across Grandma Davis's chest, his hands ready to assume the same position.

"Switch—after—my—next—set," Nurse Chandler said rhythmically, giving a final set of compressions with both hands placed squarely between Grandma Davis's breasts.

"Let me check a pulse and see the monitor," the respiratory therapist barked. He placed three fingers against Grandma Davis's neck to feel the carotid artery.

"The monitor still shows no rhythm," Nurse Chandler shouted.

"Nothing here either." The therapist returned to squeezing the bag.

Jonathon immediately arched his back over the lifeless body and, with arms straight, drove the heels of his hands into Grandma Davis's sternum. Resuming the previous meter, he called out, "One—and—two—and—three—and—four—and—five—and—"

"Give another epinephrine," Nurse Chandler shouted, in command but still winded.

"That's a total of three, with two atropine given!" one of the nurses shouted back.

"Who's on call for us?" Nurse Chandler asked.

"Mittlestedt," a different nurse said. "He should be here any minute."

"Okay, we've gotta keep going until he gets here."

Alcohol filled the air under Jonathon's nose as another alcohol wipe was torn open and rubbed across the hastily made intravenous site. He felt the cool, clammy skin of his friend and prayed as he counted out loud, *Lord, how about now? Would you use me here?*

He thought about the blue-and-white tea cup and the visits at the computer. He remembered Grandma Davis's encouragement to speak honestly with Noelle and her mention of his own spiritual gift.

This is an incredible lady, God. Please allow her to live. We need her!

"Anybody have any other ideas?" Nurse Chandler asked.

Jonathon looked around at the nurses huddled near him. Did they all avoid his eyes?

God, I'll pray for her healing, but only if I'm sure you're asking me to. Tell me, Lord, please make it clear.

The only sound outside of counting was the hiss of the artificial bagged breaths squeezed into worn and unreceptive lungs.

Before he realized it, tears dropped onto his hands. "We gotta do something!" Sobs of frustration overwhelmed his vocal cadence. He desperately sharpened the depth of his chest compressions. Davis's sternum was spongy with each blow, evidence of cracked ribs.

"We *are* doing something," Nurse Chandler said in a controlled tone. "We all are, Jonathon. You need a break?"

He licked his lips, tasting the salt of his tears. "No, I'm alright." Two more tear drops splashed onto Grandma Davis's chest. Wiping his eyes on his shoulders, he resumed the count and eased his chest blows, "One—and—two—and—three—and—four—and—five—"

The door banged open with Dr. Mittlestedt entering, dressed in a finely tailored charcoal pinstriped suit. "What happened here?" he bellowed.

The room fell quiet but for the sound of sibilant breaths and Jonathon's chest compressions, his count now being said under his breath. Nurse Chandler spoke up to tell all that was known, "Mrs. Davis suffered an unwitnessed collapse with CPR initiated as soon as she was found. Protocols were followed for the rhythm of asystole, including two doses of atropine surrounded by three doses of epinephrine."

"You've been at this how long?" he asked.

One of the nurses looked at her clipboard. "Thirty-five minutes now."

Exhaustion began to creep over Jonathon. His own adrenaline was wearing off, and the obvious became clear. Tears at his eyes were drying.

Dr. Mittlestedt bent over beside Jonathon and laid his fingers against Grandma Davis's neck.

"Stop CPR," he commanded, his eyes on the monitor.

Jonathon obeyed, leaving his hands in place, ready to resume.

"That's it." Mittlestedt stood, looking toward Nurse Chandler. "Looks like you've done everything possible."

"I believe so," she responded.

"After this long, there's no chance the brain could have stayed oxygenated," he said more to himself than anyone else. He looked at Nurse Chandler. "See if you can find out about any family, or at least her physician. I guess we need to call someone." He spoke coolly, business-like.

"Carmen should know by now. I'll get you what she has."

Dr. Mittlestedt was at the doorway and nodded at Jonathon. "Those were good chest compressions." Then he looked at Nurse Chandler and spoke quietly. Jonathon could read his lips: "What's he doing here?"

Nurse Chandler returned to her nurses. "Let's move the body to room 150 in case the family wants to stop by. And nice work, gang. We did all we could." She then pushed Dr. Mittlestedt out the door just as Jonathon caught another stare from the doctor before it closed. She was going to give the doctor an earful.

Little was said as they took off the electrodes and redressed Grandma Davis. A gurney was brought in, and Jonathon helped lift her skinny body. Ten minutes later, a nurse poked her head in to ask if Jonathon could come help her lift another patient to bed, and he left the room.

Walking down the hall, he wrestled the coldness of death. The nurse beside him whispered curiously, "Did you think about doing your stuff on her?"

He shook his head and looked away from her, fighting the cry waiting just behind his eyes. "Let's get your patient moved." He hurried away down the hall.

Chapter 21

*T*he overcast sky kept the sun tucked in longer than usual on Thanksgiving day, and Noelle enjoyed staying under the covers. Even the aroma of roasted turkey couldn't draw her out of bed. It wasn't until she heard her brother clanging around in the bathroom that she felt guilty about sleeping in.

She groggily entered the kitchen in her lavender flannel pajamas. "Can I help?" she asked her mom.

"Your eyes are barely open, girl," her mother replied, apron tight across her waist, slicing onions.

"I've missed all the fun." Noelle smiled and turned, walking into the living room as a hot pad hit her in the back.

"You get dressed, and I'll put you to work," her mother laughed.

Noelle didn't change direction, falling into the soft velour of a recliner beside an oak roll top desk. Her mother continued to converse, raising her voice to be heard from the kitchen.

"I was worn out yesterday, didn't even hear you come in from the swim party. Did you have a good time?"

"It was fun, Mom. My suit was great too. Thanks for helping me get it."

"Don't forget, the payback is today. Would you set the table?"

"Sure. Just give me a minute."

"Did you see there's a letter for you in yesterday's mail? I never looked at it until late last night. Must be from a new friend at school."

Reaching beside her, Noelle found an envelope on the top of the desk and read the handwritten return address. All it stated was a street she recognized as near the St. Louis University campus.

She slid her finger under the seal and pulled out a greeting card featuring a beautiful tangerine sunset at the beach with two young adults looking toward the ocean. One was a slender woman with arms crossed, sitting on the end of a long log. At the opposite end of the log stood a sleek man, facing the same

157

direction with a hand extended to the lady. Inside, the short sentiment was in calligraphy: "Will you forgive me?"

Below it, a large handwritten "D" was followed by an inch scribbled line. Noelle froze.

"Who's it from, honey?" her mother yelled over the top of a mixer.

She broke from her chair and avoided the kitchen to go around a back hall to her room. "Just somebody from school," she called more quietly. "I'm going to get dressed."

She landed back on her bed, legs crossed, door closed. Intently ripping the card into small pieces, she made a pile before her, followed by bits of the envelope cascading over the small mound of useless confetti.

What is it with him? How bad does he want to ruin my life? She felt a painful shiver down her spine as she tried to squash a memory of pain and humiliation. Like trying to manhandle a ball under water, she kept feeling awful images slip up into her mind.

I won't let him; I can't let him. She forced her mind to the alter ego. *Jonathon—Jonathon loves me.* She pulled him into focus, remembering the pool party, dwelling on his parting at the door with her. He had held onto her arm and squeezed it. He had wanted to embrace again; she knew it. He loved her.

Jonathon, you're too good to be true.

But maybe he wasn't. *He's been a great friend, but could I love him?*

Bam! Just thinking the word "love" conjured another snapshot from the dreadful tryst with Dave. She shoved it back under.

Jonathon gets so quirky; will he ever get a life? With his future so bleak, where would I be? And his religion…we just avoid it now because he knows it makes me mad. I AM a Christian, Jonathon. I am—

Bam! Like a cheap pornographic video, another clip flashed through her mind. *No! It wasn't my fault!* she wanted to say aloud. *God, don't You know? It wasn't my fault!*

Her fists slammed down, sending bits of a coastal sunset fluttering across the bed.

*****

Jonathon helped move a patient into bed and stepped back into the hospital hall, his gaze immediately turning to where Grandma Davis had died.

The long hall was quiet, empty. Her body had been moved to room 150, the last room of the north hall. Though he needed to return to his patients, he wanted to see her one last time. Deciding to check on little Justin and his mother first, his eyes caught a figure at the end of the hall. The individual was just leaving room 150.

And he wore an olive green trench coat.

Jonathon hurried down the hall, fighting the urge to call out, knowing he could catch up with him. The man stepped to the exit door which opened to a small concrete patio and grassy side lawn. The only other time the door was used was for rare patients forcing their freedom to smoke a cigarette outside the building. Parking was on the opposite side of the hospital, so guests almost never used the door.

With Jonathon five paces away, the door closed. Breaking into a short run to catch the guy, he banged it open, ready to finally yell.

Instead, he smacked into the chest of his target, jolting both of them as Jonathon reflexively reached his arms to the heavy-coated shoulders to steady himself.

"Oh, man! Excuse me!" Jonathon regained his footing and stepped back, readjusting his white uniform.

"I apologize," his voice was deep and soft. "I shouldn't stand so close to the door."

"No really, this was my fault. Are you okay?"

The man, in his early twenties with an athletic, six-foot-tall frame, did not appear fazed. Up close, Jonathon could see his hair was dark and thick, with light bronze highlights as it waved across his head. Even in the absence of a smile, the man's lean face was inviting and handsome.

"Yes, I'm fine, thanks. No harm done."

"I couldn't help but notice you were coming out of Gran—er, Mrs. Davis's room. Did you know her?"

Before answering, his blue eyes looked to the rain clouds in the sky. "Yes, we've been friends for some time." He didn't appear too emotional over her death.

"I'm sorry," Jonathon said to be courteous. "Word sure travels fast."

"I was surprised too. I was told that she had collapsed, and didn't know this was what I would find."

"Do you know her family? They may be coming up soon. I know we're trying to call them right now."

"I've never met them." He turned to walk onto the lawn. "Perhaps it would be best if I go."

Jonathon wasn't ready to end the visit. "I got to know Grandma Davis just the past month, but she's an amazing lady."

He turned back. "That's for certain. I have enjoyed many long visits with her."

He didn't act like the kind of guy who would sit around visiting with old ladies. "So how did you meet her?"

"A mutual friend, actually. He asked me to visit her, and our friendship took off from there."

"I'd like to tell her family you stopped by. What's your name?"

"Michael. Michael Sunday." With that he turned again and stepped onto the grass just as the rain started to fall.

Jonathon persisted. "I heard you met my mother."

Michael stopped, but remained undeterred. Turning his head, he called to the side. "She was quite worried about you. I just wanted to reassure her. Do you mind?" He was smiling in profile, his face lined perfectly. Despite mourning the loss of his friend, he remained pleasant.

"No. I'm just curious as to how you know me."

Michael idly strolled across the lawn as the rain showered down.

Trying again, Jonathon called out, "How do you know me?"

Thunder boomed and a cloudburst opened. Jonathon was unsure if he was heard, but Michael turned and waved, then broke into a light jog as he headed across the street. Before being drenched himself, Jonathon headed back inside.

He needed a towel to wipe his face and stepped into room 150. Mrs. Davis was laying in the flat bed, sheets tucked carefully under her chin. The expression on her face could have been mistaken for a peaceful sleep if it wasn't for her blanched skin shaded by a hint of light blue. Chloe, an LPN, was placing her shoes in a brown paper bag.

She eyed him and commented, "You're wet."

Grabbing a towel from the bathroom, he mopped his head. "Quite a downpour out there."

"Why were you standing out in the rain?"

"I was talking to that guy who was in here with her." He nodded over to Davis's body.

"What guy?" Chloe looked puzzled.

"That guy in the green trench coat. He's an old friend of hers and was in here just a minute ago."

"No one's been in here, Jonathon. I've been here since her body was brought in."

"But he just said he was up here visiting her. He said he'd been called to come when she collapsed."

"He wasn't in here." She shrugged her shoulders. "You better get dried off."

Jonathon came out of the room to peer out a window beside the exit door. The streets were empty, not a soul in sight. It was Thanksgiving, after all. Thunder clapped again as the rain pelted hard, and he said a prayer for his new friend Michael.

*****

A knock sounded at Noelle's door. The clock on her nightstand said she'd been in there twenty minutes. Grabbing a handful of the paper confetti, she threw it in a trash can beside her bed as she called out, "Just a minute." Glancing at herself in the mirror, she thought her red eyes weren't too ugly, at least there was no makeup to smear.

She opened the door while rubbing her eyes, finding Manny on the other side. "I was more tired than I thought," she said. "I laid down for a moment and must have gone back to sleep."

"Yeah, right. Can I come in?" It was not a question of whether he believed her; he had something else on his mind.

She stepped back into her room and sat on her bed, throwing her covers off to hide other pieces of the torn card and envelope. "C'mon in," she said as nonchalantly as possible.

He closed the door and stood across the room by her desk, eyeing her high school trophy, assorted photos, and school newspapers, still scattered across the top. He picked up the purple and gold sweatshirt and without looking at her, spoke. "Something's happened to you."

"What?" she asked as if she hadn't heard.

"What happened in St. Louis?" He turned to face her. "I can tell, Noelle."

She widened her eyes. "I don't know what—"

"I'm your brother, Noelle. I may not have your brains, but I know you. You're different."

Michael J. Huckabee

She got up and took the sweatshirt from his hand, folding it and returning it to a drawer. "It's a been a tough semester, worse than you know."

"Nope. That's not it. It's more than college life. Like with you and Jonathon last night. You kept your distance. You didn't treat him like you used to."

"So." She sorted the newspapers back into a stack before putting them in another drawer. "Your point is?"

Standing at her side, he looked down at her. "You've hooked up with someone. That's what I'm thinking."

He was wrong, but she was tired of defending herself and didn't respond at all.

"Don't let Jonathon go, Noelle. I don't think you could find better." Manny's voice was quiet but strong.

"That's not it, Manny." She hesitated and turned her back to him. "I ..."

He waited, but she only finished with a sigh. Then she started over. "It's not what you think."

"So you haven't given up on Jonathon?"

"No. I'm just not sure."

"As long as you're still giving him a chance."

She nodded once and changed the subject. "What's this about you going to church? Has something happened to you?" She grinned and admired him beside her in the mirror.

"Those guys at the pool were great. One guy—his name was Jared—we had a great time at the movie. Anyway, a little church never hurt anybody. Why don't you come too?"

"I'm leaving to go back to school Saturday. Anyway, I'll stick with Mom and Dad, thanks. You're not getting religious on me, are you?" She made a circle out of her hands and put the halo over his head.

He elbowed her. "What's wrong with that? Seems like you could use a good dose of God to help you these days. I'm going to check it out. It's something about Jonathon. I want what he's got." He smiled back at her.

"I know what you mean. Sometimes I want it too. It's just not that easy."

Chapter 22

*T*he foe continued to bore through the biochemical build of its victim, tenacious tentacles wrapping themselves with reckless abandon around unknowing recipients. The cancer reproduced at a phenomenal pace, each cell containing the DNA matrix of death. Searching in every direction, dendrites stretched through soft tissue of skin and adipose cells, abruptly encountering dense bone. The skeleton proved to be no impediment, but rather, was the mark, as microscopic molecules wove effortlessly through to the boney core. Rather than a blockade, the calcific structure served as a protected shaft for the enemy, providing security from the few blood cell sentries sent to observe the invasion. Inside the barrier of bone, the proliferation exploded with newfound freedom, finding channels of flow to every extremity. The assailing army now maneuvered to its meridian; the silent stalking striving for a fatal strike.

Jonathon grabbed the clipboard with the patient roster before hearing the full nursing report of the day.

"Glad to have you back," Carmen declared, passing by him on her way to the clerk's desk. "Didn't know if you'd be willing to come after the day we had yesterday. Some holiday, huh?" She didn't wait for an answer but continued down the hall.

He pushed his glasses up and scanned the list of assignments. Several overnight admissions made his load even heavier than the day before. He read the patients he was to care for out loud: "Holdman, Stuart, Chadwick, Moret, Polling, Smitherton—"

Double-checking himself, he read the last full name under his breath, "Henry Smitherton." A handwritten abbreviation said, "b. obst."

"Bowel obstruction. What else could go wrong with that man?" Jonathon said to himself.

In nursing report, he learned that Henry was admitted late last night with abdominal pain, and X-rays confirmed that the bowels were blocked. While sometimes an obstruction may occur due to extended constipation or medication, the X-ray report suggested evidence of a possible tumor, and he was scheduled for an MRI today. The nurses all shook their heads in agreement, knowing that for Henry, it was probably the worst scenario. Mary grabbed a pack of Winston's laying in front of Charlene and frowned at her. "That's where these will get you."

Making his early morning rounds, Jonathon hesitated before entering Mr. Smitherton's room. After their last discussion, he was prepared for the man to request a change in nursing staff. He opened the door and greeted him like every patient.

"Good morning, Mr. Smitherton, I'll be your nursing aide today."

Mr. Smitherton was awake in bed, the morning TV news blaring. He did not appear in great distress. "So we're back at it, Jonathon? With your help, let's keep it short and easy this time."

I see, it's "let's pretend nothing happened."

"We'll do all we can." Jonathon offered a cheerful smile and got one in return. He stayed strictly business. "Your pain must not be too bad."

"Not bad at all. Something sure kicked in compared to last night."

"That's great. Keep us posted. Is there anything you need?" He looked over the IV fluid bags hanging beside the bed, then moved to the bathroom to empty a full urinal.

"Nope, no complaints," Mr. Smitherton responded.

"Okay. Dr. Mittlestedt should be making rounds in a short time. Let me know if I can help you."

Exiting Mr. Smitherton's room, he headed three doors down to his next patient when he saw Dr. Feddersen bustling down the hall, carrying a tray of test tubes and needles from the hospital lab.

Jonathon hoped to crawl into a hole but instead turned his head and moved quickly down the opposite side of the hall. It was of no matter, as Dr. Feddersen never noticed him, pursuing a mission of his own. He knocked once on Mr. Smitherton's door and immediately entered, closing the door behind him.

Returning to the clerk's desk, Jonathon asked Carmen why Dr. Feddersen would be playing lab tech.

"That's how short we are, Jonathon," she replied. "They were going to make the new guy in the lab—you know, Larry's replacement—have to carry the whole holiday weekend of morning shifts. He's a nice guy—name's Cameron. Older guy, but still has kids at home. Anyway, Dr. Feddersen called last night and said he'd cover the lab this morning for a couple of hours to let Cameron sleep in and enjoy his family. Isn't he the greatest? He's giving up his own holiday to let another family have their father home for a bit more of the holidays. There's not another administrator like him in the world."

"Yup, that's wonderful." Jonathon held back his enthusiasm and headed back down the hall past Mr. Smitherton's room to his other patients. He slowed as he went by Mr. Smitherton's door but could not hear any sound. Just as he started to enter the patient's room two doors down, Dr. Feddersen came out of Mr. Smitherton's room. He gave a darting glance down both halls, seeing Jonathon but ignoring him. Thankfully, he was thinking of something other than the rehiring of his nursing aides, and rushed back to the lab.

Shrugging his shoulders, Jonathon stared at the physician/hospital administrator descending to a lowly phlebotomist's position. Impressive, perhaps, but it seemed a bit overdone. He watched Dr. Feddersen continue down the long hall, tray in one hand and—Something flashed in his other hand, like a glint of silver. Jonathon squinted.

That's a syringe, a silver syringe.

The last time he had seen one of those was when Larry Crenshaw, the now deceased lab tech, gave that midnight injection to Mr. Smitherton.

*****

Inside the lab, Feddersen efficiently worked at the receiving counter so he could return to finish drawing blood on the remaining hospital patients. Wrapping the empty syringe in the foam pad, he inserted it into the metal cylinder, loaded the container into the cardboard carton and placed the entire package into an insulated bag. As he lifted the bag off the counter, he flipped open the courier box to lay the bag beside a second one that he had placed late last night after Smitherton's first dose.

Troy had recommended a total of three doses, six hours apart.

Before closing the courier box, he reached over to add two tubes of blood drawn from Mr. Smitherton, one from six hours ago and one he had just drawn. Beside the tubes, a sheet of bubble wrap laid on the counter top, and he realized it was supposed to go around the cylinder. Troy would have a fit if the syringe did not return exactly as it had been prepared.

He left the box propped open and unzipped the insulated bag. Picking up the bubble wrap, he began to reopen the cardboard carton to pack it accurately. The lab door opened behind him, and he nearly dropped the packed syringe.

"Hello?" Mittlestedt's voice sounded just before he appeared in the doorway.

"Right here, Jack." He suddenly felt flushed, a drop of sweat beading on his brow. Mittlestedt entered the lab like he owned it, sauntering past the receiving counter to a blood chemistry analyzer the size of a large microwave.

"This is a new one, isn't it?" Mittlestedt asked nonchalantly, laying a hand on the five thousand-dollar machine. "Hospital must be doing okay to be updating the lab with one of these."

Martin smiled politely, fighting the temptation to enter the ego war. "It's working for all of us, Jack. Already paid for itself in about two months." He pushed the syringe carton behind his lab tray. "So how can I help you?"

"Just wondering, beings you were here, if you could shed some light on your policy for rehiring fired employees." He sat down on a stool and picked up a tube of blood—Smitherton's blood—turning the tube back and forth, watching the fluid pool at each end of the vial.

"You mean Jonathon Thompson?" Feddersen asked, knowing the answer.

"Or anyone else in a similar position. Wasn't he fired for a serious breach of his duties only a few days ago?"

"We needed aides, Jack. It's a holiday. He promised to behave himself."

"We don't need his kooky nursing methods around here, Martin. What would prevent him from going at it again?"

Feddersen wanted to grab the vial of blood out of Mittlestedt's hands, but didn't dare leave the syringe containers behind him. "I've talked to Chandler. We're both sure he won't."

"Sometimes I wonder who's running this institution." Mittlestedt set the tube back in its rack. "That kid could close our doors if he acted up again. You should talk to him directly, Martin. Make sure he knows where he stands. Chandler's too sympathetic." He stood from the stool and stepped toward him. "I'm going to finish my rounds, and then I need to take a lesion off one of my patients back in the ER. It looks like melanoma to me, and it might be deep. If you're available in about a half hour, I might ask for help in sewing it back up. I'll have them page you if I need you."

He walked out the door without getting a response, and Feddersen was just as glad. Mittlestedt bragged way too much and would never call for help.

But the offer presented a new idea: a patient with a potential naturally occurring cancer.

*****

Jonathon stopped by Mr. Smitherton's room for his routine check a couple of hours later. He busied himself changing towels in the bathroom and stepped out to check his patient's IV bag, even though the med nurse would typically monitor the fluids.

"Still doing okay, Mr. Smitherton?"

"I suppose. I'm feeling a little queasy, but it might have been the Cream of Wheat."

That gave Jonathon an excuse to talk some more. He grabbed the bedside blood pressure cuff and strapped it around Mr. Smitherton's arm. "Let's just see how your vitals are doing. Does your stomach get upset easily like this?"

"Not really."

The door opened and Denise Harrison entered. "Hi, Daddy—oh, I'm sorry," she pealed, noticing Jonathon with his stethoscope in his ears taking the blood pressure.

Mr. Smitherton waved with his other hand, but stayed silent until Jonathon was through.

When he finally spoke to his daughter across the room, his voice sounded weaker. "Denise, you remember Jonathon from before, don't you?"

"Sure, he's one of your favorites, right, Daddy? Good to see you again, Jonathon. How's our patient this morning?"

"Breakfast may have taken him down a notch, but otherwise he's doing fine." Jonathon carefully covered any sense of concern, but jotted a blood pressure of 100/68, noting that Mr. Smitherton's last pressure earlier that morning was recorded higher at 158/88. Looking over the past twelve hours, his blood pressures had never dropped this low.

"So tell me more about this queasy feeling, Mr. Smitherton." He reached for his patient's wrist to check a pulse.

"Nothing bad," Mr. Smitherton answered. "Just feels like there's a knot in my stomach."

Jonathon obtained a pulse of ninety-six, noticing that previous pulse rates had been between sixty and eighty beats per minute.

"Did it have anything to do with Dr. Feddersen's visit?"

Mr. Smitherton's face was already pale, but the question made his eyes widen and dart to Jonathon. "Don't start this, please," he whispered.

Whispering back, Jonathon pretended to be preoccupied with wrapping up the blood pressure cuff. "Tell me, Mr. Smitherton, did Dr. Feddersen inject you with something?"

Smitherton's forehead glistened with sweat, his voice barely audible. "I can't say—not with Denise here…I'm really starting to feel lousy."

"I'll get some help," Jonathon offered.

At the same time, Mr. Smitherton bolted upright in bed, grabbing his stomach. A fearful look swept across his face. In the next instant, he vomited.

"Oh no!" Jonathon ran to the bathroom to grab a towel and returned to Mr. Smitherton just in time to witness another lurch. He fought the acrid smell to help his patient with one hand, reaching the emergency call button with the other. Amidst the fresh remnants of partially digested cereal floated flecks of dark red matter. Blood.

"May I help you?" Carmen's voice came over the speaker.

"Carmen. I need some help right away!" He turned to Mr. Smitherton. "Can you walk to the bathroom?"

In answer, Mr. Smitherton leaned forward to heave again. Jonathon cradled the towel as best as possible to catch it.

"Mrs. Harrison, get a wet towel from the bathroom, would you?" Jonathon remained calm, and Denise immediately responded.

At the same time, Martha Chandler and another nurse entered the room.

"Right place at the right time, eh, Jonathon?" Nurse Chandler said, placing a hand on Henry's back.

"His BP's dropped and his pulse rate is high, Martha," Jonathon spoke quietly.

"Okay, we're fine. Could you check on your patient in 126?"

"Sure you don't need me here?" Jonathon was surprised to be dismissed so quickly.

"We'll be fine. Thanks for helping him." Nurse Chandler took the wet towel from Denise and wiped Henry's forehead.

Stepping back, Jonathon saw he wasn't needed, as the other nurse was checking Henry's blood pressure again. He left the room and paused in the hall. Nurse Chandler followed him out the door. "Didn't mean to kick you out, Jonathon. We'll take care of him. Just before you paged, Dr. Feddersen caught me. I can't have you taking care of any of Mittlestedt's patients. He apparently doesn't approve of your holiday employment. Dr. Feddersen said he'd work with it, as long as you weren't having to cross Mittlestedt. It's that or I let you go home."

"That's not much of an option."

"That's all I've got, except to say we need you. Will you go see how you can help in 126?" She didn't wait for his answer and stepped back into Mr. Smitherton's room.

Ripping his stethoscope from around his neck, Jonathon glared at the closed door as if his hesitation would bring Nurse Chandler back out to apologize.

It didn't. He headed to room 126.

*****

Dr. Feddersen knocked on ER door 3 and heard a voice respond, "Yes?"

He entered long before Dr. Mittlestedt was expected to come back. "I'm Dr. Feddersen, the hospital administrator here. I understand Dr. Mittlestedt is checking a spot on you, and he might have me help him. Mind if I have a look?"

"No, that's fine." The patient was in a gown, sitting on the examination table. "It's here on my back."

The lesion was irregularly shaped like an unsymmetrical hourglass, a half inch at its greatest width, raised and firm like a used eraser. It was black as coal with a subtle twist of brown at the smaller end.

Dr. Feddersen gently rubbed his finger over it, then pulled out a small plastic ruler and measured the exact size.

"Thanks much, that's all I need. Dr. Mittlestedt should be back shortly, and he'll call if he needs me. Let me just leave you with my card, as I have some experience treating these types of lesions. Your doctor's a good man; you should follow his recommendations. But if you have any questions, I'd be glad to help you. By the way, what was your name again?"

Chapter 23

*T*he old gray Chevette was parked alongside the curb at Noelle's home. Earlier hoping she might call, it was now half past nine and Jonathon took it upon himself to not just phone her but to show up. He stayed in his car for a few minutes with eyes closed, saying a prayer for confidence.

His eyes popped open with the sound of leaves being crunched underfoot. Through the fogged over car windows, he saw an image approaching from the house. A rap on the glass came before he could step out, and he leaned over to crack the passenger door.

Yanking the door wide open, Noelle appeared with a smile.

"What's steaming up the place in here?" She bounced into the seat. "Are you taking me out?"

"Uh, sure. I was wondering why you didn't call." Jonathon rubbed his chilly hands together.

"I was just going to when you drove up. Manny and my folks gave me a half hour before I promised to be back to play cards. Let's go."

"Where to?" He started the car and flipped the defrost to high.

"Just drive. Let's talk."

As he headed away from residences and town, she asked about his day, and heard about Mr. Smitherton. "I am so sure he's being treated with something different," Jonathon asserted.

"You mean some sort of nanotechnology medicine?"

"That's all I can figure. He keeps getting deathly sick, but he always seems to come around."

"And you think this Dr. Feddersen is behind it?"

"Yup."

"Tell me more about him." She was sincerely interested.

"He's got everyone thinking he's the saint of the hospital. He brought us out of debt, works overtime, fills in for people whenever he can, even compliments the employees—all of them but me, now."

"That all sounds good."

"Yeah, but he's connected with NanoMed, and after today, I think he might be treating patients behind our backs—doing some testing that no one else is aware of."

"But you said yourself, nanotechnology may be miraculously curing people. I'd be all for somebody heading that direction."

"But he's sneaking around, Noelle. I'm sure of it."

"Have you heard of blinded research studies? Some patients get real medicine and some get a placebo, but nobody knows which is which. The best research is called a double-blind study because neither the patients nor the researchers know who's getting the real thing. It prevents the players from manipulating the results. Maybe that's what they're doing, Jonathon. You go in there asking too many questions and you'll mess up their research."

"It's more than that, Noelle. They're messing with Mr. Smitherton's life."

"You don't know that. He might be a very sick man. They may be saving him. Do you think Dr. Mittlestedt is in on it too?"

"I have no reason to doubt it. He and Dr. Feddersen seem to be plotting this together."

"But why here in Windwood?" Noelle asked. "This type of research should be done at a major medical center."

"I wondered about that too. But think about it, Noelle. If it is truly illegal, what a great place to set up shop and not get caught. What I read about nanotechnology says much of it can be developed with household chemicals and materials fed into small but high-tech computer programs. This can happen in anybody's garage."

Noelle was in thought as Jonathon turned onto the two-lane highway leaving town. There was very little traffic; the only other light besides his headlights came from the half moon and stars as he drove away from Windwood.

"It's a gorgeous night," Noelle said and turned herself in her seat to face Jonathon. She bundled up in her brown suede jacket, pulling the fleece collar close around her neck.

"Are you warm enough?" he asked.

"Toasty. It feels great. Your little Chevette always did heat up fast."

"So you're ready to leave for school tomorrow?"

"Part of me wants to go, part wants to stay," she said casually, watching him drive.

171

"Which part wants to stay?" Jonathon looked over at her, and she grinned back.

"My mind says to go. I've got a lot of work to do to be ready for next week." She pulled her hands into her sleeves. "But my heart says to stay."

His gaze stayed on the road, but she saw his hands tighten on the steering wheel. The muffler beneath them rumbled louder than usual in the otherwise silent night.

"Doesn't your heart want to go to med school?" Jonathon's voice was quiet, almost soothing.

Noelle sighed. "I'm going to tell you something, Jonathon. Please just listen." She rubbed her moist palms on her jeans before tucking them tightly back in her jacket sleeves. "At school a guy asked me out."

She thought Jonathon might flinch, but nothing happened. "It wasn't a big deal, but now he keeps calling me. It's not going anywhere, that's definite. But I'm going to have to face him. I'm not looking forward to that."

"Why is he so interested in you?"

"I have no idea. We're both in chemistry, and he invited me to a party after lab one night." She reached over to turn down the heat. Leaning back, she added, "There's nothing there for me, I'm serious."

"Is he hassling you?"

"No—well, maybe a little." She wanted to be honest with him. "He showed up at my place right when I was leaving. And he wrote me a card."

"That seems nice. But is he rude to you? Are you scared of him?"

"No, not like that." The end of her sentence hung in the air, begging for more.

"Has he hurt you?"

She stayed silent, relaxing her arms, hoping it would make him think "no."

He waited for an answer. Hearing none, he asked another question. "So why are you telling me?"

"You asked me why my heart didn't want to go back," she replied. "That's part of it. I don't want to see him."

"Do you want me to take him out?" he said, straight-faced.

Noelle slugged his shoulder. "Oh, would you please?" She was smiling, thankful for the change of focus. "Keep it simple; keep it clean."

"Consider him gone." He kept his facade of seriousness.

She slugged him again. "You don't even know who he is."

"Don't need to. I'll know him when I see him. He'll have *that* look." Jonathon smiled playfully.

"Having my own hit man ought to help me make friends at SLU. What would I do without you?"

Jonathon slowed the car and pulled off on a gravel road indicated by a mile marker as five miles outside of town. It was pitch black beyond his headlights. When he turned them off, the stars beamed brightly across the clear night sky.

"So Noelle, what about us?" He continued to stare out the windshield to avoid her eyes.

"What do you mean, 'us'?"

"I've been praying about you and me a lot, asking if this is God's will. I can't say He's given me an answer, Noelle. But I think He's encouraging us to check it out."

It felt peculiar, but they spent a moment just looking at each other. Noelle had never seen him so handsome.

"I've got to be able to share my heart openly with you," he continued. "That means talking about everything. Nothing's off limits anymore."

"You mean like healing?"

"I mean everything, but especially...talking about God."

He paused and looked away, staring out the window again.

"Okay, Jonathon. I'm game."

"Then I want to pray with you, right here, right now."

She liked his lead. He didn't drop a beat. He almost expected her agreement.

"Well, okay. If you want to." Her palms turned sweaty again. *Why is this so hard?*

Jonathon stepped right into it. "Lord, here we are, and we want to seek You first above all else. You know each of us so well, and God, we don't want to mess up. I pray for Noelle as she goes back to school, that You would protect her from this guy and his interest in her. Even turn him the opposite direction, God, so he wouldn't even come close to her. May Noelle feel safe, knowing that You are in control, and may You guide her in her studies and thinking. She's got so much knowledge, and that has to be from You, Lord. Sift her mind now, so she can collect what is most important and be prepared for her classes."

Shifting in her seat, Noelle made more noise than she wanted to. Her mind raced. *Why is he doing this to me? I don't pray like this, out here in the dark, alone. God doesn't want to hear this, not this way. We should be in church.*

She tried to hold her eyes closed without success.

"And God, I want to pray for us. I don't know what's happening here, but tonight I commit my friendship with Noelle to You. I pray You will help us grow together in You, that our relationship, no matter what direction it heads, would have You at its center. I need You, Lord Jesus. I need Your wisdom and guidance in being the right kind of friend to Noelle."

He sighed and remained quiet. Noelle looked at him as his head was bowed over the steering wheel. A moment later, he cocked his head, his eyes still closed, as if he sensed a new thought. He began to pray out loud again.

"Noelle's going through a lot, but I think something is really weighing her down. Lord, I ask You to take that from her, or allow someone to help her. Lord, let me help her if I can. But whatever this is, I pray that You will touch her and meet her, right where she needs You."

He stopped speaking but held his head pointed up, his forehead furrowed with his eyes still closed. He was concentrating hard, still in prayer.

"We seek you, Lord. You are the awesome Creator. You made all we see, the stars, the moon. You made this lousy car, God." A smile surfaced on his face. "So Lord, because you made all things, I know You are all powerful and can help Noelle. Take her heart, Lord and mold it to be more like You. I need the same thing. We want to be like You."

Dropping his head, his voice softly trailed off, remaining in silent prayer.

Noelle scrutinized Jonathon for speaking to his God on her behalf. Something changed. She found herself comfortably warm, relaxed, like she'd just received a deep massage. Her anxieties were absent, and she felt a sense of gladness that she'd never experienced before. She knew he was really praying to God for her. She didn't expect it, but a tear formed at her eye.

Leaning back, Jonathon opened his eyes and turned his head toward Noelle. She met his gaze, leaving the tear glinting off her cheek in the moonlight.

He reached over, gently placing his hand on her arm. It was easy, natural for her to reach her arms to him and he bent toward her. Wrapping her hands across his shoulders, she leaned forward, her moist eyes dampening his chest.

"Jonathon, that was so special." Hugging him tightly, her tears mixed softly with her voice. "No one's ever done that."

He placed his arms around her, confined to the short space of the car's bucket seats. His hands reached over her coat in a simple, safe embrace.

"Thank you," she whispered.

In return he squeezed her waist between his hands.

She flinched sharply, a pain shooting deeply toward her spine.

"What?" He broke his embrace, surprised.

She adjusted herself in her seat. "I'm sorry, Jonathon. It's not you. I've just got a sore spot. It's healing, but it's just a little touchy. Don't worry." She patted his hand with hers. "I better get home."

Just then, headlights shined in the rear of the car. Someone turned onto the gravel road beside them. Jonathon noticed it was a Concorde, kicking up dust and gravel as it passed them and zoomed down the road.

"That's Dr. Feddersen's car. Wonder what he's up to."

"Take me home, Jonathon," she said, disinterested in his suspicions.

"Yeah, you're right." He shifted the car. "Your family's waiting for you." His hand gently slid to her knee. "Thanks for giving us some time."

Reaching out her hand, she curled her fingers around his. "Thanks for praying for me."

Neither hand moved as he drove her back to town.

*****

It had been a massive counterattack. Compared to the microcosmic menace of melanoma, the scathing scalpel loomed large, the exacting slice excising a quarter-sized circle of tissue surrounding the small black blemish. The incision went wide and deep, providing an ample perimeter to purge any remaining portion of cancer. Crimson blood briskly flowed from hundreds of severed vessels, pooling in the pocket gouged by the surgeon. The enemy's foundation was eradicated, thousands of individual cancer cells now swirling helplessly in the bloody abyss. Sutures were placed to shore up the surrounding skin, burying the deadly cells inside the wound.

But vestiges remained.

The cancer had extended beyond the reach of the scalpel. The cell clusters, now cleaved from the parent, exploded with angry growth, arising from multiple sites: bone, tissue and organ. Where one tumor had been uprooted, ten more, each an enraged clone, exponentially expanded underground.

Feddersen found Troy at the computer in the lower level lab. The room was brightly lit, giving no indication of the late hour.

"Show me how, and I'll run these myself." Feddersen set the courier box on the counter and began turning the knob on the combination padlock. "What are the numbers?"

Troy didn't respond, entranced with the computer screen as he typed. Feddersen's patience waned and his anger burned, but he didn't ask again.

Another minute passed before Troy spoke, not looking away from his screen. "Eight, fifteen, and two."

Feddersen flipped through the numbers and popped open the box. He lifted out the two insulated bags.

"You seem a bit in a hurry," Troy said calmly.

"It's my life. I'd like to do all I can to keep it." The words were thick with spite.

"Not to worry. You're making history, Marty. Did you see Smitherton's MRI?"

Feddersen unzipped the bags and pulled out the cardboard containers with syringes. Quoting the sterile radiology report, he said, "Four-centimeter mass at head of pancreas, consistent with adenocarcinoma, biopsy advised." He began to open the syringe containers.

"I'll get those," Troy said, just as expected.

Feddersen donned latex gloves and pulled out the two vials of Smitherton's blood. "Show me what to do."

"I appreciate your offer of help, but it's probably best that I—"

"You've given me pancreatic cancer, Jerry. Screwed around with my life. Let me try to save it. I want in on this whole thing."

Troy still stared at the screen, but his fingers weren't typing. "Spin down the blood; we just need the serum. And flip on the Chemstat."

Feddersen placed the tubes of blood inside a large refrigerated centrifuge so they'd swing opposite each other. After closing the lid, he set the timer as the spinning began with a low rumble, accelerating to a high pitched whir. Turning around, he reached to flip the switch behind a silver box laying on a counter with wires and tubes poking out from the front. Lights on the panel blinked on and a mechanical female voice reported, "power on, ready for testing control sample."

"It might be best for you to go home and rest," Troy said from his terminal.

"Smitherton looks horrible."

"He always does."

"He's vomiting blood. They're transfusing him two units tonight."

"So we bring him back from the brink of death. You've seen it before."

Feddersen slapped his hand on the counter. "Jerry, stop it! We're talking about my life here! What's happened to you?"

Troy turned from the screen, his face relaxed into a slight smile. "We're on the verge of our greatest miracle, Marty. Everything's going as expected. You and Smitherton will give the final evidence. Why do you think we suddenly have a problem?"

Shaking his head in disbelief, Feddersen paced to the back of the room. "Okay, just tell me what we're checking tonight."

"First we'll get the chem analysis," Troy loved to talk of his work, always speaking as a team. "Let's particularly look at his liver enzymes, amylase and lipase levels. Then we'll get a count of the NL4600."

"Is it intracellular?" He knew that would make it harder to measure.

"No, NL4600 is measured by a free index." Troy was in his heyday and stood from his chair. "It's actually a suspension of thousands of miniature, self-contained computers, each one smaller than a white blood cell. We call these nanites. Each one is programmed to travel to pancreatic tissue and identify the foreign DNA code of a single cancer cell. The nanite sentinel carries a synchrotron. That's an atom-sized magnet that reorganizes the orbit of electrons."

Marty wrinkled his forehead.

"Stay with me now. The disturbance in the electron orbit triggers an emission of photons. The photons form a beamline of radiation, destroying from five to ten cancer cells. Smitherton shouldn't feel a thing, but the cancer cells are selectively annihilated. The nanite's function is lost in the action, and a remnant returns to circulation, now about the size of a viral particle, to be removed from the bloodstream by the liver, just like any other toxin. In the blood samples you've provided, we'll measure how many defunct nanites are found and proportionately determine how actively the cancer is being destroyed."

Feddersen could not help but be amazed at this phenomenon. "How much have you given Smitherton?"

"The first injection of NL4600 last night was three ccs, containing exactly 66,000 nanites. You repeated the same amount this morning after you drew the blood, right?"

"Of course. So he has 132,000 nanites in his system?"

"Not if they're working like they should. I would expect we'll find about 50,000 used up in extinguishing the cancer before the second dose. If that's true, we should have an NL4600 level of between fifty and seventy."

"What if it's higher?"

That's good, meaning the nanites are detonating at a higher level, and we'll increase the injection." Troy referred back to his computer screen. "At this point, we'll plan on just the three injections."

"And if it's lower?"

"That's not likely, but it would mean the nanites are not detonating, either by malfunction or inability to identify the cancer cells."

"So why is he bleeding in his gut?"

"There's several reasons. What would you suggest?"

"I knew it. You're not sure." Feddersen paced away from the computer, considering the possible diagnoses. "Apart from the NL4600, I can think of a few reasons. He could be bleeding from tumor evasion into the gastrointestinal tract or possible metastatic disease. Could be a stress ulcer that's out of control. But c'mon, Jerry, could the injection trigger it?"

Troy was back to being glued to his computer. "Anything's possible, but it's highly unlikely."

"But possible?"

"Only if there was a major error in the program."

The centrifuge clicked off, the hum slowing to a low rumble before silence filled the lab. Feddersen stepped back to the machine, waiting to open the top hatch, waiting to check the blood tests, waiting to do something—anything. Not until he rested his hand on the hatch's handle did he realize he was shaking. Under his breath, but still loud enough to be heard by Troy, he repeated, "I see. Only if there was a major error."

Chapter 24

*L*egion swelled in lethal growth at ground zero. With the mother-lode violently removed, the melanotic cancer proliferated with fury, flanking out in every direction like fire across a dry field. With such a voracious flare, the purpose was plain, the goal in grasp; the keeper of death was knocking.

Jonathon hopped out of bed the next morning with a smile on his face. It had been the most perfect evening of his life. His sleep had been sweet, and he woke late without an alarm. His mother was already at work for the day, and he hadn't even heard her shut the back door.

His mind replayed the night one more time: the car ride, Noelle's willingness to pray with him and their embrace. She was sensitive, ready to go with him before God. She reached out to him, accepting the affection he offered. When he took her back to her house, he stepped out of the car and wrapped his arms around her again. She returned the same response tenderly. He was careful to avoid the sore spot on her back, and that made the embrace even more delicate, protected. A simple hug, but it sent him skyrocketing.

Nothing was on the schedule for the whole day, a perfect Saturday. Even the morning clouds framed a grin under the sun as it peaked through just enough to take the bite out of the cold. Turning to his morning scriptures, he found words that spoke to his feelings. He prayed with a portion of Psalms, praising God for caring so much for him, even the numbered hairs on his head. He thought long about Noelle, praying for her return to school, praying for them.

After a Pop Tart, he ran to the library, determined that this was his day for answers.

"Hi, Joey." He entered, seeing his young friend at the counter. "Must be Saturday—you're manning the desk."

"You got it." Joey closed a comic book and threw it under the counter. "The computers are all up, just waiting for you."

"You're a hacker." He smiled at Joey and walked over to the monitors to open his screen name.

"Jonathon, I found something you might like." Joey had followed him over, holding two books in his hands. "I ordered them myself; thought the library could use them. Maybe we'll get up to date on this stuff. They're by that Drexler guy."

He handed Jonathon two hard-bound books. The top one was titled, *Nanosystems*. The author was listed as K. Eric Drexler.

Joey explained more. "That's supposed to be the text on molecular nanotechnology. The description said it's basically an expanded version of the guy's doctoral thesis. Did you know he earned the world's first doctorate in molecular nanotechnology?"

"I didn't know you were that interested."

"Just doing my job. I looked through those websites we found, and this stuff is kinda cool. The other book here is *Engines of Creation*. I looked through it a bit. It even talks about using nano-stuff in cryonics."

"Freezing people?"

"Yup. It's incredible."

"You're a nano-nerd, Joey."

"Proud of it." Joey walked back to his counter.

"This is a big help. Can I check them out?" Jonathon watched him pull out his comic book and return to reading.

Without looking up, he replied, "Already did. Due in two weeks."

"You're awesome, Joey."

Jonathon jumped online, wrote a welcome back note to Noelle, and signed off. Leaving the library with his books, he was set for a long read. There was just one more stop.

Driving out of town, he followed the trail he had made last night. He turned off the highway five miles from Windwood onto the same unnamed county road. The dust hung in the air behind him as he drove the gravel road, harvested cornfields on either side.

He had all the time he needed, so he just coasted along the fields, looking for any side roads. It had to have been Dr. Feddersen driving down the road the night before.

Jonathon swerved to miss a skunk in the road, but that was the only life he found. He carried the stench for two miles. After about twenty minutes he came across a small herd of mule deer in the field ten yards away.

But that still wasn't what he was looking for.

Driving another twenty minutes, he reached a ninety-degree bend in the road and slowed to make the sharp corner. Just after this, a farmhouse came into view in the distance.

Jonathon turned off the road onto a lane approaching the front of the farmhouse. He could tell the home hadn't been lived in for years.

No, this isn't what I'm looking for.

He turned his Chevette around, looking over his shoulder as he backed up. It was then that he noticed the metal buildings behind the farmhouse. The garage door of one of the buildings was open. Inside he saw the shiny green gleam of a car.

A Concorde.

Bingo.

He returned down the lane, back to the dirt road. Turning right, he resumed his travel on the dusty path, going even farther away from the highway. After another fifteen minutes, he stopped, far out of sight of the farmhouse.

He sat in his car on the roadside, skimming through portions of the Engines of Creation text for nearly a half hour. Then he laid the book aside and drove slowly back up the road, keeping the dust down. Pulling into the cornfield a half mile from the rear of the farmhouse, here he could obtain a clear view of the two outbuildings.

He picked up the Drexler book again and resumed his reading, glancing up regularly to watch for the green Concorde.

*****

Mr. Smitherton was alone as he laid in his hospital bed. The sheets were tightly wrapped over his thin frame, making him feel like a sardine peeking out from a roll-top can.

The nausea hadn't left, so he remained still. If he moved too much, a wave would crash over him, sending his stomach into spasms and emesis. It had been a half hour since he last tracked to the bathroom; he tried to stay quiet to break his old record.

If he could have a few less interruptions, he wondered if he could sleep, but the nurses' activities kept stirring him. Maybe this time would be different. He rested his eyes, tuning out the noise of laughter in the hall, announcements over the public address system, and a distant crash of a breakfast tray dropped in an unknown room.

It was working; he was going to sleep.

Minutes into his slumber, the door to his room breezed open, followed by Mary, the medication nurse.

"Good morning, Mr. Smitherton. How are you doing today?"

He pinched his eyes tight, fighting back unpleasant utterances.

"Here's your meds this morning," she continued. "It's your fluid pill and the one for pain." Her voice sang in a routine that made it all seem so childish.

Forcing away the queasiness, he squeezed a hand out from under his sheet and grasped both pills in his palm. After he swallowed them, she held a cup of water with a straw to his lips.

"Here's a good chaser," she awarded him with a second song. "Anything else I can get for you, Mr. Smitherton?"

He started to shake his head, and stopped. "My cassette," his voice croaked.

Mary had already turned away and asked again. "What was that?"

"Get my cassette." His voice was raspy but audible.

"Oh, you want to do some recording again? Sure, let me get that for you." She reached into a closet and pulled out a small cassette recorder. "That's such a great gift you're making, Mr. Smitherton. I wish I could get my dad to record his reflections on life. You're leaving quite a legacy for your family. Here you go. Where's your cassette? I'll put it in for you."

He pointed to his suitcase and she found the cassette in the front pocket. Loading it in the player, she laid the small box on the bedside stand and moved it over his bed.

"Anything else?" She hardly paused. "Fine, I'll see you a little later."

Henry reached a hand to grab the small microphone on a cord attached to the recorder. He pushed the red button and brought the microphone up to his lips.

"Denise," his voice was rough and cracking. "You've heard me say this before, but this may be the last time I can speak." He fingered the microphone, assembling his thoughts quickly as the tape continued to roll.

"This is the worst I've felt. I just don't think I'm going to make it. They're supposed to be curing me of cancer…this time. Anyway, I hope you know now how I've done this for you. The money's been good, and I'm so thankful…so thankful you could use it. It was more than that, I know. I didn't want them to hurt you. They said they might, and I couldn't put you…"

His hand dropped to his pillow, his strength ebbing, the nausea rising. He rolled his head to the side to reach his mouth closer to the microphone, his voice now a whisper.

"After you hear this…you've got to give it to the police. And tell… Jonathon, the aide up here. Tell him…he was…right."

The tape continued to roll, but he had to fight the nausea with silence. Extreme fatigue rose to consume his need to vomit. Sleep overwhelmed the sickness—a welcome relief.

He wished to sleep forever.

*****

By late afternoon, Feddersen found his suspicions true.

"We've got a problem, Jerry. Smitherton's NL4600 level is twenty-three."

It was a simple reagent test. The computerized Chemstat machine would mix a small sample of Smitherton's serum with a couple of chemicals that only reacted with the virus-sized nanite remnants. A photometer would then read the serum and detect the concentration of the reactants.

"Did you double check it?" Troy had constantly worked at his computer except for answering questions on how to run the procedure. Feddersen purposely walked over to him multiple times during the past three hours, trying to determine what was so captivating. Twice he found him surfing the web, clicking off as soon as Feddersen approached, changing to some sort of software program filling the screen with lists of numbers and characters.

"Is that the first sample?" Troy didn't look away from his screen.

"I'm not an idiot, Jerry. The first sample was from before he'd received any injection. It measured zero, just like it's supposed to. I've run both samples three times. The second sample, after Smitherton had received the nano-juice, reads twenty, twenty-three, and twenty-three. That's way too low. It's not working."

"I'll have to repeat it." Troy sighed and shook his head as if he was working with a fool.

"Of course you will. Get over here and do it."

Troy's fingers stopped typing. Feddersen was standing at the table across the room, his hands firmly supporting his weight as he leaned over the counter toward his partner.

As Troy stood, he faced Feddersen for the first time. "I don't like your attitude, Marty. You've been here all night. Perhaps you should leave, get some rest."

"You just don't get it, Jerry," Feddersen boiled inside but kept the lid on. "You've shot me full of this stuff, poisoned me. It's not working, and you think I've got an attitude problem? I'm dying, Jerry. It's called murder. Now help me."

"We had no choice." Troy's voice was quiet and firm. You needed data and I needed volunteers. Now, I told you I'd repeat your tests. Go home, Marty. You need to take care of yourself."

*****

Out in the cornfields, Jonathon made it through most of *Engines of Creation*. Though he did not completely understand the text, the tale was nevertheless incredible: atom-sized computers with the power of a mainframe, combined with microscopic levers, sensors, and power cables forming a new class of "smart materials." A re-engineered bone could be strong enough to withstand a fall out of a building. Surgery would be obsolete, as programmed computers could be injected into the human body to perfectly execute the operation in minutes, without pain or bruising. Bodies could be reconfigured; in fact, men could bear children.

It was mid-afternoon when he saw the green Concorde drive away, leaving a long and lingering cloud of dust. Jonathon waited another half hour before pulling out of the field, with plans to return to the library to scour the websites.

The digital camera, hidden in the seed corn sign along the road, identified and recorded the departure of both cars.

*****

When Noelle unlocked the door to her small studio apartment in St. Louis, she immediately felt beckoned again to enter the world of freedom, escaping the trappings of Windwood.

Except this time she was not running away.

184

Her room looked the same as she left it, papers scattered on the floor, a pile of dirty laundry at the bathroom. She dragged her bag through the door, knocking over a fast-food cup of days-old Mountain Dew.

Flipping on her computer, she wandered into the small galley kitchen, grimacing at the sight of the sink filled with every dish she owned. Stepping back to her keyboard, she logged onto her e-mail.

With fifteen new messages to read, she selected the one marked from jon4jc@juno.com. It stood out from the crowd like satin amongst burlap.

"Noelle, last night was the greatest. When I got home, I went out to the swings. BTW, they held me just fine. You should have seen the stars—brighter than ever. It was because of you. I hope you had a great time with your family. We've got to talk, and I want to call you Sunday after Manny and I go to church. Pray for him, Noelle. And I'm praying for you. And for us. Get lots done for school, and remember, I'll handle that guy who's bugging you as soon as you give the word. Take care of your back, cuz there's a big hug waiting here for you. Love, Jonathon."

She smiled and hit "reply," but stared at the screen without typing. Reaching a hand to her back, she felt underneath her blouse. The two band-aids were still in place over the small dip in her lower spine. It wasn't nearly as tender as yesterday.

The phone rang and she picked it up, hoping to hear her mom's voice.

"Hello, Noelle. Welcome back!" The man's voice was deep, cheery, and unwanted.

It was Dave. She pushed the off button on her phone without saying another word and stared at her computer screen.

Chapter 25

*J*onathon cracked the door to his house late after spending the evening at the library with Joey, connecting to several informative websites on nanotechnology. Successes in research were reported all over the world. France, Germany, the United Kingdom, Canada, Switzerland, Korea, Taiwan, China, and Japan all had active nanotechnology research programs. American nanotech hotspots included Chicago, Dallas, Houston, NYC, Boston, Los Angeles and the Silicone Valley of Northern California. The time flew by, and afterward, Jonathon took his young researcher out for a burger to reward his efforts.

He entered his home in nearly complete darkness, except for the flickering light from the television in the living room. His mother, wrapped in a scratchy gold blanket, sat in the rocking chair. Her face glinted gray to the flashing scenes of *Star Trek,* her eyes glued to the screen.

"Hi, Mom."

"It's the tribbles one, your favorite. Sit yourself down."

Sinking into an easy chair across the room, he glanced at the furry little critters adorning the Starship Enterprise. He was sick of this episode, must've seen it twenty times.

"Yup, that's a classic." Hungry and tired, he was already missing Noelle. He'd rather be anywhere but watching tribbles, yet he had to tell his mom.

A commercial finally interrupted the torture. He seized the break. "I'll have to miss church in the morning."

"Working more? They can't live without ya." She stayed riveted to the Dodge commercial.

He pondered leaving it at that, but by the next commercial he had convinced himself that she'd find out. He had to tell her. Now.

"I'm going somewhere else, Mom."

"That blame community church?" The tribbles were back on, and her gaze would not leave the set.

"Windwood Community, right. A friend is going with me—Manny Lewis."

"You're not bringing him to your own church?"

"Not this time, Mom."

She started rocking. Tribbles were dropping out of air ducts on the brig. Captain Kirk was buried to his waist in the woolly devils.

She was silent. She was crushed.

*****

The hot water beat against Jonathon's back longer than usual the next morning. He delayed his routine, making sure he didn't cross his mother's path any closer than necessary. In his morning prayer, he asked God again if he was making a mistake, but the answers in his heart only encouraged him to bring Manny to church.

Should I have offered to bring him to my church?

But he knew Manny would have hated that.

Should I have suggested Manny go to Windwood Community by himself?

He never would have done it.

Am I putting too much emphasis on church, anyway? Going to church can't save you.

But might it help?

Maybe I'm being selfish, just looking for an excuse to go to Windwood Community Church myself.

And what's wrong with that?

But he wondered how he would handle his mother.

Love her. Give her time.

She would be leaving the house in ten minutes. He had been standing in his room for the past half hour, fully dressed in khaki pants and a gray pull-over sweater, praying and praying again.

Okay, I can do this.

Stepping into the kitchen, the odor of strong coffee filled his senses. He poured himself a glass of orange juice, standing right behind her as she sat at the table reading the newspaper.

"Morning, Mom."

The paper rustled to the next page. "Morning."

It was too short of a word; he couldn't tell how mad she was yet.

"Thanks for letting me go this morning." He drank half his orange juice with his back to her. It didn't taste as good when all he could smell was coffee.

"They'll suck you in if you let 'em."

"I'll be careful, Mom."

Getting up from the table, she folded the paper and eyed him as she took a last sip of her coffee.

Walking out the back door, she didn't utter another word. Jonathon heard the car engine start and said out loud to himself, "That didn't go too badly."

He downed a second glass of juice before leaving to pick up Manny. Jonathon reached the Lewis home ten minutes later, with Manny at the door waiting.

A whiff of strong cologne flooded the car as Manny got in.

"Who are you trying to impress?" Jonathon smirked and pinched his nose.

Manny fixed the collar of his dark blue silk shirt, then fingered the crease in his black slacks. "What do you mean? This is what I always wear to church."

"You're so sophisticated."

Manny grabbed his own nose. "Have to do something to cover up the smell of this old car."

"Least I've got one."

"I'm saving up for my dream machine. I'd never settle for a tin can like this."

"You wanna walk to church?" Jonathon grinned and gave Manny a shove before driving away.

Walking through the front doors of Windwood Community Church, Jonathon deftly led his friend past the greeters and pre-church crowd into the sanctuary. Down the aisle near the front right center sat several of the college-age crowd from the swimming party.

Hillary was among them and leaped up at the sight of Manny and Jonathon. "Hey, guys! You made it." She wrinkled her nose and laughed. "Who's got the Old Spice?"

Pinching his nose, Jonathon pointed at his friend.

Manny slugged him back. "It's called 'class.' Sorry you're missing yours."

Several of the group greeted them, and Jonathon caught Manny's eyes as they both were again overwhelmed with such a welcome. After not more than a

Healing NOELLE

Healing NOELLE

few minutes, the music started from the platform, and room was made for Manny and Jonathon to sit in the midst of their new friends.

The stage was different from the worship musical; this time six vocalists lined the wide platform. Jonathon saw Melinda Camelson among the six as she leaned back in her wheelchair, clapping her hands over her head at the start of the music. The band was tucked in the left corner with two drumsets; a keyboard; a piano; and string, electric, and bass guitars forming a tight circle of players creating a powerfully driving beat. Almost immediately, those surrounding Jonathon and Manny were on their feet, clapping to the music.

Jonathon joined in like it was natural, noticing Manny hesitate for a moment before clapping along himself. He knew Manny would never think of church the same way ever again. He smiled to himself.

Words to the song were projected on a large video screen above the stage, and the singing rang out with exuberance. The vocalists each sang with individual mannerisms, all reflecting an inner joy and a vision beyond the scope of the room. Jonathon watched Melinda particularly, still fascinated by the sweetness inscribed across her face. The room was thunderous in clapping and alive with song, transcending the rational intellect to an inner place of awe and wonder.

They'll suck you in, his mother's words quietly echoed in his mind. *Maybe so, Mom. Maybe so*. He allowed the music to swallow him.

The music varied from broad strokes declaring the power and might of a holy God, to thin lines of intricate harmony declaring His majesty in creation. John Camelson appeared on stage at one point to share several memorized verses of a Psalm that cried out to the mercy of God, and the music resounded again in affirmation that only Christ was worthy of praise. The tremendous worship led into a time of prayer where one of the vocalists offered a personalized adoration of Christ. No sense of hurry drove the prayer as more time was spent in quiet than in words.

The heart of the congregation was offered before God in worship, and Jonathon felt his own heart released from the cares of the past days. A sense of expectation naturally followed, that God would now fill any void left from worry. He even left behind any concern about how Manny was doing. It was up to God now. As they were seated to hear the sermon, Jonathon did not fear the open vulnerability of his soul.

The pastor was neither handsome nor eloquent, but he was without equal in passion. Jonathon marveled not so much at the man's words, but at his

189

Michael J. Huckabee

sincerity. It was clear that he was sharing out of a relationship with his Lord that left him as a transparent vessel. When he spoke of Jesus Christ, his eyes would light with intense compassion that could only represent a heart that had fully experienced God's love. Jonathon was drawn to the man without acknowledging a word that was said. He had never before seen a life so transformed into a manner of bold surety and peaceful kindness.

At the end of the sermon, the pastor offered the front of the church for anyone seeking to pray. The band began again, a soft melody that Jonathon soon recognized as a hymn sung often in his own church, "Beneath the Cross of Jesus." To the instrumental sounds, nearly twenty or so individuals walked from their seats to the front, kneeling randomly along the three steps that made a half-circle around the stage.

Jonathon had only seen an altar call on television and held an aversion to it. How strange to ask people to enter such a personal moment of prayer in the midst of such a public occasion, yet there were those who responded. Emotion seekers, that's what these people were.

They'll suck you in, his mother's words rang again.

He contended with his own desire, questioning this type of prayer while at the same time wondering if it held value. He reasoned that this should be reserved for those who were truly hurting...truly in need of speaking to Christ in this holy setting.

The instruments closed the first verse of the hymn, and the worship vocalists reappeared on stage. The pastor stepped forward, motioning for the band to keep playing. At the microphone, his words stumbled out, again unrehearsed, but genuine.

"Brothers and sisters, pray for those who have come to the front to seek a special audience with Jesus Christ. But there remains something heavy on my heart." He sighed and hesitated, as if reluctant to share. "I sense a burden on one of you here that Christ desires to take. You have yet to know Him as your Savior, and you must wait no longer, for He desires to hear your prayer today." His voice broke. "At this moment He stands at the door of your heart, but you're holding back. You are here, and you know who you are. I only ask you to let Christ in. Open the door."

He turned away from the microphone and walked down the steps.

Jonathon leaned forward to see the pastor kneel at the floor beside the stage, apart from the others already in prayer.

Maybe I should go up and pray, just to encourage the pastor.

190

The band quietly finished the second chorus of the hymn, lingering on the last progression of chords. No other movement followed.

No, this is the manipulative stuff Mom hates. This isn't for me. It couldn't be; I'm not that far from God. We talked just this morning.

A stillness hung across the sanctuary, the only attention drawn to the people praying unobtrusively along the front, hunched shoulders silently communicating conviction, petition or restoration.

But maybe I need that special time of prayer. Maybe the Lord wants to tell me something about my healing gift. I don't want to miss it.

Melinda Camelson lifted her microphone and softly sang the words to the hymn, blending almost unnoticed with the instruments as the words came into view on the screen overhead. The song spread gently across the auditorium, voices bringing unity of thought through the music.

Suddenly, Manny stood upright out of his seat and bustled down the row, knocking several knees together as his large frame shoved its way into the aisle. Jonathon caught a glimpse of his face, a countenance bearing an explosive mixture of godly fear and frank guilt. Manny took long strides to the front and banged down on his knees on the steps.

Tight as a ball, his face nearly touched the floor. The subtle tremors of his frame gave evidence of tears and brokenness from a young man recognizing he had turned away from God. Jonathon watched in amazement as he knew his friend was being transformed in this very instant. It was the holiest of moments, seeing a man confessing a contrite heart as Jesus Christ renewed his soul, right before his eyes. Manny was being saved, born again, redeemed, joining the believer-hood of Christianity.

An older man stepped forward to Manny, bending to his knees and resting a hand on his shoulder in prayer for a brother.

Just down the row of other kneeling bodies, Jonathon caught the eye of a friend standing there, Michael Sunday. He stood in front of several kneeling, but his gaze was on Jonathon. With cheeks glistening from tears, Michael offered a warm smile, then took several steps to find a place among the kneelers, bowing with them in prayer.

A warm flush came over Jonathon. He felt tears in his eyes, but more than that, an abandonment to everything other than gaining an intimacy with Christ, like he saw in Manny. Without hesitation, he rose to his feet and marched down to the front himself, finding an area between others praying.

191

Chapter 26

*M*r. Smitherton died.

It came as no surprise to Dr. Mittlestedt and the nursing staff. More amazing to them was that he had made it this long.

Even Denise seemed well-prepared. Her father had lapsed into a coma while she had been in church that morning. The hospital called her at noon and she came up immediately, making it for his last breaths. "It was okay," she told the nurses. "We had said our goodbyes to each other. He had been a great father and lived a full life. It was his time."

Mary handed Denise the cassette tape, explaining what a special gift of love this was. Denise was surprised, touched that her father would provide something so personal and intimate. That just wasn't the way he was. She said she didn't know how soon she could listen to it.

Mary understood. It might be hard right now. But someday Denise would find it to be a wonderful memory of her dad. Just hang onto it.

Even the hospital administrator, Dr. Feddersen, stopped by while Denise was at the hospital. It was a short visit, but he made a kind reference to how much he had appreciated her father. The nurses later told her how Dr. Feddersen especially liked Henry. He seemed truly shocked to hear of his death. According to the nurses, he looked especially tired and drained. He usually worked all day Sundays, but left the hospital immediately after speaking to Denise. They were sure he was sincerely broken up over his friend's death.

But that's just how Dr. Feddersen was. He cared about everyone—just like they were his family.

*****

Healing NOELLE

The green Concorde immediately escaped back to the farmhouse. Feddersen leaned his eye into the iris scanner and banged on the wall with his fist to hurry the elevator along. He cursed at how slow it moved.

It was time. Way past time.

Seething, he yelled for Troy as soon as the elevator doors opened.

"Yes?" the calm response returned from the garden room.

Stepping out of the office, Feddersen crossed the hall and entered the room lit by the bank of ultraviolet lights across the rear wall. The odor of moist, rich soil filled the air, like a freshly plowed field. Troy's back was to him, his broad but short shoulders huddled over the back wall shelves, black dirt scattered at his feet. He turned around, clutching one of the pots that used to hold the peculiar hyacinths. The lights shined brightly overhead, casting a shadow over Troy that magnified the dark pits of his eyes. His hands were caked with mud, his canary yellow shirt smeared with broad swatches of muck that had also soiled his black slacks.

Infuriation rose in Feddersen, but the shock of seeing his partner covered with grime stopped him from lashing out. This didn't seem like Troy. "What are you doing?" he asked, holding his anger at bay.

"Planting." Troy spoke as if talking to a four-year-old.

"I've got bad news. We've got to talk." When Troy didn't look his way, Feddersen slapped the wall beside him and barked, "Now!"

Troy raised his dingy hand and wiped it across his mouth, leaving a trail of mud that he ignored. "Bad news? There's no such thing." He turned back around. "Take these hyacinths. They bloomed. In their prime I cut them down. Enjoyed them for Thanksgiving, right? Well, now they're limp and brown. I had to pitch them. Is that 'bad news'?"

"Jerry, listen to me."

Grabbing a second pot, Troy pulled out the old flower bulb and tossed it over his back. It landed near Feddersen's feet, dirt flying across the floor.

Troy dug his hand back into the pot, twisting and turning it as if searching for something amidst the dirt. "So the flowers are gone. Too bad, some might say. But we'll just replant them. In the same soil, no less. See, it's the soil."

"Jerry, listen. Smitherton—he's dead."

"We just put another bulb in. That's all. The soil gives life." He cupped his hand with dirt and held it up over his head. "Here's the source of life, Marty."

"He's dead." Feddersen raised his voice. "The nanites killed him."

193

Michael J. Huckabee

"We just need another bulb." He reached for a third pot, plucking out the bulb and tossing it recklessly against the wall. He massaged his hands in the dirt, both buried to the wrists in the pot.

"You've lost it, Jerry."

"No, indeed. I've found it." He worked the soil up so it spilled over the pot. One hand reached up to scratch his scalp, then plunged back into the dirt.

"Did you recheck Smitherton's tests?" Feddersen tried a reality point.

It made Troy stop digging for an instant. "Yes, and I owe you an apology." He turned around and swiped a hand across his forehead. The mud made his appearance grisly, scary.

"You were right, Marty. You performed the tests accurately." He clasped his blackened fingers together and touched them to his lips, reluctant to speak. Opening his hands, he gestured to his only friend. "I'm sorry I questioned you." His voice broke and he turned back to his pots, sniffing loudly. A hand flew up to rub his nose, another pot was dug into, the bulb thrown out, the hands thrust into the dirt, rubbing and searching.

Dumbfounded, Feddersen stepped back out of the room. "I'll be back in a few minutes."

He slowly walked to the office near the elevator and stood at Troy's desk, looking for evidence of alcohol or drugs. Thumbing through two short stacks of paper, all he found were a few bills and an assortment of data sheets, pages with four columns of six-digit numbers used for tracking DNA sequences. He sat down in the burgundy leather desk chair and quietly opened a side drawer filled with manila files. The first file was an inch thick and labeled "Smitherton." Inside, the top papers were Chemstat lab reports. The three test reports Feddersen performed last night were already filed. Two more reports were on top, showing dates and times from early this morning, and the results were twenty-two and twenty-three.

Almost exactly what I got on Smitherton's tests last night.

Beneath those papers were more documents: lab and X-ray reports, copied papers from the hospital, and more data sheets. Closing the file, he slipped it back into its spot in the drawer. He glanced through the next few files, all labeled with codes similar to the NL4600, but differing in characters. Inside these files were pages of data sheets filled with repeated columns of six-digit numbers. The filing system was impeccable, everything in its place.

So why is Troy so confused?

194

He reached to the back of the drawer where a thick file was lodged slightly cockeyed. Pulling it out, he found the first several pages to be all Chemstat lab reports. Behind them were more data sheets. Thumbing through the sheets, a few held pencil marks of circles and lines, nothing but hieroglyphics. He began to put the file back when one of the front sheets slipped out of the file. Readjusting the sheet in the open file, his eyes fell upon the Chemstat report date: it read today's date. The time was a few hours ago, and the result was fifty-six.

Placing the large file on the desk, he pulled out the report behind the front page. It was from two days ago. The result was sixty-two. Behind this, a third report from just last week read fifty-nine.

Shuffling through the top reports, all the readings were just a few days apart over the last month, with the results always between fifty to seventy, the normal range for the nanite measurements.

Behind these reports, Feddersen pulled out the data sheets to study them more closely. The columns of six-digit numbers filled each page, with no text or identifying data, except the top of each page giving the code of "ME2700" on the first ten or so pages. Behind these, the title was "ME2600" for several more pages, and "ME2500" followed after that. As he tracked through the pile, he found the columns of numbers gave varying reports, but the sheets all looked identical in format with the exception of the title systematically reducing its number by one hundred. He left the file open on the desk before him and leaned back in the chair, still staring at the pile of reports.

The sound of two feet shuffling behind him caught his attention, but he made no move to cover his actions. Rather, he spoke quietly. "Jerry, you can't go on like this. You're not making sense."

"It's perfect sense." Troy's voice was practical, not defensive.

Feddersen didn't turn around, not wanting to look at a crazed face. "But what do we do with Smitherton dead?"

"Plant another bulb," Troy repeated.

"Is that what I am, just another bulb you're growing?"

"We all are, really. It's the soil. Don't worry so much, Marty. We just need to adjust your soil."

Feddersen whipped his chair around and reached out to Troy, grabbing his left arm. The surprise left Troy as no match for Feddersen's taller height. All he could do was push away with his opposite arm and shout. "What are you doing? Don't be a fool, Marty."

Troy struggled, his sheer weight almost toppling them both, but it was a weak effort compared to the hold Feddersen had. Once he got his footing, Troy was helpless.

Feddersen immobilized Troy's arm under his own and grabbed the yellow cuff of the shirt sleeve, ripping it open and pulling it up to the elbow. Red needle marks dotted Troy's arm at his elbow's inside crease.

"I thought so," Feddersen exclaimed, releasing the arm and walking back across the room. "What have you got?"

Troy stood, streaked in mud, holding his squatty shoulders back with self-assurance. Before answering, he rubbed his hands together like he was cleaning them, dried mud and dust falling away. Satisfied with his makeshift hygiene, he reached down to his left pant leg, lifting the slacks up to his knee.

An impressive oblong cavity the size of a cigar was exposed on Troy's mid-calf, a wide scar six inches long sealing the floor of the depression.

"Melanoma?" Feddersen asked.

"Diagnosed ten years ago—Clark stage II-B. I'm alive because of those nanites." He dropped his pant leg and stood again.

Feddersen reached back for the file and tapped the lab reports. "But you're still needing treatment? Still taking injections?"

"Unfortunately, I under-dosed myself initially. I can't fault myself; it was the first case of nanomedicine used in a human with cancer." Troy began rubbing his hands again, picking at the dirt still stuck to his skin. "I utilized the correct DNA sequence but dosed the nanite injection too low. By all appearances, the melanoma was eradicated, but a few cancer cells slipped through and shifted their DNA sequence, mutating, unrecognized by the nanites. It metastasized to three lymph nodes, but I have been able to arrest the growth with routine injections. The only problem is, it keeps changing. The mutations now force me to modify the nanite composition about every month."

"But," Feddersen hesitated, wondering if Troy knew the obvious, "the cancer keeps spreading, metastasizing to other organs."

Troy scratched at a smear of dried mud on his bald scalp, not answering.

"And it's metastasized to the brain." Feddersen closed the file on the desk without waiting for an answer.

"Jerry, I think I can help you, but you're going to have to let me in. I need to know how you do this."

Troy looked up, his face chalky from the dried mud. "I can teach you."

"What if I brought you a patient with a nodular melanoma, just diagnosed?"

"Malignant nodular melanoma?" He lit up. "What stage?"

"Let's say a Breslow depth of five millimeters, Clark staging II-B at a minimum. I would wager it's a stage III, maybe even IV."

"Perfect. Melanoma's straight forward early on. The DNA pattern is redundant. The nanite program is easy to determine."

"Easier than Smitherton?"

"Much."

"Easier than pancreatic adenocarcinoma?"

"Of course."

"If I brought you a naturally occurring nodular melanoma, at least a stage II-B, would you be able to treat it and then be better off treating you and me both?"

"It's just a matter of dosing. Too little and you get a migrating, mutating cancer like I have. Too much, and we get Smitherton. We've got it down to a tight range of dosages. One more and we'd have an answer."

"Go get washed up, Jerry. We've got work to do."

"You've got a patient with melanoma?" Troy's eyes gleamed with excitement, as if this new focus somehow sent his madness into remission.

"I'll have her here within twenty-four hours."

*****

No one could have pulled Jonathon away from Manny that afternoon after church. Hillary and several of her friends took them both out for dinner, and Manny was almost crazy. He'd start laughing with the simplest of jokes, with a smile that burst out across his face to the size of a clown's. However, if someone talked to him about what had changed in his life, he'd be on the brink of tears, speaking tenderly of Jesus Christ and how much He cares for all people. Jonathon found the enthusiasm contagious as Manny acted like a blind man first experiencing the glorious sights of the world. It was a joy to be around him, hearing his fresh questions about what it meant for Christ to be Lord of his life. The other guys from the church talked openly with Manny; the discussions were penetrating and heartfelt. Jonathon marveled at seeing a life transformed before his eyes.

It wasn't until the middle of the evening when Jonathon came home. His mother was gone, but she had left a message for him that read, "Chandler called to say Henry Smitherton died today. Funeral is Wednesday." He had to know more. He immediately left for the hospital.

*****

Noelle hesitated before she answered her ringing phone. Since Dave's call yesterday, she worried that he would call again. She guardedly said hello.

"Hi, Noelle."

She sighed with relief. "Manny, I'm so glad it's you."

"What? You were expecting the grim reaper?"

"No, it's nothing. Just nice to hear from you—you never call. How's Mom and Dad?"

"Fine as always. And everything's okay back at school for you?"

His tone was caring. She found herself liking her brother more these days than ever before.

"I'm loathing tomorrow," she answered. "It's going to be a long day, but sure, everything's fine."

A pause on the phone made her realize Manny had called for a purpose.

"Something happened to me today, Noelle."

"Yes? What is it?"

"You know I went to church with Jonathon?"

"Oh, yeah. So you want some brownie points for that?" She laughed, waiting for Manny to pop back with his own sarcasm.

"It was incredible, Noelle." He didn't laugh.

"I became a Christian this morning, Noelle. I prayed to Jesus, told Him I was sorry for making such a mess of my life, and asked Him to be my Lord."

"What?"

"You gotta listen to this, Noelle. It was a great church, the music was powerful and the people so kind. There was such a sense of love, a love that can only come from God. I finally realize that's what I've been missing in my life. God's been trying to show me how much He loves me. Today I really felt like I was in His presence, and Jesus..." his voice dropped. "I know that He died for me. For me, Noelle."

She couldn't believe it, but her brother was crying.

"Manny, are you sure you're okay?"

He spoke in the midst of his tears. "I'm better than that, Noelle. I am saved, fully loved by the Son of God. It's the most incredible feeling I've ever known. You've got to believe in Jesus, Noelle. Confess your sins." She could hardly understand him as the words were uttered through his choked voice.

"Have you told Mom and Dad?"

"Tried to." He took a deep breath and seemed to gain some control. "They were nice about it. I'm not sure they get it though. But you've got to know. It's what Jonathon believes too. More than just church stuff, this is about Jesus being alive! He healed me, back when I had cancer. I'm sure of it. And now He forgives me, forgives you. He loves us, Noelle. Loves us so deeply. Do you know that?"

"Of course I do." Noelle had to respond affirmatively as her brother started crying again. She had to comfort him somehow.

"Trust Him, for your life, Noelle." His words were squeezed between tears and sighs. "Do it. Tonight."

"I'll think it through, Manny. Listen, I better go, but thanks for calling."

"Tonight, Noelle." He was broken, wholly and completely.

"You take care of yourself, Manny."

She hung up, worried about him. She thought about calling her folks. They might know what really happened. But Manny would probably answer the phone.

Then she thought about Jonathon. *Was this one of his crazy ideas? Was Jonathon into something...cultic?* She fought with herself. *No, he wouldn't be so foolish. He's always been stubbornly conservative, never into that emotional trash. And, the way he was to me last night, so tender.*

She fingered the cordless phone, sliding the volume control on the ringer. *He's supposed to call. Maybe he can tell me what got my brother all upset. But, he'll think it's great, I'm sure. I don't know if I want to hear it. Maybe he's back to thinking he healed Manny.*

But what's wrong with my brother?

She crawled into bed with the phone still in her hand. It was a chilly night in her apartment, and she pulled the comforter close around her. She was exhausted, and chemistry class came early in the morning. She counted up all her studies and paperwork from the day and felt spent. The call from Manny took her last bit of energy. She had to sleep.

I've never felt so tired.

She slid the ringer volume to silent and rolled over in bed.

Michael J. Huckabee

Death stole into still more organs, staining healthy tissue black with cancerous streaks. The body raised a rousing defense, an urgent and broad immunologic response from every physiologic system. Diving boldly into the cancerous webs, white blood cells sacrificed thousands while millions more were promoted to enter the battle. Helper cells individually locked themselves to the enemy with a relentless grip that guaranteed their mutual destruction. The initial response was valiant, but the cancer soon waged the war on multiple fronts, surrounding detachments of immunity fighters and swallowing them in single gulps. Forced to recruit more ranks, the body's alliance drafted immature cells anxious to join the resistance, but they were no match for the vast stronghold of melanoma. The droning efforts of the human corps wore down its own defenses. Fatigue and weakness robbed the body's strength, allowing the cancer to flourish.

Chapter 27

*N*oelle slipped out of her morning chemistry lecture two minutes early to avoid any possible encounter with Dave. While he sat at the front of the class, she sat conveniently near the back door. He hadn't looked her way through the whole class. She knew because she'd stared at him the whole hour.

This is never going to work. Maybe I should have Jonathon take him out. She smiled at her own lame humor.

Walking back to her apartment, she planned the next three hours before it would be time to return for biology lab. She needed to study and finish a couple of papers, but she mostly wanted to check her e-mail.

When she walked into the apartment her phone was ringing.

"Hello?"

"Noelle, this is Dr. Mittlestedt's office," the female voice was pleasant. "Can you hold for him?"

"Yes, of course." She was expecting his call but didn't know she would hear this soon. While waiting, she turned on her computer and clicked on her e-mail so it would connect as soon as she hung up.

A voice on the other end of the line cleared his throat. "Noelle, Dr. Mittlestedt here. You're back at school already?" His question was stiff; he very well knew the answer.

Stepping into the kitchen, she filled a cup with water as she responded. "I came back Saturday, actually. I had too much work to do here. My incision looks good though. Sutures have all stayed in place."

"Good. That's good." He hesitated, and she could imagine he was rummaging through her chart at his office. "Let's see, when we were going to pull those out?"

Doesn't he remember? She placed her cup in the microwave and set it for two minutes.

Michael J. Huckabee

"You said Friday that I could have someone here do that in a week." She patted the small of her back to feel the bandage covering her sutures. "I thought I'd go to student health and have one of the nurses do it. I really appreciate you taking care of this over your holiday, Dr. Mittlestedt."

"Of course. Well, that's why I'm calling. We've got to look at it again."

A twinge of discomfort hit her stomach as if she hadn't eaten for two days. "No problem. I'll be back in Windwood in three weeks for Christmas break. I made an appointment to see you then. I think it's for December 17." Finding the last Chamomile tea bag in the cupboard, she started to tear the foil covering.

"It needs to be sooner than that, like this week. Tomorrow, if possible. Noelle, it looks like melanoma."

The half-opened pouch fell from her hands; the wall catching her as she leaned to the side. The gnawing ache suddenly stabbed her gut, stealing her breath.

She grabbed her belly to push the pain away as her voice faltered. "You're serious, aren't you?"

"I'm afraid so, Noelle. It's okay if I call your mom, isn't it? We need you to come back immediately. It looks like the same type of lesion your brother had, called nodular melanoma. This type spreads rapidly."

"I..." She left the kitchen and stepped into the living room, searching for something to hold her up. "I better talk to my parents."

"Yes, you do that. I'll call them right now. Make arrangements to see me as soon as you're back. The receptionist will get you in quickly." He spoke abruptly, wanting to get off the phone.

"Sure." Her voice started shaking. "I understand."

"I'll see you today or tomorrow, whenever it works for you. Let me call your folks now." She heard the click of a disconnection before she could respond.

Noelle knew he was way too abrupt. It was cruel. Leaning to the wall, she superficially analyzed his behavior rather than deal with his message. Hardly comprehending what was happening, something deep within her began to rise, a natural inclination that she fought, like holding back an ocean wave.

The microwave dinged in the kitchen.

No, it can't be. Not cancer.

She dropped to the floor in a flood of tears. Her body folded over itself, collapsing like a sand castle in the tide as she sobbed uncontrollably. Anguish overflowed, now unheeded. Goals were consumed, dreams vanquished.

202

It wasn't more than ten minutes when her phone rang again.

As soon as she answered it, a soft and loving heart spoke from the other end. "Noelle, honey?"

"Oh, Mom. I've got cancer, don't I?" She held back her sobbing to hear her mother's response.

"Dr. Mittlestedt just spoke to me. Now don't jump to conclusions. We've got to walk through this together."

"Is it bad, Mom? What did he tell you?"

"You know Dr. Mittlestedt; he didn't say much. He needs to see you, honey. Let's take it one day at a time. Your father's still in Denver on business, so Manny and I will leave to come get you. He's just over at Jonathon's, so as soon as I reach him, we'll take off. I don't want you driving by yourself, and we should be there by five."

"No. I can't believe this." Questions continued to leak out of her: *Will I have to quit school? Am I going to be in the hospital a long time? Will they use radiation on me?*

An inner resolve served her thoughts by plugging the hole. There were no answers yet.

Her tears hesitated as she wrestled the immediate task at hand. "No, I can drive, Mom. It makes no sense for you to come." She wanted to sound more thoughtful than Dr. Mittlestedt did on the phone. She wanted to command something, make a decision.

"Let me drive home, Mom. I'll call you on my cell along the way."

"I'd rather we come get you."

"But then we'd have two cars here. It would be a hassle." She thought through it again and convinced herself with surprising clarity. "If I leave now, I'll get home in time to see Dr. Mittlestedt yet today if I need to. It's just five hours, Mom. Let me just come."

"I'm reluctant, honey. But if you're sure…I want to know I can speak to you on your phone. Check to see if it's charged and call me back as soon as you're about to leave."

It felt good to have some control. She asked one more question that brought back the brink of tears.

"Mom, do you think I'll have to quit school?" She wished she hadn't asked it.

"One day at a time, honey. Let's get you home."

*****

Feddersen hunched over Troy, watching the computer screen. Pity mixed with suspicion as he guarded himself, watching for any signs of confusion in his partner. They had worked together all morning, Troy giving instruction on how the research data was kept on the various responses to the nanite injections. Feddersen picked it up quickly, marveling at Troy's genius in creating the system. While the brain tumor could create mental disorientation, it seemed to be intermittent, with Troy's methodical functioning still the norm.

"Let's take a break," Feddersen said. "I'm on overload."

"Okay, let me show you something completely different." Troy's fingers danced across the keyboard, then he reached for the mouse and made the pointer land on a small icon on the screen. "This icon reviews the images on our security cameras. I try to check it daily, but I'm behind a couple days." He double-clicked on the icon.

The screen blinked blue followed by three columns of six photographs, all showing vehicles that had driven past the surveillance cameras over the weekend. Dates and times were stamped below each one, with all shots featuring various angles of a green Concorde. One other car was in a lone photo on the screen: a gray Chevette.

"I need to smile and wave when I drive by," Feddersen quipped. "So who's driving the gray car?"

"Never seen it. We can easily check on it, but I doubt if it's anything to worry about. Probably a high school kid cruising the country roads."

At the bottom of the screen a small box blinked with the word "MORE." Troy brought the mouse down to the box and clicked. The screen flashed again with a new series of six pictures.

Troy let out a low whistle. The gray Chevette showed up across the screen in every shot. The two middle frames pictured the car off the road, parked in the cornfield.

"Who is that?" Feddersen muttered.

To answer, Troy double-clicked on one of the photos and the computer initiated an online search, completed in less than five seconds. A data screen displayed a license plate number followed by a name, address and phone number. The name was Jonathon Edward Thompson.

"It's that Thompson kid again." Feddersen slapped his hand on the table top.

"I thought you said he was gone," Troy spoke calmly.

"He's gone from the hospital, yes. But how'd he know we were out here?"

"I have no idea, but he definitely knows about our little place." Troy flicked his finger on the mouse and returned to the screen with the six photos of the Thompson car. "Look at the clock times. He was out here for almost six hours on Saturday."

"Think he should go?"

"He needs to be already gone." Troy made a wide circle with the mouse, sending the pointer in large loops around the six framed, identical Chevettes.

"Are you up to it?" Feddersen sternly looked at Troy. "It's got to be done carefully."

"I'm fine. It'll be cleaner than the Crenshaw boy. I've heard those Chevettes don't handle rear impacts very well. Something about exploding gas tanks."

"I just need to know you'll do it right, Jerry. I've got to make arrangements to get the girl here."

"You've got to have more confidence. You do your job and I'll do mine."

I'll have the girl here by nightfall. What about you?"

"That's reasonable. By nightfall then."

*****

Manny was at the Thompson's house early that morning, before Jonathon was even out of bed. Elaine answered the door and, noticing a Bible in Manny's hands, kindly welcomed him. With the aroma of brewed coffee filling the kitchen, they both sat for a cup as he easily poured out his story of his new spiritual awakening. Like reacquainted old friends, both were in tears by the time Jonathon stumbled into the kitchen.

"What's going on?" Jonathon muttered, still half-asleep.

"Oh bless the Lord! Bless the Lord!" his mother exclaimed. "Look what God's gone and done in your friend, Jonathon."

Manny's wet cheeks turned into a meek smile, and he sniffed loudly.

"Looks like God's wringing him out to me." Jonathon threw a box of tissues on the table. "You're both a sopping mess."

"Them are tears of sweet Jesus, son. You let 'em flow, Manny. They ain't hurtin' nobody."

"Yeah, you're right, Mom." Jonathon reached over Manny's back and gave him a bear hug. "This guy's a new creation, and I love the new look."

Manny reached his arms up and grabbed Jonathon's neck to return the hug.

"Help, help!" Jonathon feigned. "He's strangling me!"

Jonathon kept his grip and slid to Manny's side, slipping his head out and pulling him over in his chair. They crashed to the floor, Manny quickly flipping himself over in a wrestling move that planted him spread-eagle over the top of Jonathon, a half-Nelson hold around his neck.

"Boys! You're gonna kill each other!"

"At least we know where we're going," Jonathon squeaked out.

"Yeah, I'll be able to take you down in heaven too," Manny heaved.

"No way! 'The weak will become strong.'"

"Both of you knock it off." Elaine looked away and sipped her coffee before grinning. "It's the joy of the Lord, don't cha know? That's your strength."

Manny relaxed his grip and Jonathon unwrapped himself. "You're a wise woman, Mom."

"Thanks for the coffee, Mrs. Thompson." Manny took a gulp. "Jonathon, would you have time to help me with something I found in the Bible last night? I just want to be sure I'm getting it right."

"And you're coming to me? I'm no expert, but I get a kick out of your questions."

Manny grabbed the Bible he brought with him. "Hillary has me going through the Book of John, and it's been great. I'm in chapter fourteen; here it is, verse twelve: 'I tell you the truth, anyone who has faith in me will do what I have been doing. He will do even greater things than these because I am going to the Father.' Now what's that all about?"

Jonathon leaned over to read the text again out of Manny's Bible.

Manny asked, "Does that really mean I can do what Jesus did?"

"Hey, Mom, take that one." Jonathon leaned back in his chair. "I'll bet you have a great answer."

She set her coffee cup down. "I just might. But he ain't askin' me, is he? He's asking you, and I'm waitin' to hear what you're gonna say."

She wasn't going to say a word, Jonathon knew it.

"Okay, here are my thoughts. I've wrestled that verse too." He leaned forward. "I remember that Jesus is being asked by His disciples for proof that He is the Son of God." He pulled the Bible around so he could read it. "Yeah, and here Jesus responds by saying that they've seen His miracles, which should be evidence enough. Then He shares that if we act in Christ's name, God will empower us so that it brings Him glory." He pushed the Bible back to Manny. "It's not that hard, really. If what we do, we do in the name of Christ, God will see that it gets done in a way that honors Himself."

"Out of the mouths of babes," Elaine muttered.

"What do you mean, Mom? Don't you agree?"

"Yup, I agree with you, alright. I just wonder then, why don't cha live it?" She got up from the table and took her cup to the sink, standing behind Manny. "If God's tellin' ya what to do, giving ya the power to do it, why aren't cha doing it?" Her eyebrows wrinkled up as she looked straight at Jonathon. Neither young man spoke a word.

"Well, I best be going to work." She rinsed her cup and laid it on the counter. "Make it happen today, boys. Do what God's tellin' ya to do."

"Okay, Mrs. T. We'll do it." Manny jumped up.

Jonathon stayed in his chair and waited until his mom was out the door. "It isn't always that easy, Manny."

"You just said it's not that hard." Manny poured himself another cup of coffee.

"It's not hard to understand. But it's hard to know what to do, at least for me." Jonathon slid back in his chair. "Lately I just can't tell what it is God wants from me."

"You're kidding me. I see God using you all over the place. Why, if you hadn't prayed for me to be healed, I probably wouldn't even be here. And if you hadn't gotten me to go to church? Where would I be? Still coasting to hell?"

Jonathon sighed. "Beings you brought it up, it's about this healing. I thought maybe I had a connection to God on it. But last night a guy in the hospital died. I prayed for his healing a month ago. I thought it had worked, but now he's gone. I never saw God get any glory. Then there was the mayor; I messed up there royally. And just last week I prayed for this lady who was dying, Grandma Davis. She didn't make it." Jonathon rubbed his eyes with his fingers. "If I ever had it—some kind of spiritual gift—it's gone now."

"So how'd you know to pray for those folks?" Manny asked.

"Well, usually I got a strong sense I was supposed to. Like with you, Manny. I just knew in my heart God wanted me to pray for you. God even makes my spine tingle, and sometimes my chest burns. That's how I know."

Michael J. Huckabee

Manny looked as if he wanted to laugh, but held it when Jonathon didn't crack a smile. "And is that what happened these last times?"

Jonathon paused to think back. His hesitation answered the question. "You just read in the Bible that we need to act in Christ's name." Manny put his finger on the still open Bible. "So did Christ tell you to heal those folks?"

"Not exactly. But who could say that this wouldn't bring God glory?" Jonathon argued. "Seems like anytime God heals would bring Him glory."

Manny's mahogany eyes narrowed and he spoke softly. "I'm not sure. Isn't that up to God—not you?"

Jonathon started to speak, then stopped.

*****

Noelle was on the road in no time as she'd hardly unpacked her clothes from the Thanksgiving trip. Tossing the same suitcase, dirty clothes and all, back in the car put her on the road in fifteen minutes. She called her mom just as she was leaving St. Louis, and the sound of that stable and comforting voice gave her the resolve to get home quickly. The unanswerable questions had to wait, so she turned up the CD player and kept herself from contemplating the future.

The cell phone rang a half hour later, much earlier than when she and her mom had planned to talk.

"Hello, Noelle? This is Dr. Feddersen, remember me? We met in the emergency room last Friday when Dr. Mittlestedt biopsied that skin lesion on your back."

"Sure, I remember you."

"I just called your mother, and she gave me your phone number. She thought it might be a good idea if I talked with you. I might have some good news."

Noelle turned down her CD player. "Go ahead."

"I've reviewed your pathology report, and the type of tumor we've found may respond well to some new treatments. I don't think you need to be quite so concerned."

"Why didn't Dr. Mittlestedt tell me about this?"

"He and I have been chatting about you, and the first report didn't tell us what we know now," he lied. "He wanted me to call you as soon as possible."

208

"I guess that is good news. Thanks for calling, I should be back in Windwood about 3:30 or so."

This was too easy. She was giving him all he needed.

"My goodness, you're making good time. Is your car reliable?"

"It's a Chevy Cavalier. It gets me around."

Simple small talk.

"Drive safely and again, don't worry too much about the melanoma. It should all work out fine."

"Thanks, Dr. Feddersen. Will I be seeing you again?"

"There's a good chance, Noelle. Nice talking with you."

Chapter 28

*N*oelle's immune system was overthrown. The cancer mobilized in massive maneuvers across her body, blackened cells boldly drawn to blood, bone, and brain. These sites boasted a frenzied feeding ground, replication flourishing at a frenetic pace. Yet, in the midst of defeat, the only symptom Noelle acknowledged was a vague fatigue. There was no other indication of the incredible invasion that had been induced inside of her.

Manny spent the morning with Jonathon, talking through two more pots of coffee. They parleyed from the heart, Manny sharing his concern over his parents and sister not understanding his new faith in Christ, and Jonathon opening up about his suspicion that Feddersen and Mittlestedt were involved in illegal research in nanotechnology.

"Is there something I can do to help?" Manny offered. "If what you say is true, those guys are going to kill somebody."

"I'm wondering if they already have." Jonathon felt like he should lower his voice. "I have my suspicions, but I can't prove anything."

"C'mon, that's cloak and dagger stuff. Let's figure out a way to expose NanoMed before anyone gets hurt."

"And how would you suggest we do that?" Jonathon wished it was so simple.

"Let's go out there; snoop around the place."

"There's not much to see."

"How about if we get inside?" Manny's eyebrows curled up.

"And what if they find us?"

"No big deal. We're just messing around. Let's take advantage of our youthful ignorance."

Jonathon rolled his eyes. "I think it's too risky."

Manny stared into his coffee cup. "Okay, then. Here's what we do." He sat up and pushed his cup away. "Let's pray about it."

"Actually, that's a great idea." Jonathon realized his friend's faith was deepening daily. "You surprise me, Manny. That should have come from me."

Manny smiled sheepishly and folded his hands in front of his chest, hesitating just long enough to be sure Jonathon was bowing with him.

While it was no polished prayer, Manny sincerely asked God to lead Jonathon in wisdom and strength. At the end of the prayer, he added, "And Lord, if You'd let me have a hand in this, I'd like to help my buddy here. If You'd be so good as to allow me to help him bring this NanoMed into the open so Your truth would shine, I'd be grateful. Thanks for using Jonathon in my life, Lord. Your ways are perfect, and I know You're leading both of us down Your path."

It was as comfortable as the whole morning's visit, and Jonathon knew a greater friendship with Manny after this time of prayer than he had ever experienced with anyone else.

They left Jonathon's house at noon to go over to the Lewis home for lunch. What they found took their appetites away.

Manny's mother was sitting at the kitchen table, the cell phone clutched in her palm and a pile of balled Kleenex beside her. She acted surprised when Manny stepped in, and stood quickly, turning her reddened eyes away.

"Mom! What's wrong?"

She kept her back to them with her first words. "It's Noelle." Slowly turning, her head stayed low. "She has melanoma, Manny."

"What?" Manny was in disbelief. "When did this happen?"

"She had Dr. Mittlestedt do a biopsy on her back last week. She just got the results today."

"Are they sure?" Manny demanded.

Raising her head, tearing eyes met her son's. "She's kept it a secret, Manny. She didn't want us worrying." Though she spoke with strength, her face was drawn tight. She grabbed a fresh tissue. "Dr. Mittlestedt took the spot off her back last Friday. What they don't know is how far it's progressed. He only said it might be more difficult than yours. Then a Dr. Feddersen—I guess he's a consultant for Dr. Mittlestedt—called Noelle later to say it might be okay. I guess we just have to wait until she gets here."

Jonathon felt out of place, with a hundred questions of his own that he couldn't ask. "Maybe I should go, Manny."

Mrs. Lewis answered. "Jonathon, please stay. I'm about to call Noelle, and I know she'd like to hear from you."

"I don't know what I'd say."

"Tell her to buck up," Manny interrupted, "and plan to have her friend Jonathon pray for her right away. That's the cure."

"Yeah, well…" Jonathon mumbled. "I'm not so sure."

"Encourage her, Jonathon. She'll want to hear your voice." Mrs. Lewis pushed the buttons on her phone, and Noelle answered right away.

"Hi, dear. Where are you now?" Her mother paused to hear Noelle's answer. "Just passing Travecky? That means you're less than three hours away." Waiting for another response, she then said, "I've got someone here to talk to you," and handed the phone to Jonathon.

"Hi, Noelle." Trying to sound cheerful, his words came out cracking. He turned his back on Manny and Mrs. Lewis, feeling like he was about to cry.

"Jonathon!" Tension filled Noelle's voice. "What are you doing over there? Did they call you?"

"Whoa, Noelle. It's okay. Manny and I had just stopped by when your mom told us the news." His eyes welled up as he fought for control.

She calmed down. "Quite a bummer, huh?"

"How are you doing, Noelle?"

"I don't know, Jonathon. It's like I'm in a time warp—like everything's on hold." She sounded solid, steady like her mom.

His tears abated. "There's a lot of people here waiting to help you in every way." He grabbed his head, frustrated with sounding so trite. "How's the road trip?" He smacked his head as soon as the words left his mouth.

"It's fine, traffic's not bad." She was polite, but her voice wavered. "Jonathon? Would you do me a favor?"

"Anything."

"Would you be there when I get to town? Be at Dr. Mittlestedt's office?"

"Sure, if you want me there."

"I just don't know how my mom will do. I need someone to lean on."

"I'll be there, Noelle."

She changed the subject quickly. "That Dr. Feddersen called me this morning. He said he thought I'd respond to some new treatments."

"That's what your mom said." Jonathon tried to sound confident. "Guess his opinion couldn't hurt."

He chose his words carefully, with Manny and his mother staring at him. "I need to let you talk to your Mom. Just be careful, Noelle. Are you stopping along the way?"

"No, I want to get home. I'll go straight to Mittlestedt's office."

"Good, I'll see you there. Probably be about 3:30."

"It'll be good to see you, Jonathon."

"Same here, Noelle. We'll all be here for you." He felt the twinge of tears again, quickly handing the phone to Mrs. Lewis before stepping into the hall.

Manny followed him, reaching his hand to Jonathon's shoulder. "How'd she sound?"

"Good." He shook off his sadness. "She's hanging in there. But there might be a problem." He nodded for Manny to come further into the hall away from Mrs. Lewis.

"Dr. Feddersen has suggested Noelle could get some new treatments."

"You think it would be nano-stuff?"

"Possibly. I can't trust him. I know what I saw. His treatments are illegal and dangerous."

Manny thought it over. "It's a stretch, Jonathon. Should you call the police?"

"They'd laugh me out of town."

"I don't think there's anything we can do until she gets here."

"I'm more tempted to drive out to that building in the country like you said, Manny. Just see if there's any sign of activity. See if Dr. Feddersen's car is out there."

"Couldn't hurt."

"I might run out there now, but Noelle asked me to be at Dr. Mittlestedt's office when she gets here. Do you think your mom would mind if I come?"

"Not at all. She'll appreciate the company. This has got to be driving her crazy."

"She's quite a lady, handling all this."

Just then, Mrs. Lewis came into the hall. "Noelle is quite a lady."

"Actually, Mom, he was talking about you." Manny put his arm around her. "Do you mind if Jonathon comes to the doctor's office with you? Noelle asked him to be there."

"That's just fine. I've wanted to spend some time with Jonathon myself." She turned to him with a smile behind her red eyes. "Can I get you guys something to eat?"

213

I've got an idea," Manny said. "I'm going to run out and get something for Noelle, a welcome home gift, maybe some candy or something. Why don't you have lunch together—get to know my mom better."

"That's sweet of you, Manny," his mom replied and kissed his cheek lightly.

"Are you sure I shouldn't come with you?" Jonathon asked, unable to hide his nervousness.

Mrs. Lewis put an arm behind Jonathon and gave him a little push. "You go sit down in the kitchen and let me make you a sandwich. Tell me what you did to Manny to make him so nice all of a sudden." She laughed.

Manny raised his eyebrows with a smile and gave Jonathon a thumb's up. "Let me drive your car. I'll make that trip out to the country for you."

Jonathon hesitated, then threw his keys at Manny. "I couldn't get out of this if I wanted to."

"All right, let's just see what that heap of yours can do." He jingled the keys in his hand. "I'll be back in a couple of hours."

*****

December was not one of Manny's favorite months. Hot, humid summers were his life, full of sweaty roofing jobs that funded his jet skiing. He waited until the bitterest cold day to bring out a winter coat, and then only wore it to appease those around him. The icy wind of below zero temps had not yet hit Windwood, so today Manny ran out to the Chevette wearing a T-shirt without a thought of the twenty-degree chill.

Just before entering the car, he nodded to a parked grain truck sitting just down the block. It was rare to see such a large vehicle around the neighborhood, but he offered a friendly wave typical of Windwood, and the driver gestured back with a lift of his fingers straight up from the steering wheel.

Starting the car, he revved the engine a few times while he rubbed his shoulders for warmth. He pulled out of the driveway and headed to Highway 6, choosing the trip to the NanoMed research building first. Jonathon was too worried, and Manny hoped to be able to call back in twenty minutes to tell him he found the green Concorde safely tucked away.

He ground the stick into second gear, getting used to the Chevette's clutch. As he drove away, the grain truck rumbled behind him. With a better look at the driver in his rearview mirror, he saw a balding, round-faced man.

Heading out of town, he counted the mile markers along the highway to find the five-mile corner. Traffic was light, but the grain truck lumbered behind him, closer than Manny would have liked. The Chevette did not claim much acceleration, but Manny tried to open it up to gain some distance. Still the truck stayed less than a car length behind him.

The five-mile corner came into view and Manny flipped his turn signal on, glad to get out of the way of the truck.

Pulling the Chevette onto the dirt road, he shook his head when the truck behind him turned the same way. "Who on earth is that?" he asked.

Slowing to about thirty, Manny found the truck staying right on his bumper, and he shrugged. "Okay, then. Go on around me." He slowed and pulled over to a stop on the gravel shoulder.

The grain truck lumbered over just behind him and stopped, idling noisily.

Manny looked behind him, unable to make out anymore than the bowling ball head of the driver; his face was in the shadow of the truck's cab. Manny raised a hand as if to say, "What gives?"

The driver raised a finger off the steering wheel again, same as his previous greeting back in town.

Heart pounding, Manny stuck his arm out his window and waved for the truck to go around.

The diesel engine behind him lazily knocked away. He sat in a stalemate, afraid to pull forward.

"Okay, Mister." Manny popped open the door. Pausing, he hoped to see some kind of response. All he felt was a blast of the cool December breeze. Stepping out of his car, the brisk air raised goosebumps across his skin. After two steps toward the truck, large gears grinded noisily and the truck slowly pulled forward. It widely arced around him and proceeded down the gravel road, exhaust fumes befouling the air. The driver's head bobbed up and down as the truck picked up speed passing by.

Hopping back into the car, Manny turned the heat on high and tried to relax. "Some sense of humor."

The truck ambled down the gravel road, and Manny was fine just waiting. Not until the truck had shrunk to a match box size in the distance did he pull his car back onto the road. "Hope the guy got his kicks out of that."

Manny headed down the road, cracking his neck in all directions as he stretched the tight muscles. He laughed at himself and his anxiety. It felt freeing to be alone in the country. Kicking up gravel behind him, he grinded only slightly at fourth gear and sped up to fifty miles per hour. Occasionally washboards in the gravel rattled the loose hatchback door, inviting dust to enter. The taste of grit in his mouth only made Manny feel more rugged and unrestrained.

It wasn't long before he saw he was gaining on a small cloud of dust ahead of him that could only be the grain truck. As fast as he was approaching, the truck had to have reduced its speed. Looking at the stark fields around him, Manny hoped the truck was slowing to turn off onto a dirt path into a field.

The straight stretch of gravel did not offer any crossroads. He fast approached the truck, deciding to remain at his speed and pass. He swung wide with a fleeting thought that the truck might swerve out at him just as he was going around. Rather, he passed the truck easily, seeing again the driver raise one finger in greeting as Manny passed. Racing the Chevette to a faster speed to distance himself quickly, a wake of dust shot up from behind him as he sped away, making him smile with gratification.

The old hatchback's acceleration lacked power to gain much speed, and Manny felt the steering wheel rattle in his hands as he pushed to go faster. Glancing in his rearview mirror, it remained filled with the hanging cloud of dust he created. He floored the gas pedal, but the speedometer wavered at sixty.

Even as he pressed his toes hard against the floor, he saw the familiar grill of the truck emerge through the dust fog behind him. The truck wasn't more than a half car length behind him.

He stomped his foot on the already floored gas, hoping to squeeze more velocity out of the car. The truck loomed fully out of the dust behind him, just inches from his back bumper.

Wham! His car lurched forward and to the right as he was rammed. Manny clung to the shaking steering wheel, correcting a narrow skid and pulling to the left to move out of the line of attack. A slight taste of blood told him he'd bit his tongue.

The truck veered left to follow him with amazing precision. Manny saw the next impact ahead of time, bracing his extended elbows as he squeezed his hands around the wheel.

Wham! The hit was the same as the last, forcing a short loss of control that Manny was again able to compensate for. His mind wandered momentarily to why he wasn't being hit harder. A good swift rear end from the truck would certainly send him out of control. He looked out the side window, seeing loose gravel and deep side ditches in both directions.

Still flooring the pedal, Manny saw his speed inch up to over sixty-five. In desperation, he prayed out loud, asking God to end this madness. The truck's grill filled the rearview mirror again, another hit imminent.

Suddenly the truck backed off and became smaller in the mirror. Manny jammed his foot hard on the gas to gain another inch of distance, not understanding why, but thankful for the abrupt change.

One second later he saw the road sharply bend in a ninety-degree turn to the right.

Jerking the wheel while instinctively slamming on the brakes forced a blind skid that shot the car off the gravel road. Loose gravel in the shoulder tossed the car treacherously toward the ditch, forcing a high-speed flip end over end in two revolutions. The Chevette's doors popped open on the last pitch.

Manny was already unconscious from a blow his head took against the front windshield. His body flew out of the car ten yards farther into the cornfield.

The grain truck rolled to a stop. Jeraldo Troy stepped out, donning gloves to bear the freezing chill of the afternoon. He sighed long, a cloud of breath visibly escaping his lips, then reached back into the truck and brought out a shovel. Using it as a staff to steady his steps, he crossed the ditch and walked into the field.

*****

Manny wasn't back at the Lewis home when he had promised. It was two hours that went faster than Jonathon expected, what with Mrs. Lewis asking him all about his work at the hospital. Then she added her own stories of Noelle when she was a young girl and related the story of Manny's scare with cancer. It was therapeutic for her, remembering special moments with her children, but after two hours it was time to go to the clinic and Manny wasn't back yet.

"That's okay," Mrs. Lewis said. "We'll go down to the doctor's office and find Noelle. Manny will probably meet us down there."

There was no choice for Jonathon. Covering his concerns, he told Mrs. Lewis, "Yeah, he's probably out for a joy ride."

Chapter 29

*J*eraldo Troy whistled through his teeth, a nondescript ditty that he made up as he went along. The dirt was only beginning to harden in the early winter's cold. Slapping his shovel against large clods left from the plowing a month ago, he scooped up the dark soil and scattered it over Manny's body. It was short work to cover the form, sprawled face down. No more than a six-inch blanket of soil served to hide it.

When Feddersen returned, they would get the Chevette hauled into one of the sheds. He returned to his truck and tossed the shovel in the cab.

Not until the engine revved and the truck drove off did a small funnel of dirt cave above Manny's right hand. No one was there to see the weak movement of fingers.

*****

Noelle was an hour late and wouldn't answer her cell phone. Mrs. Lewis kept finding possibilities. "Maybe she stopped to get something to eat. That's a lot of driving. She probably just took a break. I'm sure she'll call. She's just like her father. He's never home when he says he'll be."

Jonathon stepped out of the single-story Family Health Specialties, Inc. clinic building to stand along the street. With Manny taking his car, he was trapped with Mrs. Lewis, who apparently soothed her anxiety by talking.

He gazed down the street, looking for evidence of his missing friends. Even the sight of a green Concorde would at least answer some questions. He strolled the sidewalk, pulling his arms tight across his chest in the chilly breeze of the afternoon. When a minivan pulled into the clinic parking lot beside him, he found himself gawking as a mother and three kids unpacked from the car, as if expecting to see Manny or Noelle climb out behind them. The mother bustled the kids to the clinic door, looking twice over her shoulder at Jonathon, the last time with a look of discomfort, before he realized he was staring and turned away.

The parking lot kept a busy pace, and Jonathon tried to be more discreet as he watched cars enter. He stepped over to a large five-foot granite sign resembling an over-sized tombstone. The names of Drs. Mittlestedt and Wells were deeply engraved on its face, and his fingers fit inside the broadly inscribed letters as he traced their names subconsciously.

"God, where's Manny? And where could Noelle be? You've got to help me, Lord," Jonathon prayed. The questions resounded in his head as he turned and leaned back against the stone. "I need to know You're there, God." He slapped his hands against the hard rock. Bending his knees, he sunk down to sit at the base of the sign. "I'm not sure You're there."

*****

Dr. Feddersen carried Noelle's limp body across the black and white tile of NanoMed's office. The floor-length windows of this room faced east, so the late afternoon sun only dimly lit the room, obscured even more by the ranks of green plants lining the floor and hanging from the ceiling along the windowed wall.

After laying her gently on the black leather couch, Feddersen folded her arms across her belly. She sighed deeply in her medicated slumber. He watched her for a moment, seeing her rest comfortably, before stepping to the kitchen for a drink.

Opening the refrigerator door shot a band of light across the otherwise dark galley kitchen. Feddersen left the door wide open, perusing the few items of an opened orange juice carton, a nearly empty tub of margarine, and three half bottles of wine. He winced with the reminder of the poisoned wine and suddenly felt distrustful. In the silence he leaned back to his right to listen for the breathing sounds of Noelle. A faint snore came from the office area, and he reached for the wine bottle furthest back, recognizing the cheap label he'd brought for Thanksgiving. Closing the refrigerator door, the kitchen turned black again. He felt for the cupboard handle above the sink and opened it, finding a goblet inside. As his eyes adjusted, he peered to his left into the deepest darkness of the dining room. The glint of two eyes appeared in the shadowed form of a body.

Michael J. Huckabee

"Jerry, you're spooking me again," he said before flipping on the dining room lights to reveal Jeraldo Troy sitting at the dining table. "What are you doing here in the dark?"

"Just enjoying the silence. It's a great afternoon, isn't it?" His voice was relaxed and slow.

"Wine?" Feddersen offered, trying to stay nonchalant.

"I've had my share, thanks." Troy fingered his empty crystal. "Don't let me stop you. The Chardonnay you brought wasn't too bad, considering the grocery label."

Feddersen poured himself half a glass from the bottle he still held. He fought against his distrust of Troy as he recalled the fateful drink. It was best to stay congenial. He needed Troy to save his life. "Our patient is out in the office, sleeping like a baby."

"Any trouble?"

Feddersen was relieved to see Troy's clarity. He might have been slightly inebriated, but he was tracking. "Very smooth. I found her driving along the interstate and followed her just before she came into town. She was heading to Dr. Mittlestedt's office, but I called on her cell phone to tell her to go to the hospital instead of the clinic, as Mittlestedt and I needed to see her there. Her family would be waiting there, I said. Worked like a charm. As soon as she parked, I pulled up alongside her and had her sedated before she left her car. Too easy." Feddersen took his first sip, letting the wine tingle across his tongue before swallowing. "How about you?"

"Not a problem. Jonathon Thompson will not be found for some time. Certainly not before he's able to contribute his finest nutrients to the next corn planting. I can't wait to see what the yield will be for his field."

Feddersen choked on his sip of wine. "What does that mean?"

"The boy has returned to the dust from whence he came."

"Tell me more."

"He was involved in a tragic traffic accident. Just up from here, actually. I think he was coming to see you, perhaps. It couldn't have gone better had he walked up to our front door. He missed the final corner, crashed his car into the field. I buried him out there. Best fertilizer the ground could ask for."

"Thompson's buried in a farm field?"

"Just up the road. I'll show you. We'll have to move his car."

"Are you sure you're making sense, Jerry?"

"Never clearer. Drink up."

220

"But what about his car?"

"As I said, we'll have to move it."

"You're sure you're not drunk?" Feddersen's voice was firm. "Where's Thompson's car?"

"It's out in the field, right beside that final turn east of here. We can get it later."

Feddersen lost interest in the wine and set the goblet down. "We'll get it now, Jerry."

"Relax. We're about to make history."

"If Thompson's car is wrecked out in the field, we've got to get it now. Someone's going to come looking for it." He wished he could trust Troy.

"Let's go see your patient." Troy got up from his seat and walked through the kitchen to the office. He leaned over the couch and gently brushed Noelle's hair across her forehead. "Ah, yes. This will do just fine. I'll need three ccs of serum, so we best draw two vials from her. Do you want to do the honors?"

"Definitely." Feddersen followed him, seeking to take charge. He stepped over to the office desk and opened a drawer with blood-drawing equipment. "Then we must get the car. How long will it take before you'll have her coded?"

"I should be able to run her DNA matrix in under an hour, then make the nanite configuration specific to her melanoma type. It'll take about three hours to develop the synchrotron structure so that it fits the nanite; that's the hardest part. After that, it takes only minutes to copy 100,000 replications, and we'll be ready for her first injection."

"That's four hours," Feddersen responded. "I'm going to dose her once more with the Rohypnol; that'll keep her out for almost six hours. We can get the car while she sleeps. When she wakes up I'll keep her relaxed with some Valium. Any chance those drugs will interfere with the nanomeds?"

"Not at all." Jerry stepped near the plants and leaned over to reach behind the large schefflera. He flipped a button on a stereo receiver hidden there and Tchaikovsky filled the room. "There, my little ones." He caressed a green leaf the size of a dinner plate. "Keep our patient comfortable," he told the plant.

Feddersen had his latex gloves on and wrapped a rubber tourniquet on Noelle's arm. She barely flinched when the needle was inserted into her vein, and there was no response whatsoever when he withdrew it after obtaining two glass tubes of blood.

Michael J. Huckabee

"There you go, Dr. Troy," he said with feigned professionalism. "Reassure me now. You're able to work cautiously, right? Accurately? These are our lives at stake, both yours and mine."

"Of course, Dr. Feddersen." Troy smiled broadly. "It's the young lady's life at stake too. And millions of others facing death from cancer. Let's save us all."

"Let's do."

*****

At the Family Health Specialties clinic, Jonathon leafed through the fourth copy *Newsweek* magazine, this one from six months ago, hardly reading a word. It was 5:30, and the clinic receptionist fussed around at the counter, rustling and filing papers, noticeably uncomfortable with he and Mrs Lewis still sitting there waiting for Noelle. The last patient came out from the doors leading to the clinic exam rooms and scheduled her appointment for next week.

"I'll need to let you out," the receptionist announced and followed the patient to the front glass door to unlock it. She closed the door and locked it again, looking at Mrs. Lewis. "If your daughter comes, I'll be glad to open it for her. This just helps us get the doctors out before dark." Smiling sympathetically, she returned to her counter, busily typing on her computer.

Mrs. Lewis had run out of conversation an hour ago, but was just as polite as she spoke across the waiting room to Jonathon. "I suppose we should go and let them finish their work. I just keep thinking she'll be coming any minute."

"I'll take you home whenever you're ready." He tossed his magazine on the stack beside him. "I'm in no hurry if you want to wait a little longer." He picked up the Lewis's cell phone that he had used for the past hour. Pushing redial again, he heard three rings followed by the recording that Noelle was not in the service area. He could repeat the message verbatim.

A large shadow appeared at the clinic entrance and pulled against the locked handle. Jonathon heard a deep voice holler, "Open up the door! Open up!"

Mrs. Lewis jumped to her feet. "Tom!" She ran to the door. "I'm so glad you're here!"

The receptionist went straight to the door, and Jonathon recognized Noelle's father. He stood, staying where he was in the waiting room.

After the Lewises embraced, Tom Lewis asked the inevitable. "Where's Noelle? Still with Dr. Mittlestedt?"

"Tom, she never came." Mrs. Lewis was in tears, barely able to speak. "We haven't heard from her in three hours." She looked over at Jonathon and motioned for him to come.

"You remember Jonathon Thompson."

After briefly shaking hands, Jonathon explained. "I've been keeping your wife company, but I'm not too good at it."

Mrs. Lewis patted his shoulder. "You've listened to me for long enough, Jonathon. Best set of ears I could have asked for."

"Where's Manny?" Mr. Lewis asked.

"We're not sure," she responded. "He took Jonathon's car and was supposed to be back by now." She acted as if this was nothing unusual.

"We better go find Noelle." Mr. Lewis directed the course of action.

"First let's get Jonathon home," proposed Mrs. Lewis. "Noelle will probably just come straight home." She lingered on her undying optimism.

"You head home, and I'll drop Jonathon off." He held the door open as his wife and Jonathon left the clinic.

"Call us tomorrow and we'll be sure to get Noelle right in," the receptionist offered before locking the door after their exit.

It was dusk as the winter wind greeted them with a cold blast. Mrs. Lewis quickly thanked Jonathon and headed to her car. Jonathon followed Mr. Lewis to his sedan at a quick pace.

As they both got into the car, Jonathon thought it best to share more of what he knew. "I'm worried about Noelle, Mr. Lewis."

"Yes, of course." He started the car and pulled quickly out of the parking lot.

"I think she might be…in trouble."

Mr. Lewis responded abruptly. "What do you mean?"

"Dr. Feddersen called Noelle and offered her a special treatment. I have reason to think that his treatment may be quite dangerous."

Mr. Lewis made his car turn quickly and drove forty-five in a thirty-five zone as he headed to Jonathon's home. "Go on."

"He's into some new technologies called NanoMed. It's got to be illegal. I believe he has used it on patients at the hospital, and there's evidence to suggest it has killed one of them."

The car sharply turned another corner, a block from Jonathon's home.

223

"Mr. Lewis, I think he wants to use Noelle as his next guinea pig. He might have her even now."

Mr. Lewis's face was unreadable. He pulled the car over in front of Jonathon's house.

"So?" Jonathon begged for a response. "Do you think you should check into it?"

"Remind me, Jonathon. Is Dr. Feddersen the hospital administrator?"

"That's the guy."

"And isn't he the one who blew the whistle on your miracle-working with the mayor a couple of weeks ago?"

"Oh." Jonathon's heart sank. "It isn't what you're thinking, Mr. Lewis."

He ignored Jonathon and continued. "And didn't Dr. Feddersen have you fired at the hospital over your little praying incident?"

Jonathon was silent, but his eyes pleaded with the man. *You've got to believe me.*

"I think you should think through your accusations, young man." Mr. Lewis's voice was stern. "It isn't fair for you to attack others like this just because you've been hurt." He popped the car door's unlock button to punctuate the end of his conversation.

Stepping out of the car, Jonathon continued to search for words. "I do—I do care about your daughter."

The car started to pull away, and all Jonathon could do was slam the door.

Chapter 30

*J*onathon entered his darkened home, slamming the front door the same way he had slammed Mr. Lewis's car door. His mother was gone, which meant there was no car at home. Pausing only to grab his Kansas City sock hat, he exited through the back, the screen door whacking against the house with a bang.

"Okay, Michael!" The call snapped at the crisp night sky. "Michael Sunday! It's time for you to show up again!"

The stars twinkled back at him. A slight, brisk breeze made the tip of his nose burn.

"Sunday, where are you?" He taunted the darkness. "C'mon, you always pop up. Now'd be a good time." Cool wetness formed in his eyes as he stretched the sock hat over his ears.

"I don't get it! Time for another magical entrance, isn't it?" A wavy circle formed in the frozen grass as he stomped around the backyard. "Time to burst in and save the day! You must have some new miracle you want me to do. What trick is up your sleeve this time?" His voice cracked as he demanded, "Michael, where are you?"

Sitting down on the swing, he shivered, tucking his hands deep into his jacket pockets.

"I'm so confused, Michael. This would be the perfect moment." Tears didn't withhold his speech as they dropped from his cheeks. "You've made a fool out of me again. Here I am, yelling at the moon. Are you just going to let me scream at nothing?"

His legs slowly rocked the swing. Reaching up to grab the swing's chains, he buried his head in his own shoulder. "You can't do this to me, Sunday," his voice was muffled through his coat. "You can't do this to me…God."

The heavens were silent and dark. If the night had eyes, the sliver of the moon suggested they were closed.

The absence of sound intensified Jonathon's yearning to hear something, anything. A faint rustle came from the tree tops circling the yard where the few remaining leaves dryly clung to their branches. A car passed by a block away, its aged muffler gruffly sounding out, then trailing into the distance.

Jonathon sniffed and rubbed his eyes against his collar. *Don't you care, God?*

No whisper, no sign, nothing. No response.

You're the God of the whole universe. Can't you help me? The tears were gone, replaced by a dulled affect. *I'm on my own.*

He stood and walked back into his house. He needed a car. Flicking on the kitchen light, he found a note from his mother. "I work til close tonight," it said. That meant after midnight. He needed wheels now. Reaching the phone book, he flipped to the Ws. He hesitated, closing the book with one finger marking his place. "I can't do this," he muttered. A small voice in his head agreed with him.

Pacing the hall, he weighed his options wondering where he could get a car. He shook his head as every name that came to mind wouldn't work. Out loud, he told himself and the inner voice, "I have to do this."

He opened the phone book to where his finger marked the page. Finding the listing for Joseph Wells, MD, he reached for the phone and stopped himself again. The address was less than a mile away.

Grabbing his black flannel gloves, he stepped out the front door and headed down the street on foot.

*****

The truck's headlights illuminated the upside-down gray Chevette, appearing like a giant aluminum can squeezed in the middle. The car rocked back and forth as two men pushed against the bashed in passenger side. As it had crashed on the downward slope of the ditch, it didn't take much force to roll it right side up. Feddersen pulled out a set of heavy chains from the back of the truck and handed one end to Troy. "Hook this on the front frame. Let's go."

Troy dutifully took the chains but stood still, staring at his partner.

"On the Chevette," Feddersen explained. "Wrap it on the frame under the front bumper." He pointed back to the Chevette and kneeled down to put the other end of the chain around the truck's rear frame.

Troy stepped over to the Chevette, grasping the chain tightly.

226

Feddersen threaded the chain underneath the truck's frame and hooked the end, pulling it taut. He stood and flicked on his flashlight, pointing it toward Troy, who stood straight up beside the Chevette's bumper, still holding his end of the chain.

"Hook it up, Jerry! We gotta go."

Troy glanced up and then returned his gaze to the chain. He knew something was wrong.

"Jerry, you okay?" Feddersen walked to the Chevette, keeping the flashlight trained on his partner. Lifting the chains from Troy's hands provoked no response. Feddersen asked again, tersely, "Jerry? You okay?"

"I'm...fine." It sounded like more of a question than a statement. Troy touched his forehead. "I can't remember. What was it you needed?"

"You're blanking out." Feddersen banged the chain loudly as he wrapped it underneath the car. "Come with me," he barked. "We're going back to the truck."

"Yes, that's good." Troy was suddenly ninety years old and grabbed Feddersen's arm to walk with him.

"We can't keep this up." Speaking under his breath, Feddersen sighed resignedly. "Let's get the car home."

"Yes, get the car home." Troy echoed.

His arm suddenly went stiff in Feddersen's grasp and he stopped walking. "How about the body?"

"You buried it, right?" Feddersen faced Troy. "It's buried here."

"Yes, that's right. I remember. I buried him."

"Where, Jerry? Where did you bury him?"

"Why—" Troy's finger pointed to the darkness outside the beam of the truck, "Over there. I believe."

"Show me, Jerry." Feddersen clenched Troy's arm harshly. "Take me to it."

The flashlight shined up at Troy's face, revealing a bewildered look of helplessness. He hesitated, then started walking to the right of where he had pointed. His voice was halting. "It should be over here."

Stumbling together over the heavy dirt clods, the flashlight poorly illuminated the uneven ground as they walked beyond the shine of the truck lights.

"Where, Jerry? Show me where," Feddersen coaxed.

"Here." Troy pointed just ahead. "It's here."

Feddersen walked Troy to the spot he pointed to and kicked around. There were small mounds of plowed up ground, but nothing resembling a grave.

"This can't be it, Jerry. Where did you bury Thompson?"

Troy was silent, turning his head both directions.

Feddersen grabbed Troy's shoulders roughly. "Jerry, show me where. Where's Thompson?"

"I buried him. I know I buried him."

Shaking his shoulders, Feddersen shouted in exasperation. "Where? You've got to show me." He released his hands.

Troy turned in a slow revolution. He had no clue.

"You stay right here." The words were angry and sharp. "I'm going to look around."

Kicking against any rise of dirt in the field, Feddersen walked in a broad circle around the Chevette. His flashlight flicked back and forth, the uneven ground creating shadows that forced him to stop several times to explore a possible grave. After a full circle, he was back to Troy with nothing.

"I buried him. I did," Troy mumbled.

"No one could have survived the wreck, but there's gotta be a body." Shaking his head, Feddersen laughed sarcastically with no amusement.

"I know I buried him," Troy droned.

"How would you know anything?" Feddersen spit the words. "Get back to the truck."

After checking the chains once more, Feddersen pulled the car out of the field with some difficulty. The car's tires were ruined. Once on gravel, Feddersen shortened the length of chain leaving only two feet between the vehicles. The Chevette would have to be literally dragged back to the farmhouse, a short half mile away. Out of breath when he got back into the truck, it took several minutes before he could speak to Troy.

"You're losing it, Jerry," Feddersen finally said as they slowly bumped along the road. "That cancer is knocking out your brain cells. It's eating them one by one."

"I know I buried him. I know it."

"How are you going to get the girl's blood work done acting like this? You gotta get it together."

"I can do it." Troy's voice was mellow. "I know I can do it."

"How long do these spells last?"

"I'm okay. I need to go to the lab."

"You're not okay, Jerry. You say you buried a body we can't find. You were absolutely worthless back there. You're not okay."

"Get me back home," the words were sternly quiet. "I'm okay."

No further conversation was shared.

Driving into the NanoMed complex, Feddersen entered the open door of the farthest metal outbuilding, dragging the Chevette behind him. They stepped out of the truck leaving the car still chained, and exited the building, closing the overhead door. Troy headed robotically to the lab.

Feddersen ran into the office to check on Noelle. Feeling her pulse, he could hardly distinguish her rhythm against the racing beat of his own heart. She didn't flinch as he held her wrist, palpating the slow methodical pulse of a drug-induced rest.

Hurriedly wrapping nylon rope he'd brought from the outbuilding, he bound her hands and feet. She remained unconscious throughout, indicating the depth of her slumber. He was taking no further risks.

He rushed down to the lab to find Troy.

＊＊＊＊＊

Jonathon rang the doorbell and stood at the door of a newer, two-story home. The oak door held an oval stained glass etched with a bouquet of mixed flowers. Through the glass, he could see a body approach. He was so thankful when Hillary Wells stood in the doorway, a surprised look on her face.

"Jonathon!" she exclaimed.

"Hi, Hillary. I hope you don't mind my dropping by."

"No, not at all. Step in," she offered.

"No. Listen, I don't have much time." He frowned. "I just need to ask a big favor. I mean big. That's why I came here, because you've got to believe me."

"Sure," Hillary said cautiously, noticing his reddened eyes.

"I need to borrow your car, just for tonight."

"My car?" She hesitated at his earnestness. "I'm leaving in about a half hour. Otherwise it'd be no problem. Why do you need it?"

His response was terse. "You gotta believe me if I tell you."

"I believe you, Jonathon." His taut shoulders relaxed and she caught the curve of a smile appear subtly on his lips before his face became stern again.

"I'm convinced Noelle's in big trouble, Hillary. She's disappeared, even though I just talked to her earlier this afternoon. She was supposed to meet me and her parents almost four hours ago, and she's gone. She doesn't answer her cell phone and, without going into the whole story—you've gotta believe me—I think she's been taken against her will."

Hillary would have laughed out loud if Jonathon hadn't spoken so sternly. She wondered if this was an elaborate prank or if he was serious? Shivering in the brisk air, she folded her arms and waited to hear more.

"I have a hunch, Hillary. I think I know where she might be and if I can get there, it will either confirm my suspicions or I'll know I'm wrong. I need a car to get out there."

"Sure, Jonathon. I'll take you there."

"No, Hillary. I can't have you come with me. It might be dangerous. I know it all sounds crazy, but you've got to believe me."

"That's a lot to swallow, but," Hillary tried to sound trusting, "how about Manny? Can't he help you?"

"Manny's disappeared. With my car." He paused. "I think he's in just as big of trouble."

She grimaced. "You're scaring me."

"That's why I can't have you come with me. Listen, call the Lewises if you want. They'll tell you Noelle's not home and that they haven't seen Manny since he borrowed my car this afternoon." Dropping his head, a sigh escaped his lips. "I tried to talk with Mr. Lewis about it, but he thinks I'm a nut."

Hillary saw his dejection and grabbed his coat sleeve. "Step in here; it's freezing!" Pulling him into the doorway, she closed the front door.

"I'll help you, Jonathon. I believe you."

"I can use your car?"

"Try this. I'm worried about what might happen to you. I want to make a deal."

His head turned away.

"Wait, hear me out." Grabbing both ends of his coat collar, she pulled them tightly together. "I said I'll help you. But you need someone with you. Let me call John Camelson. I'll bet he'll go."

She saw his eyes look to the ceiling in frustration and slapped his chest. "Don't be a jerk, Jonathon. You need help. If what you say is true, you can't do this alone." Dropping her hands, she turned aside, her back to him.

"You need someone with you," she repeated herself.

Silence fell behind her. She faced him again.

"If it's this dangerous, I don't want you out in my car alone." She smirked. "It's too nice of a car."

His head was down. "Okay. Call John. If he can come, that'll be fine." There was no smile in return when he raised his head. "He's got to believe me too Hillary."

"He will, Jonathon. He will."

*****

Staying as close as a shadow, Feddersen watched every move Troy made. Mentally, he seemed more clear back in the lab. He knew where the vials of Noelle's blood were placed, and he centrifuged them himself under Feddersen's watchful eye. Troy's conversation made more sense now as he taught Feddersen everything he knew about creating nanites.

Except for making notes to himself, Feddersen never took his eyes off Troy. The next four hours were critical to their survival.

"So when do you give yourself your next injection?" Feddersen queried.

"I take my dose twice a week now, Mondays and Thursdays."

"You had a dose today?"

"Yes." Troy was adeptly measuring diluted samples of serum into cuvettes. "Place three micromilliliters into cuvettes five through eight."

"I thought maybe that was why you had a spell out in the field." Feddersen drew the serum into his pipette and delivered samples to each of four thimble-sized plastic chambers, modeling Troy perfectly.

"Never seems to be any connection. I don't know what triggers them." Troy grasped the aluminum rack that held his series of cuvettes and handed it to Feddersen. "Now take your samples and line them up behind mine. Set them in the receiving tray beside the computer. Let's take a look at our patient's DNA."

Feddersen followed suit with his samples. "Does it happen every day?"

Troy stopped his work and looked to the floor, speaking impatiently. "I don't know, Marty."

"It's frightening, Jerry. What if you make a mistake? What if we can't find Thompson's body?"

"Stop it. There's been no mistakes." Troy squeezed his fingers with each hand. "We'll find it tomorrow when the sun's out. I know he's buried. Now stay with me."

Troy moved to the keyboard, his fingers gliding over the keys as he explained how to access and initiate the DNA matrix identification program.

Scratching feverishly with his pencil on his notepad, Feddersen tried to record the pathways and passwords, rarely asking a question. He couldn't help but stare as Troy's fingers typed slower than usual, but not for the sake of his partner.

Troy's fingers were trembling.

Chapter 31

*T*hrobbing bass rhythms pounded Noelle's mind. Her muscles, wanting to fight, would not respond. She wanted nothing more than for somebody stop that awful noise!

The colors were fluorescent and slightly blurred, but the dream was otherwise similar to the last one—except for the banging racket. It was a curious sight, like peeking through a long, giant kaleidoscope with the images exaggerated and three-dimensional. At the distant end of the tunnel was Jonathon, smiling and surrounded by an ever-changing array of magnificent opulent colors that brightened and faded sporadically.

But her head hurt from the booming bass sounds; a beat without cadence, spoiling an otherwise splendid scene. She could see Jonathon's lips move to call her name and he grinned, his head floating nearer as he unhurriedly approached.

She tried to move her head toward the jarring din, but even her neck was limply paralyzed. She was helpless, unable to speak, lift an arm, flex a knee. Staring back at Jonathon made her feel a weak smile, his eyes lit with energy and his smile buoyant. If she could just stay with him, perhaps the painful sounds would dull.

Come, Jonathon, come! She wanted to shout.

His head bounced as gently as a lollygagging balloon without a breeze, his lips still repeating her name, though she could not hear anything but the thudding bass. Oh, but if she could stretch out a hand, beg him to come more quickly. He would certainly take care of her.

The noise thundered even harder, impossible to ignore, each stroke now lancing sharply as if trying to burst the image before her. The jewels surrounding Jonathon glowed like intensely burning coals. She squinted, surprised to see Jonathon's expression blur as the hues of red immersed his face in fiery colors. He blinked twice, his eyes changing each time, losing their glimmer, losing their joy. Eyebrows furrowed as his black locks were swept up in a hot breeze and cropped. In an instant, his whole image changed.

No, not you! I told you to stay away. I don't want to see you!

The face had changed to David, with dark pits for eyes and an evil curl to his lips that moved to say three words over and over. She did not care to hear, but her eyes, still locked open, could not avoid the sight. The bass echoed with stabbing reverberations. As David's head loomed closer, she read the lipped words, "just once more."

His bare muscular arm reached out to her, nearer, nearer. Mixed smells of alcohol and pungent cologne brought back the memory she tried to forget. Advancing, his face filled her vision, yet his outstretched hand still did not touch her, prolonging the inevitable pain and agony again.

Nnnooo!

Bound by invisible shackles, she could not even force tears while the anguish swept through her mind. To shudder, to scream, to escape were all impossible as her emotions were incapacitated. The booming sounds crowded every sensation, now with David's face menacing inches before her.

"Just once more."

Piercing eyes shaped into black caverns of endless depths. His hot breath blew against her lips. With every source of strength she fought her immobility.

"Just once more."

Her eyes could not close to hide the hideousness of the insane attraction. She could not even grimace against the taste of his lips.

Whack!

Her faced slapped hard against cold tile. A new burning pain arose from her cheek. Instinctively waking from her dream, her eyes opened to find David gone and a more surreal but actual image before her. She stared at the mahogany legs of a leather couch. She was lying face down on the floor.

The scene had drastically changed. It was real this time.

Except for the pounding. There was still pounding.

She lifted her head toward the sound and saw a blur of green plants lining a far wall of windows. A shadow of a figure was outside the glass, beating against the window. The noise, no longer thunderous, was the irregular bass sound she had been hearing throughout her nightmare.

Trying to rise from the floor, she found her hands and feet bound.

Her memory gave no help; she had no idea where she was, how she got there, or why she was tied. She looked numbly back at the figure behind the window still pounding away. A hint of nausea trickled past, followed by a wave of exhaustion. The drugs in her system took her emotions captive, holding her amnesia and forcing sleep. Fighting vainly to keep her eyes open, she had to rest her head back on the floor.

The last thing she heard before losing consciousness again was the sound of crashing glass, followed by a weak but familiar voice, crying out her name.

Manny fell through the wall of glass, knocking over potted plants on his way to the floor. Landing with a thud, he cried out as he hit his left arm against the tile. An intense pain shot from deep within his wrist bones into his fingers, convincing him his forearm was fractured. Rising from the glass and dirt, he cradled his arm. The warmth of the room evaporated as cold winter air blew through the broken window frames behind him.

Touching his face, he felt fresh blood from glass cuts, nothing but scratches. A swollen bruise remained on the back of his head, unchanged from his car wreck. Tasting blood now mixed with the dirt he'd been spitting out of his mouth for the past couple hours left his stomach queasy. After being buried back at the crash site, he had risen out of the dirt and followed the road the truck had taken to these buildings. Circling each structure, he had found the windows on the back side of the office, seeing Noelle bound and asleep on the couch.

"Noelle!" he called again, crunching glass under foot as he walked across the room to where she laid on the tile floor. Her only motion was the slow respirations of her sleeping breaths. Kneeling at her body, he gently rolled her over.

She looked unharmed except for the red swelling near her cheek, due to her fall off the couch.

"Noelle, wake up." She remained unresponsive and limp. Manny looked across the room, knowing he couldn't lift her with his fractured arm. Instead, he stood to find a knife to cut the ropes at her hands and feet.

*****

A howling siren blared through the basement of the NanoMed laboratory.

"Keep working, Jerry. I'll lock the doors behind me. Some fool's trying to be a hero."

"I thought you'd sedated her. Don't let her get away." Troy's voice was unalarmed, in deep concentration at his computer, tailoring the code for the microscopic molecular killers to perfectly recognize the DNA pattern of Noelle's melanoma cells.

"I'm sure she's out. She had enough to put a gorilla down." Feddersen ran to the elevator, questioning himself as he muttered. "It's gotta be someone else."

After peering into the scanner to call the elevator, he dashed to Troy's desk, grabbing the .38 caliber pistol he knew was kept in the bottom drawer. Fiddling with it briefly, he found it still had a full chamber of bullets. It had been years since he had even touched a gun. A med school friend had taken him to a shooting range once. He'd hung the best of his target sheets on his wall above his bed for months afterward, proclaiming the beginner's luck of his bullseye aim. All he remembered now were the brief instructions he was given: squeeze the trigger, don't pull. Whatever than meant.

The elevator raced him up two stories to the ground level.

*****

John Camelson was home when Hillary called. The urgency in her voice easily convinced him to come right over.

Hillary hung up the phone in her kitchen and went back to the entry way where Jonathon faced the back wall, staring at a painting of a field of cows.

"He said he could be right over."

"That'll work," Jonathon said reluctantly. Meeting her eyes, he added, "Thanks, Hillary." He lingered for a moment before heading to the door.

"They live just a couple blocks from here, so he'll just a minute," she offered.

"I'm going to wait for him outside. I wanna be ready."

"Are you sure I shouldn't call the police?"

"It's only a hunch, Hillary. I've got to pursue it myself first."

"Are you going to be okay?"

"Now I am." He paused before exiting the door. "Don't worry."

She grabbed the door handle. "I'll pray."

The screen door closed and he walked down the steps to the road, slapping his hands and rubbing them together in the chilly air. Turning back, he saw Hillary at the front window offering a wave. He pressed his hands together as if praying and pointed up. She nodded back and walked away to answer his call to pray.

Moments later the screen door opened again behind him, and Hillary ran down the steps. Her blue parka was lined with white fur, the hood bouncing at her back as it cradled much of her golden hair. She radiated both an adventuresome spirit and a delicate beauty.

"Here's my cell phone, fully charged. I'll expect to get it back tomorrow." Her grin was warm and reassuring.

Taking the phone, he put it in his coat pocket. "Thanks, Hillary. That'll be great."

She nodded. "I'm worried about this, Jonathon. Worried about you." Her smile dimmed.

"No need. You've given me a cell phone, a ride, and your prayers. I'm in pretty good shape." He started to jog in place and grinned to bring her smile back. "Just need to work up a sweat to combat this freezing cold."

Shrugging her shoulders, she eyed him bobbing up and down. Her momentary loss for words was replaced with her smile.

The silence, though uncomfortable, didn't last long. Approaching car lights slowed and pulled over, the Camry's passenger door popping open.

"Hop in, Jonathon!" an eager greeting came from within.

The rugged features of John's face warmed Jonathon immediately. There was safety in confiding with these friends.

"You don't know how good it is to see you." Jonathon indulged in the heated car, allowing his icy fingers to melt.

"Hillary told me it was important, and you caught me on a free night. Where we heading?"

"Take Highway 6 east, about five miles out of town. We've got a ride of about forty-five minutes or so. Is that okay with you?"

"Plenty of gas, plenty of time, Jonathon."

John did not push and seemed content to know little or nothing. It gave Jonathon reason to confide in him more.

"We might be heading into a little trouble." Jonathon rubbed his fingers together, his circulation returning.

"Why's that?"

"It's a long story."

"I'm ready. You want a piece of licorice?" John reached to his side and pulled out two red twisted cords of candy.

"No thanks." Sitting upright, Jonathon spoke excitedly. "Hang with me. I've gone over this so much in my mind, but I'm still not sure all the pieces fit.

But we're going out to hopefully find Noelle. She's a friend of mine, and I think she's in trouble. Her brother is Manny—he's the guy I brought to church last week."

"The guy who gave his life to Christ?"

"That's the guy. His life's changed for real. It was very cool. Anyway, Noelle's got some kind of skin cancer, a melanoma. It's very serious, and she could die from it. But I think she's being used by a doctor for some lame research project. Nanotechnology, it's called. Dr. Feddersen is the hospital administrator. You know him?"

John's voice showed his wariness of the whole conversation. "Uh, I've heard of him. Never met him."

"You're already lost, aren't you?"

"I missed something somewhere, Jonathon."

"Let me slow down. You need to hear this." He went back to Henry Smitherton, relating the strange illness that he had, and how he had miraculously recovered but acted so scared about telling anyone what happened. He related the story of Larry Crenshaw in the lab, and how he had died the day after being seen injecting an unknown medicine into Mr. Smitherton. He shared about his visits with Dr. Feddersen and the NanoMed connection, explaining what he had learned about nanotechnology. Then he brought Noelle back into the picture, sharing why her cancer may have provided a target for Feddersen.

"So now Noelle is missing. Manny used my car to go look for her and now he's disappeared too. That's why I think it may be trouble."

John was silent, quietly chewing his licorice. It made Jonathon nervous. Only the smooth rumble of the engine was heard for several seconds.

"It's more than Noelle, isn't it?" John's voice was unassuming.

"What?"

"It just seems to me like you've got more against this whole thing than worrying about Noelle."

Jonathon sank back in his seat. He responded softly, "Noelle's in trouble. She needs my help."

"Maybe. Even probably." John's eyes stayed fixed on the road in front of him.

"You mean about my healing gift." Jonathon stated it without a question. The obstinate stare didn't flinch.

Jonathon looked out the side window himself before he continued. "Sure, it bugs me a lot. I thought I had a special gift from God, and now it won't work." He hesitated before muttering words almost against his own will. "Now, when I could really help someone—someone special—it looks like it's gone."

"Hm-hm." It was only a grunt of understanding, but it encouraged Jonathon to say more.

"You thought I had an ability to heal, didn't you?" Jonathon watched John respond by nodding his head once. He wasn't clear if it truly meant "yes."

"I know I saw God use me to heal people. Like Manny. He had cancer—melanoma, like Noelle. I prayed and he got better."

Jonathon remembered Noelle's always sarcastic response. She would say in her early teen years, "The doctor did surgery on Manny. Don't you think that had *something* to do with it?"

"And there was Mrs. Wittenburg. She was dying of a heart attack and I prayed. She's fully recovered." His eyes continued to dream outside the window. "Although, she got better as the doctors were working on her." He continued to mentally flip through his memory. "That girl with asthma downtown. She couldn't breathe. She was blue," he argued with himself. "After I prayed, she was better. But her mom had just given her the inhaler."

Luck? Chance? Jonathon questioned himself.

"Two years ago—the baby that was thrown out of the car," Jonathon continued. "She was good as gone before I prayed." He looked back at John, who had not moved his gaze from the road. "But I had tried to do CPR on her. Was that what saved her?"

John drove down the gravel stretch without responding.

A handful of failures flashed across Jonathon's mind with accusative fingers pointing at him. They were all folks he had prayed for: Henry Smitherton, dead; Grandma Davis, dead; Mayor Royce Horton, cancer. And maybe the one that hurt the most: Aunt Emma, dead.

"But my aunt Emma. That was the first one. Her finger was healed."

"How old were you then?"

"Four."

"Sure you don't want some licorice?" John pulled out another piece. "Help yourself."

"I'm fine."

"So how do you remember what happened?"

"My mom told me about it." Jonathon spoke defensively. "But I remember it too."

John didn't answer and kept driving straight on the gravel.

"So what you're saying is you don't think I can heal?" Jonathon's voice was soft.

"Not at all." For the first time, John glanced at Jonathon. "But what do you think?"

"I don't know anymore." He couldn't look back at John. "Let's get out to NanoMed. We have to find Noelle."

Ten minutes passed without any words between them. An eighth of the moon inched up through the vast darkening sky, a handful of stars poking out through patchy clouds. The car cruised past mile after mile of empty and lifeless fields of dirt.

"You're saying it's more than miracles." Jonathon's sullen voice broke the monotonous rumble of gravel beneath them.

"And you're saying you want to heal," John responded.

"So what if I can't?"

John completed the question. "Does that mean your faith in Christ is a wash?"

"It shouldn't."

"Listen, Jonathon. I think I know your heart, only because it reminds me so much of my own." He glanced over, a caring warmth in his smile. "I went to Russia a few years ago with a mission team from our church. I had it all figured out, what we would do, what God would do, and how we would make a difference in the church over there. It was a great plan and would surely build up the church there." He reached for another piece of licorice and took a bite. "But God had something else in mind. He completely disrupted our plan. What happened was extraordinary. Revival broke out in the town. More than I could have ever imagined."

"So you think I'm trying too hard?"

"You shouldn't have to try at all."

"I know I get caught up in the healing. But it's because I've sensed it, felt it. I know God has used me that way."

"And you want more of that."

"Of course."

"More of that feeling?"

"Yes." Jonathon caught himself. "I want to be used by God."

"I know. But we also want to choose how God will use us. Because the other option is scary."

"What's the other option?"

"Giving it all up. Not stuck on a plan of our own making. Back in Russia I was helpless. I had my own strategy that our whole team was following. When it fell apart, we were completely lost, on the other side of the world, wondering if it was all a waste of time."

"You think God forced you to give up your plan?"

"Not at all. God just had a different plan, beyond my understanding. He had to get me away from my own desire to control things so he could work through me. I would never have chosen to do things the way He did, but seeing the results, I now know that it was amazing and perfect. The best thing that could have happened."

"So I might be in God's way."

"You're exactly where God wants you, Jonathon. No doubt about that. But what is He really trying to show you? What might He be wanting to change about you?" He pulled out another piece of licorice. "Those are the better questions."

Jonathon was staring at his feet and turned to look at his friend. He reached for the licorice sack himself and grabbed a strand to chew. His taste buds leapt around the rubbery strawberry flavor. It was the first food he'd had for hours.

Pointing to a lone light illuminating a farmhouse in the distance, John asked, "Is that NanoMed?"

Chapter 32

"**P**ull over here!" Jonathon exclaimed.

"That's okay," John calmly replied. "I'll take you on up to the house."

"No, stop now! I can't let them know I'm coming. I'll walk the rest of the way."

Slowing to a stop, John pulled over, unsure but willing to let Jonathon call the shots.

"John, promise me you'll go home." He opened his door. "Your showing up here could only cause more problems."

"I don't think that's wise."

"I'm just going to look around. I've got Hillary's cell. I'll call if I need a ride, but I'm hoping I find my car out here."

"I didn't drive all the way out here just to leave you in the middle of nowhere."

"John, I can't be worrying about you. If there's something going on out here, I won't be stupid. I can call if there's any problem." Jonathon stepped out of the car. "Promise me? No sticking around?"

John was reluctant. "I don't like it, but I promise, Jonathon. Call Hillary at the hint of anything suspicious, and I'll be ready to come back out any time."

"Deal."

"And you promise to call me first thing in the morning?"

"Deal again." Jonathon leaned back into the car and held out his hand. "Thanks."

John grasped the hand firmly. "Want some more licorice?" he smiled and handed him a bundle.

Jonathon took it with a grin. "I'm asking God the better questions, John."

"I know you are."

Jonathon shut the door and watched the car drive away. It was just him and a slice of a lonely, midnight moon in the middle of the farm fields.

He turned and trudged down the road, just shy of a mile's walk to NanoMed.

*****

The wind softly wailed through large fragments of fractured windows of the NanoMed office. Manny was in the kitchen when he heard the sound of footsteps on broken glass. A row of drawers stretched open along the galley counter where he had just found the knives. Without time to turn the overhead light off, he silently grabbed a ten-inch butcher blade and dashed away as fast as the pain in his wrist would allow him. Beyond the back side of the kitchen, he hid in the darkened, small dining room. Breathing heavily from hurt and nerves, sweat formed over his brow despite the frigid air blowing through the room. The only way to silence the noise of his breathing was by holding it, crouching low under the table.

I've got to get Noelle out of here, Manny convinced himself. *I can do this.*

The footsteps were silent now, which meant the person either had left, or was entering the kitchen where he had just been. He let a long trickle of air exhale through his teeth and breathed deeply, tightening his lungs around the fresh air. The wooden handle on the knife was wet with sweat; he wiped his hand against his shirt before gripping it again. His body shook from the mix of cool air and shock, and he rested his shoulder against the table leg to try to control the tremors.

God, help me do this.

The light above the dining table flicked on, brightly lighting the room. Manny saw a hand disappear from around the wall by the light switch. His own fingers tingled from holding his breath as he gripped the knife tightly. A man's frame came from behind the wall, a pistol leveled in front of his waist.

The knees in front of Manny flexed, and the gun lowered directly at him. Manny fought against the shudder of his body under the table.

A face appeared behind the gun, narrow and scared.

Feddersen's voice squeaked with his first words, "I'll kill you right now if you try anything."

Manny exhaled fully, on the verge of passing out, and gasped for a fresh breath of air.

"Drop the knife."

He obeyed.

"Come out from under the table," Feddersen barked more clearly.

He crawled out from the table, awkwardly holding his injured arm. "What are you going to do?"

The man's face read surprise as Manny stood. "You're not Thompson."

Manny wondered if he could take the man. The guy was six inches shorter, fifty pounds lighter. If it wasn't for the gun, he thought he'd have a chance, barring his limp hand.

"Who are you?" the man insisted, waving the gun sloppily as a threat.

"Manny Lewis." He sounded tough and more composed, his breaths returning to normal. "You've got my sister over there."

"How'd you get out here?" Feddersen barked.

"I was driving the country roads when some nut ran me off the road. He left me for dead. Must have been a friend of yours?" Manny asked sarcastically.

Feddersen's face belied alarm before he spoke. "Get out there." He angrily pointed the gun toward his sister. Manny walked back through the kitchen with Feddersen several steps behind him.

"Sit in the chair," Feddersen ordered, and Manny sat down in a leather chair across from his sister on the couch. The cold leather stretched tightly against the weight of his body. He couldn't help uttering a grunt from a muscle spasm near his fracture. Feddersen came behind him and roughly tied a towel around his head, blinding his eyes.

"Move once and you're dead."

Manny could hear the sounds of his captor's movements but could not distinguish the activity. Minutes later, he thought he sensed motion close by.

The barrel of a gun touched the back of his neck. "You move an arm and there's a bullet in your brain." The voice was brusque and confident.

He immediately felt a bite deep in his upper right arm, the good side. He wanted to jerk it away from the pain, but he controlled his reflex. It burned like fire for an instant before he recognized that he'd been injected.

"Good man," the voice behind him said. At the same time he felt a rush of warmth under his skin, racing across his chest and then moving down his legs, out his arms, and up into his face. In the freezing air, it felt unusually warm, almost pleasant. Within sixty seconds he didn't feel nearly as much pain in his fractured wrist, which was his last thought.

*****

"Your dead man has come back, Jerry." Feddersen held the gun more comfortably at his side as he walked into the lab. "But it's not Thompson."

"What do you mean?" Troy turned from his computer screen, his eyes focused on the .38 in Feddersen's hand.

"It's the girl's brother. He broke through the windows of the office." Feddersen slapped the pistol onto the lab counter, feeling more powerful than ever. "He's covered in dirt and looks like he's got a fractured wrist, besides several glass cuts. He's a mess."

"He drove the car we towed in?"

"Apparently."

Troy returned to his computer screen, typing hesitantly. "So you killed him?"

Feddersen flinched. "Of course not. He's drugged with his sister."

"You'll have to kill him."

"No. We can use him. I've got some ideas." Feddersen watched Troy's full concentration go to the computer.

"We can get more from Noelle and use her brother as a control. He'd have an ideal gene match, same DNA line." He stepped over to Troy's terminal. "We can't kill him."

"Maybe you can't." Troy's fingers moved across the keyboard slowly but accurately.

Feddersen reached back for the pistol. "Listen, Jerry. I've thought through all this. He'll be another research participant. They're brother and sister; if I explain what we're doing, I think I can convince them to follow through with this. They'll encourage each other to stick with it." Feddersen leaned against the counter. "We can't hold the girl forever. This may be a perfect way to get her and her brother to team up with us. If necessary, we can give him a cancer too. What do you say?"

"Impossible. He's got to go. All we want is the girl." Troy kept typing.

"Jerry, we can't just murder every person who gets in our way. I didn't like it with Crenshaw, and I especially don't like it now. We can do this without more killing."

Eyes set on his computer screen, Troy didn't respond.

"Have you got any rolls of plastic around here?" Feddersen moved onto something simpler. "I've got to seal up the windows in the office. The guy broke through them when he saw his sister."

Troy flipped around, eyes pierced in sudden anger. "Did he hurt my plants?"

"Relax. They'll be fine." Feddersen was exasperated with Troy's obsessions. "What can I cover the windows with?"

"There's some polyethylene sheeting in the back closet. Use that. I'm coming up to check on the plants. If he's hurt any of them…"

"So are you worried about getting the girl's nanites set?" Feddersen interrupted. "How soon can we inject her?"

"It's going faster than I expected. The synchrotron has about a half hour more to match up against her DNA. Then we'll replicate the nanites and be set."

"The only thing I missed was the synchrotron program. How do you do that?"

"It's all configured in the system. Once it receives the serum sample, it only requires a click of a few 'okay' buttons, and it does the rest. Even you can handle that."

Feddersen ignored the insult, fingers sliding along the smooth, cool metal of the pistol. "You're a genius, Dr. Troy. A dying genius."

"And you're going to save my life."

"As you are mine, don't forget." Feddersen smiled. "How much nanite serum will we need to give the girl?"

"The dose is automatically calculated. I readjusted the program using Smitherton's last results, so we should have an accurate dosage. Look here." Troy clicked to a separate screen and pointed to several lines showing dosage and frequency. "Click here and it will initiate the production of the nanites in a saline solution at the precise concentration. You'll just need to draw up the correct dosage in a syringe and give the injection."

"You're a genius," Feddersen repeated. "How many doses will it make?"

"There'll be enough for the first six doses, and then you just need to rerun the program by clicking here," he pointed to a separate icon on the screen.

"So when do you think I'll need my own dose of nanites?"

"Your cancer is very early, still in microscopic stages likely. For the sake of the project, we must wait until you have symptoms, perhaps showing up in a month or so. A little weight loss, some abdominal pain, back pain, something like that." Troy spoke carelessly, like a surgeon's routine description of his millionth appendectomy.

"This is my cancer you're talking about."

"Of course. As soon as you have confirmed symptoms, we'll make the diagnosis and prepare nanite injections just like we've done today. You'll be doing it with your eyes closed by then."

Troy looked away from the screen for the first time and smiled.

Feddersen grinned back, dreams of fame and glory rising in his thoughts.

"You're crazy, Dr. Troy."

"As are you, Dr. Feddersen. Crazy, dying geniuses."

"I'm going up to check on our patients."

"To kill the boy, I trust." Troy returned compulsively to the computer.

Feddersen took two steps away, Troy's back hunched over the keyboard. He raised the pistol to the height of his waist and pointed it.

Bam!

The explosion kicked Feddersen's hand harder than he had expected. Troy's head flexed hard sideways and he sucked air to no avail. The bullet perforated his trachea after ripping through his carotid artery. Troy's eyes turned to his partner, a look of alarm turning glassy as his body fell off the chair to the floor.

"You're just not tracking with me, Jerry. We can't keep killing everyone." Feddersen spoke apologetically to the body on the floor. "This is going to work. I'll do it just the way you taught me."

He leaned over to the computer and clicked "okay" in a box on the screen. The screen flicked to a new directory titled "Final Synchrotron Scan." The built-in clock reported an estimated completion in twenty-nine minutes, twenty-five seconds and counting.

He wrestled the short but hefty body away from the computer and laid him out of the way along the back wall of the lab. The rolls of black polyethylene sheeting were right where Troy had said, and Feddersen used one roll to cover the body. Out of breath, he stripped off his now bloody shirt and stuck the .38 in his waist outside of his T-shirt.

Squeeze, don't pull. It worked.

He hurried to the office with two more rolls. He knew another visitor was not far behind.

*****

"What am I doing?" Jonathon asked himself, walking along the gravel, his only companion the slivered moon. "God, am I crazy?"

He had started a jog and quickly became winded, almost nauseated. Now at a stroll's pace, he fought with himself at his own foolish secret agent antics. *It's all probably nothing. Manny and Noelle are likely home, tucked in bed in a nice warm house.*

Maybe he should have called their folks again to be sure. Walking to an abandoned farmhouse, he had no idea what he would do when he got there. Call Hillary and make John pick him up again?

His eyes had adjusted enough to the darkness to be able to make out the gravel road ahead of him. Kicking a swipe of dirt with his feet, he stopped his trek. He wondered if he should just knock on the door when he got there and say he's lost. Or maybe he should break in?

He knelt down and scooped a handful of dirt. Suddenly feeling horribly ill-prepared, he stole off the road into the three-foot ditch, avoiding any chance of being seen. The dirt was tossed high into the darkness.

I can't figure this out, Lord. Can't figure You out.

He wrestled John's words. What are the "better questions?" Is it about healing? He wondered if he ever really had the gift of healing.

The two outbuildings loomed ahead with the farmhouse to the side. He considered exploring the sheds for any clues. All the while, every thought was interrupted.

"I need the better questions, Lord." He dropped to his knees, the hard, cold ground offering no comfort. "What am I doing here? Lord, guide me!"

The last time he prayed on his knees was with his mother. His mind wandered to thoughts of her, remembering how people would sometimes call her odd, or more politely, eccentric. Would she really have made up a story about him healing his aunt's finger? It didn't make sense that she would fabricate a story like that. Unless it had to do with his father's leaving. Was his so-called supernatural healing ability just a way of coping with disappointment and desertion? *Has it all...been a lie?*

Those weren't the better questions. His mother was clearly committed to Jesus Christ. That didn't make her more crazy. No, it didn't matter what she did.

He looked up at the black sky dotted with stars. It was how she did it. How she lived her life. That's what spoke loudly.

"But what about me? Have I just been living a lie?" He wondered if he had ever truly worked a miracle healing. Each time could be explained by natural circumstances. He stared back down at the dirt, blackness surrounding him. "I hide behind those healings. Is that all my faith counts for?"

He went back to his mom. She was content with her menial job, her quaint home, her simple life, because that wasn't the issue. It wasn't about what she did. It's about how she does it. She lives every step of her life for Jesus Christ. She's not concerned about what she gets out of it. She's not seeking anything for herself. She's following Christ.

He bent over while kneeling, arms extended in front of him, open palms firmly slapping the dirt. "Am I too concerned with what I'm doing?" It's more than whether he should be healing, whether God should work any sort of miracle through him. Yet, he realized that's all his relationship with God was about: what God could do through him.

Grabbing a clod in either hand, he held them outstretched to his side.

"Lord, here I am. I'm surrendering all to You. These are not only my words, Lord, but now it's my action, my life. I will believe in You, even when it doesn't make sense. I will obey You, even if I want to go my own way."

His hands tightened down on the clods, crumbling them to powder in his fists. "I won't seek your gifts for my personal gain. It's whatever You want, not what I want."

Opening both palms, the dust fell away.

"It's not about me anymore, Lord Jesus."

Chapter 33

*T*he windows were taped up, and the office was starting to warm again. The smell of medicinal alcohol filled the room as Feddersen drew up a new syringe and injected it into Noelle's arm.

He sat down to wait.

He'd actually killed Troy. He'd planned it for weeks and tonight the time was right. He was now leading this project. No more Troy, no more crazy mistakes.

He knew this would be better. He couldn't let himself think on it long. It was time to move ahead.

*****

The injection reversed Noelle's slumber in only minutes. Her eyes flickered, then opened fully before closing again. With a cotton-dry mouth, she licked her lips feeling her coarse, parched tongue. The first uttered word was a raspy request for water. Reaching a hand to her cheek, she felt a dull ache that smarted when she touched it. A cool glass touched her hand as a voice said, "Here."

She looked up to meet Dr. Feddersen, looking rough, hair disheveled, in a tank T-shirt that was spotted reddish brown like a catsup bottle had exploded in front of him. Rather than speaking, she took a sip. Leaning back on a black leather sofa, she noticed to her left a miniature greenhouse of plants with several knocked over. Dirt was scattered across the black and white tile floor. Nothing made sense.

"Where am I?" she asked groggily.

Feddersen's voice was calm and assured. "You're at a research wing of NanoMed, Noelle. How are you feeling?"

"My head hurts." She lightly touched her cheek again.

"Yes, you took a fall off the couch a little bit ago."

He could see she was thinking hard. "I can't remember."

"That's to be expected, Noelle. We don't have much time. Do you recall your cancer, the melanoma?"

She reached a hand to the lower part of her back. "Yes, I have cancer in my back. I came home to get it treated. Where are my parents?"

"Your parents don't know you're here, Noelle. I'm Dr. Martin Feddersen and I'm offering you a cure for your cancer, but I need your help in return."

She was a tough girl. He had wondered if she'd be falling apart by now, but Noelle was a fighter. This was going to work.

"I can start a treatment for you with minimal risks, no surgery, and it should cure your cancer."

"What about Dr. Mittlestedt?"

"Dr. Mittlestedt doesn't know about this. It's a secret research treatment. We've got to keep it that way for now. But I'm offering to save your life. No surgery. We're ready to get started if you are."

"I can't. This is crazy." She couldn't help but stare at the red stains on Feddersen's T-shirt.

"You'll be famous, rich. And alive."

"What if it doesn't work?" she asked quietly.

"Noelle, we've got to move fast. Let me help you with your decision." He pulled out his pistol so she could see it. "Behind you, I believe, is your brother."

Noelle stiffened at the sight of the gun and dug her fingers into the leather cushion. Flipping her head behind her, she saw Manny lying on the floor, his hands and feet bound with duct tape. She gasped before breathing his name, "Manny!"

"He's okay, just asleep like you've been. Here's the deal. You become a part of a research protocol that will cure your cancer, and your brother lives. I'll be with you every step of the way to be sure you're treated safely. Noelle, you'll be making history."

Eyes wide with fear, she stared at Manny, reassured to see his chest rise and fall with regular breaths. She whispered haltingly. "And if...I don't go along?"

Feddersen looked across at Manny and slowly returned his gaze to Noelle.

She eyed the pistol again, anger now mixing with fright. Her words came out quiet but firm, "Let me talk to him."

"That's possible. You convince him this is the right thing to do, Noelle." Feddersen was suddenly disarming, poking the gun back into the waist of his

251

pants. "I'll give him an injection that reverses the hypnotic effect he's under now. It's the same as what you just received. You'll be able to speak to him in just a few minutes."

Feddersen stepped over to a small desk and pulled out a syringe and vial of medicine. Alcohol fumes wafted through the air again as he prepared the injection. After giving the shot to Manny, he calmly sat down next to Noelle on the couch.

"It actually couldn't work out more perfectly. Your brother was in a car wreck on his way out here. It looks like he fractured his wrist. We can tell your parents that both of you were in the car, and I found you and brought you to the hospital. I'll admit you for observation tonight and be able to start your treatment there. Manny can get his wrist casted. Tomorrow, you both go home and take care of each other. He'll know how to help you, and you and I will see each other regularly to monitor your progress."

"What about my doctor?"

"People trade off all the time," he said candidly. "Patients go to Dr. Mittlestedt for a while, then switch to me. Later they may switch back to Dr. Mittlestedt or go with someone else. We're all used to it."

"No. I want to go home." Her voice cracked with tension. "Please—let us go."

"That's not possible."

Feddersen got up and returned to Manny, reaching in between the duct-taped hands to feel his pulse. "He should be stirring any minute." With that, Manny rolled and moaned.

Noelle jumped from the couch to kneel at her brother's side, and Feddersen stepped away.

"You're in the middle of a cornfield far from town, Noelle. No sense trying to escape." He stepped into the kitchen, still in sight of the siblings.

"Manny, wake up." Noelle said softly. He moaned again and tried to move his hands, which forced a loud, "Ow!" from his wrist pangs.

"Don't move. Your hands are taped."

Blue eyes blinked open. "What are you doing here?" he asked without knowing where here was. He grimaced again with pain.

"We're prisoners, Manny. You're taped up, and you broke your wrist in some car wreck."

Manny didn't respond. His eyes widened.

252

"Do you hear me?" She grabbed his good shoulder. "Do you understand? We don't have much time."

"Okay," he mumbled.

"There's a guy here, he's got a gun. He says he's a doctor and he wants to do some secret treatment on me for my cancer. It's illegal, Manny, but he says he'll kill you if I don't do it."

"Jesus."

Noelle thought he was cursing. "He says if I do the treatment, he'll let us go home tomorrow. But you'll have to help me with the treatments."

"Lord Jesus."

"I'm scared, Manny." She tried to hold her voice steady. "I've never felt so scared."

"They'd left me for dead." His speech was clearer, his eyes sharp. "This guy buried me out there. I told God if He'd let me find you—" He gritted his teeth and tried to reposition his arm.

"Manny," she felt tears form in her eyes, "you've got to help me. This guy's got a gun and he's serious. I don't want him to kill you." She wiped her wet cheek and brought her hand back to support his arm.

"Noelle, I'm scared too." He gritted his teeth through a spasm. "But I've gotta trust Jesus. We need His wisdom, His power." Bending his frame, Manny tried to sit up. Noelle pushed on his good side to help lean his back against the wall. He grunted and laid his taped hands gently in his lap before muttering, "That really hurts." He breathed deeply and sighed before continuing.

"I'm afraid something horrible will happen," Noelle sobbed. "Are we going to die out here?"

"Listen to me, Noelle. We're gonna follow what we know is right." He closed his eyes. "Lord Jesus, give us what we need. As Lord of my life, help us."

He grasped Noelle's arm more tightly. "Jesus is all you need, Noelle. Whether or not He heals you. Whether or not you live. This is more important than anything else. Jesus saved your soul, has a place for you in heaven. I want you to be there, Noelle." His blue eyes showed pain, but communicated more a brother's love. "You've got to be there."

"I can't do this," she spoke through her tears. "I can't let you die, Manny."

"It doesn't matter. You've got to follow Jesus. He needs to be your Lord."

Feddersen interrupted, stepping out of the kitchen. "Okay, are we set? Big brother, you know what you need to have your sister do?" He walked forward, brushing the dried blood spots on his shirt with one hand while the pistol dangled from his other. "Let's get this show on the road."

Suddenly there was a pounding at the outside door to the office. Feddersen turned his gun up and walked to the door, his hand nervously shaking the weapon.

"Who is it?" he snapped.

"You've got to see what I've found," a male voice yelled through the door.

Feddersen recognized the caller. "Hold on, I'll be right out." He pointed the gun directly at Manny, noticing him weakly propped against the back wall. They weren't going anywhere. "You two talk this out. I'm watching you."

He opened the door the width of his body. Manny and Noelle couldn't hear what he was saying, but he kept looking back to check on them.

*****

"What've you got?" Feddersen said through the cracked door. A body stood outside, covered from head to waist in a gunny sack. "What?" he exclaimed.

Behind the gunny-sacked body, a young man with shaggy brown hair poked his head around. "Quite a find, right?"

He pushed the burlap hard, knocking the body to the ground. "Oummfff!" sounded from inside the sack when it hit dirt.

"Let's take a rest here, Jonathon," the young man sarcastically spoke to the sack as it laid squirming on the ground.

"Crenshaw! Is this our visitor?" Feddersen became playful after realizing it had to be Thompson sprawled on the ground. His hands were tied with clothesline cord behind his back, his feet wrapped by the cord as well, forcing his hands to be uselessly pulled down. Feddersen smiled at Crenshaw. "You found our visitor."

Roughly kicking the legs jutting out of the sack, Crenshaw barked to Jonathon. "Say something!"

A muffled voice sounded from inside. "Feddersen, is that you?"

Feddersen ignored Thompson's question. "Good find, Crenshaw." He peeked around the corner to see Manny and Noelle still in their place, speaking intently to each other.

"Keep him down and quiet right here. I'll be back." Feddersen shivered in the cold. "You warm enough?" He flipped the collar of Crenshaw's denim jacket.

"I'll be fine." The dead man smiled back, brushing long, brown bangs out of his eyes.

Feddersen left, shutting the door.

"Crenshaw, you're supposed to be dead!" Jonathon exclaimed, briefly squirming before finding it useless. As he laid in the dirt against the exterior back wall of the NanoMed office, his only source of light shined through the burlap weave from a beacon on a tall pole beside the nearby outbuildings. It cast a dim light at this distance, shaping broad shadows as Jonathon peeked through the woven grids of the sack.

"It's cuz of you that I had to die," Larry Crenshaw replied. "Lucky for me Feddersen knew how to find a derelict to take my job that morning."

Jonathon coughed on the dust and jute inside the sack. "I don't get it."

"Crenshaw had to die. He was too careless," Larry spoke of himself. "He let a nurse named Thompson witness his injection to a patient. He had to go." He shuffled his feet in the dirt, raising dust that Jonathon smelled through his sack. "Thankfully, Feddersen didn't agree with the order, so when that insane driver came to find me on my morning run, he had no idea he was knocking off some deadbeat drunk from Kansas City. The body was so mangled, the best identification was found in my wallet that had been placed on the body. Convincing the nurses was simple, as no one wanted to enter the mess. Feddersen handled the rest."

"So you faked your own death. What good is it to you?" Jonathon asked in a muffled and disgusted voice.

"Haven't you figured out the importance of NanoMed's work?" Crenshaw answered. "This is life-changing—life-giving. Who wouldn't pass up a chance to have their name on this discovery?"

"Larry, you can't be serious. This guy's a quack."

Crenshaw kicked Thompson's legs again.

"At least Dr. Feddersen's truly healing people. He's a miracle worker. I want to help him. But you—you were running around pretending you could heal. You're the quack, Thompson."

That hurt worse than the kick in his shins. "Is he paying you?"

"Better than any hospital lab job, that's for sure." Crenshaw laughed. "And that's just seed money compared to the millions to come once we release NanoMed."

Jonathon hacked on the sack's dust again. "Where do you fit in?"

"I'm running the lab and the computer software," Crenshaw bragged. "I'll take over for a guy they have doing it now. Feddersen's been teaching me what he knows. It was going slow, but after I was 'killed,' I've been able to hide out here in the shed. He's set me up with everything I need. He's a genius, Thompson. We're going to be able to help so many people with NanoMed."

"Like what helped Mr. Smitherton?" Jonathon asked humbly, worried about getting kicked again.

"That's not fair. NanoMed did a lot for Smitherton. Saved his life several times. You should see the research Feddersen has on him. He lived years longer than he should have."

"But it was the research that killed him."

"After adding years to his life."

Jonathon conceded that and sneezed twice. "Any chance you can take this sack off? I'm not going anywhere."

Crenshaw hesitated. "You're staying around, right? Aw, it should be okay. Gotta keep you tied up, though." He reached over and pulled the sack off Jonathon's head.

Coughing again, he shook his head before breathing in the fresh but frigid air.

"So this is what nanotechnology brings?" Jonathon questioned. "Kidnapping and imprisonment?" Still sprawled on the ground with arms uncomfortably tied behind him, he raised his head to see Crenshaw standing over him and wondered about another kick.

"Listen, I'm sorry." Crenshaw was minimally apologetic. "You're the one who was snooping around. Feddersen told me you might show up out here. He warned me that we'd need to hold you, try to talk some sense into you. You could screw up the whole plan if you squealed about the research. He said he had even offered you a job out here. Thought you could be a great help to the project."

"I can't support unethical, illegal work like this."

"We're taking medicine to the next era, Jonathon. We're not just healing people. We're making them better—a higher quality of life than ever before.

We'll be able to anticipate and cure disease before it even takes hold. Why do you want to prevent that?"

"I'm not against the idea, Larry. But look how you're doing it. You've wasted a life you never even knew when they killed that guy in place of you. You call that sound and ethical? I'm lying here tied up like a broken muffler, and Dr. Feddersen's inside threatening two of my friends."

"No way." He shook his head both directions, bangs flopping. "The derelict they killed was stoned out of his mind, dead to the world. We didn't waste a life there. If that's the price of advancing this research, it's well worth it." He confidently combed his fingers through his temples, clasping his hands behind his head. "Your friends are in there helping with the project. Dr. Feddersen told me the girl has cancer, and he's going to show the world how nanotechnology can save her life."

"Listen to yourself, Larry. You're excusing the murder of another man for your own benefit. You can't seriously think that his life didn't matter. He's another human being, same as you." Despite the contortions of his body, Jonathon raised his head and nodded angrily. "And do you think my friends are here willingly? I don't think so. Dr. Feddersen's forcing them to participate in his games." He buried his eyes into Crenshaw's.

"Nah. Feddersen's not that way." The brown bangs quickly darted away.

"Okay, let's go inside and see. I'm freezing out here. If everything's above board, there's no reason you and I can't be with them, hearing their talk."

Chapter 34

*T*urning away from the door after speaking to Crenshaw, Feddersen found Noelle and Manny still behind the couch on the floor. Her head was bowed on Manny's shoulder, his good arm resting across her back in a brotherly hug.

All Feddersen saw was that Manny's hands were no longer duct taped. She must have freed his arms.

Feddersen waved his gun, about to interrupt them, but caught himself. It didn't matter. They weren't going anywhere. He slipped the gun under his belt and uselessly wiped the blood stains on his T-shirt again.

More gently, he approached the couple. "Okay, okay. Are you ready, Noelle? It's just a quick injection, and then we'll head to the hospital. Manny, we'll get your arm X-rayed right away."

Manny looked up, eyes tearing but steely when they landed on Feddersen. "We're not doing this."

Noelle turned, biting her lower lip while her cheeks glistened wet.

"What does that mean?" Feddersen raised his voice. "Noelle? What's the problem?"

"I don't want your treatment." She took a deep breath and spoke decisively. "We want to go home. Just let us go, Dr. Feddersen."

"Well, kids, you know I can't do that." Feddersen instinctively felt for the handle of his pistol. "That wasn't our little agreement."

"We don't like your offer," Manny shot back. "We demand to be released."

Grabbing his pistol, Feddersen jerked his arm forward, pointing the barrel straight at Manny. His aim shook uncontrollably. "You're not in the place to make demands!" He gripped the gun tighter, but his arm shook all the more.

Squeeze, don't pull, he remembered.

Noelle raised herself from the floor and slipped into the line of fire between Manny and Feddersen. "You can't shoot me."

"Get away, Noelle!" Manny yelled.

The gun quivered.

"I know what I'm doing, Manny." Her voice broke, but she stood firm, eyeing Feddersen. "You can't kill me. I'm your research tool."

Feddersen shifted two steps to change his angle at Manny. Noelle slid one step to her side and blocked the aim again.

"Noelle!" Manny screamed. He started to move his sore, stiff body, causing spasms in his wrist again. His position was easily blocked again by Noelle.

"Let us go, Dr. Feddersen." Noelle gritted her teeth. "We don't want to be here."

"Stop it! Stop it!" Feddersen shrieked.

*****

Outside, both Crenshaw and Jonathon heard the yelling.

"Larry, get me in there."

"What's going on?" Crenshaw put his ear to the door. It was not necessary as they both clearly heard Manny scream for Noelle with Feddersen shouting back.

"Untie me. We've got to get in there!" Jonathon demanded.

Hesitating only a moment, Crenshaw reached over and fooled with the knots at Jonathon's hands. "You're staying with me. No tricks," he awkwardly commanded.

As soon as Jonathon's hands were free, he pulled the ropes off his ankles himself. "You follow me. I'm going in!" Jonathon bolted to the door, Crenshaw on his heels.

*****

Feddersen mopped his brow, beads of sweat running down his forehead. The gun slipped in his hand despite a tight grip. He couldn't shoot Manny, even if Noelle would step out of the way. With Troy it was necessary, even required. It was a calculated loss, and no one would miss him. But Manny too? How could he escape this lunacy?

He needed the girl. Force was now the only option. Still pointing the pistol, his rational mind fought against the absurdity of another murder.

259

"Sit down, Noelle!" His voice wavered like the rest of his body. Sweat burned his eyes, forcing a squint, but he kept the gun aimed loosely at Noelle.

The door to the office burst open, Jonathon breaking in with Crenshaw following.

"Noelle!" Jonathon shouted.

Feddersen turned, eyes wide at Jonathon's entrance. "No!" he screamed. Sliding his finger against the curved iron of the trigger, his damp grip began to pull.

It took an instant, long enough for Noelle to pounce. Knocking Feddersen's arm with her shoulder, she slammed into his body. She clung to him, yanking his arm down.

With his free arm Feddersen swung, slugging Noelle's head. Her hold on him didn't flinch.

"Get back!" he yelled, prying his shoulders out of her bear hug. Still clutching the gun, he forced it away from her grip of his wrist. They stumbled, body to body, upright as he muscled both arms to shove her away.

Wrestling inadequately to a stance, Manny screamed at his sister. "Noelle!"

Jonathon sprinted forward, grabbing Noelle's shoulders to pull her away, but she clenched down more tightly. He crammed his hand between them toward the gun, creating an inch of space between Feddersen and Noelle.

The gun exploded.

Everything froze for a long instant. Jonathon's first mental question was to wonder if that was really the sound of a gunshot. More like a firecracker, with that loud of report. But it had to have been the gun.

He was convinced when he felt the burn of his hand stuck between Noelle and Feddersen. The pain grew like scalded water against his flesh. Pulling out his hand, a thick, red streak of blood crossed his palm. The bullet had grazed his hand just below his little finger.

Manny was yelling something, but his voice was distant, a scream in a tin can, unintelligible.

Reaching up, Jonathon pushed Feddersen aside easily. The man was stunned, mouth gaping. Staggering back three steps, the .38 dangled from his finger before dropping to the ground. He collapsed into the couch behind him, his eyes never closing as he stared incredulously at Noelle.

Noelle slumped forward as Jonathon grabbed her shoulders, standing behind her. Reaching both arms around her abdomen, he held her up. What he felt with his hands at her waist was warm and wet.

Her legs buckled. Holding her whole weight, he gently brought her to the floor. A dark, glistening ring of blood soaked through her shirt at the level of her navel. He saw her hands reaching for the pain, quickly covered in red.

Before he could find words, she spoke. "Jonathon, it's me and Jesus now."

"Don't talk, Noelle. We're getting help…right now." On his knees, he looked across the room and saw Crenshaw on a phone. "You're calling 9-1-1?"

Crenshaw looked up and nodded, eyes wide and scared.

"They're coming to help you," Jonathon said to Noelle with a forced effort at calmness.

Noelle's eyes were intensely fixed on his. "Jesus," she whispered.

"Shhhh." He comforted her, putting one hand behind her head, brushing her hair back with his other.

Manny crawled over beside him. "Noelle! Oh, Lord God. Save her, Jesus." He burst out in tears, reaching his arm around his sister to cradle her.

Jonathon bit his lip hard, a dam burst rising up within himself. Removing his hands from behind her head, he yanked off his coat and put pressure on her abdomen. Manny's head laid on her chest as he cried out to God, but Noelle's gaze stayed locked on Jonathon.

She mouthed the word again, "Jesus." Her eyes were peaceful while immovable.

Jonathon reached under the coat to feel a pulse at her wrist. Instead, her fingers interlocked with his and squeezed tightly.

Breaking down for an instant, he cried out with Manny, "God, heal her. Jesus, heal." Teeth clenched, he held back the tide of agony crashing inside his soul. *She can't die, Lord.* His thoughts were riveted on the only option. *Lord God, would You have me heal her? Surely…*

Her face whitened, her eyes less intense as they peered into Jonathon's soul. He felt her hand grasp weaken.

He hoped for a tingle in his spine, a sharp burn in his chest. "Lord, I pray for healing. "I pray You heal her. Not me, God—but You." He closed his eyes tightly to shut out death.

"Lord," he whispered, "You can heal her. Please, God. Work Your hand." His body shook as he arrested his own distress. Eyes opened, awaiting God's response.

"Noelle," he called softly. Her eyes twinkled briefly.

"I love you, Noelle," he whispered.

She heard it; her lips curled gently in a smile before she mouthed again one word. "Jesus."

Her eyelashes flickered once and closed halfway. His fingers held hers firmly, but the return grasp faded.

She was gone.

Her limp hand was like dough as he squeezed it, forcing even a painful response if that would allow him one more moment with her.

She was gone.

He took his eyes off hers for the first time, the blank death stare his last memory. Looking up to heaven, he joined Manny's cry. No words were said, just open groanings of anguish.

She was gone.

*****

Feddersen sat on the couch, hunched over as he stared at the three young people huddled on the floor. His face was sullen, his eyes dark and sunken. Reaching to his chest, he unconsciously felt the stains on his shirt once more. The two men's cries before him were deafening, yet it did not trigger an emotion of sadness in himself.

He reached forward to the gun on the floor ahead of him. His hand didn't shake this time as he rested it on his legs. Rubbing the shiny handle with his thumb, he questioned why it was now not nearly as wet. He clutched the gun again and raised it up, looking into the barrel.

Squeeze, don't pull.

With his mouth open, he inserted the barrel, pointing it upward. Tasting burnt gun powder and smoke, he grasped the pistol handle between both hands. The absence of any tremors surprised him.

He hesitated momentarily. It seemed the best thing to do.

Stretching his index finger out, he curved it widely around the trigger.

Squeeze—

A hand wacked his head on the right; another slapped his hands away.

262

"No way!" Crenshaw shouted and pulled the loose gun out of Feddersen's grip. "You're not getting out of this." His fist landed squarely on Feddersen's jaw, sending him back against the couch.

"You sit here and watch! Watch the death of the girl you killed." Crenshaw was sobbing as he threw the gun across the room, cracking against a planter on the far side. He stood behind Feddersen sitting on the couch and firmly grabbed his shoulders, forcing him to stay in his seat. It was another half hour before the ambulance came. Feddersen, shocked and dazed, sat limply under Crenshaw's watch.

Across the room, Manny raised up, his face drawn in pain. He used his good arm to grab Jonathon's shoulder.

Opening his crying eyes, Jonathon saw his friend and reached over with a hug. Manny's voice spoke into his shoulder. "She accepted Christ, Jonathon." He held on. "What?" His tears were momentarily held at bay.

Manny, exhausted and spent, leaned into Jonathon for support. "She prayed, just before you came in." His breath heaved with each phrase. "She prayed to Jesus. She asked Him to be her Lord and Savior."

Jonathon angled himself back to see Manny's face. In the midst of reading disaster across his expression, Manny nodded his head. "Yes, I heard her." He smiled weakly as his tears overflowed again.

Jonathon grabbed him tightly as Manny muffled into his chest, "She's in heaven."

Their cries blended together again, a strange mixture of deep mourning with faint but eternal joy.

Chapter 35

*J*onathon's mother drove him home from the police station at eleven o'clock the next morning. The night and early morning had been spent with doctors, the Lewis parents, a brief visit with the mortician, and a lengthy visit with the police. Though drained, he resisted going to bed until his mom insisted he go to his room and at least lie down. He was sure he wouldn't be able to sleep.

Snoring in ten minutes, even the mental turmoil was unable to prevent fatigue from claiming rest.

He woke with a start three hours later. The sound of a gun blast.

Eyes wide open, he raised himself to his elbows and looked around his familiar room. The house was silent. Maybe it was a dream.

That was it. It was all a dream.

Except for the taste of grit and jute yet in his mouth. His gaze landed on his clothes crumpled on the floor beside his bed, worn the past twenty-four hours. A dark maroon stain blotched his shirt and pants. The putrid odor of old blood stuck in his nostrils.

It was no dream.

He flopped back into bed, hugging his pillow tightly. His eyes clenched shut to prevent the reality of the world from crashing into his mind. Tears stored up during his sleep swelled against tight eyelids.

Dear God, bring me sleep again. I don't want to remember.

Waiting for sleep to overcome his thoughts, his heart screamed, Why? His mind refused to acknowledge the unanswerable. Chains wrapped around his heart, prohibiting further questions.

No way was sleep returning. He sobbed unconstrained, face buried in his pillow. Words were muffled, only for heaven to hear.

"Are you there, Noelle? Are you with Jesus now?"

The words quieted his tears, and he rolled over to his back to wait for an answer. Though the room was chilled by the wintry day, he let the blankets stay low across his waist, enduring the cold as if he was due this minor misery.

Lord, is she as delightful to You as she has been to me?

He waited, fully prepared for an audible response but heard nothing. Wading through flashbacks of the past evening, he sought signs of God's deliverance, evidence of His hands at work.

"Why take Noelle?" he whispered, his heart breaking through the chains of intellect. "Should this make sense to me?" It was not asked spitefully, but as a sincere question honestly posed.

There were still no answers.

Stepping out of bed, he rubbed the rope burns on his wrists. He threw on a fresh T-shirt and denim jeans and left his room for the living room.

"Hi, darlin'," his mother greeted him with a compassionate smile. "I knew sleep would do ya a world of good."

She held a cup of steaming coffee in her hands, her Bible in her lap. Sunlight streamed through the windows, warming the carpet under his bare feet. "Let me get ya some." She set her cup and Bible aside and moved to the kitchen. "Just sit yerself down," she called, and he sat in the straight chair across the room.

She returned in seconds. The hot mug placed in his hands seemed unfair. It was far too nice, too comforting.

"Never knew ya knew so many folks 'round here." She sat in her rocker, tucking a blanket over her legs and reaching her cup. "If it weren't the phone, it was the door, all for you."

He held back from taking a drink, despite a delightful hazelnut aroma sweeping across his senses. He shouldn't be enjoying this.

"Well, don't cha wanna know who came by? I even started a list, cuz I knew I'd forget somebody."

Looking up, his mother was perched forward. She would mount an attack against his silence if he didn't respond.

"Sure," he mumbled, wrinkling his lips into an unconvincing, momentary half-smile.

"That's the way, boy. We gotta keep on with life. Now sip your brew—"

She insisted on waiting until he brought the mug to his lips and slurped.

"That'll never be 'nough to warm your bones on a day like this," she fired off. "You keep sipping, and I'll start going down the list."

With an old bulletin from the church in her hands filled with names scratched in pencil, and after placing her silver-framed glasses to her nose, she began. "Let's see here…first was that nice Mrs. Chandler, the charge nurse at the hospital. She stopped by on her way to work first thang this morning and couldn't stop saying nice things 'bout cha, how proud she was of ya. She said to tell ya your job is waiting for ya when you feel up to coming back. What a nice lady—I knew they'd 'preciate ya more after ya was gone.

"After that, Elaine Wittenburg stopped by. First time we'd talked since her heart problems. That didn't come up. She mostly wondered how ya was doing and all. We're having lunch next week.

"A sweet couple came by, the Camelsons. She was in a wheelchair, real pretty lady. Said they'd met you at their church. The mister really tooted his horn 'bout cha. Talked about you being smart and all, figuring out where the nanotack was happenin'. They brought those flowers over there." She pointed to a clear vase of three red roses surrounded by yellow daisies. "They was so nice, I invited them in to sit. Stayed only a few minutes, but I like 'em. You know how I can tell good people. Those are good people." She rocked back in her chair, folding the church bulletin in half.

"Take another sip now. You need that in ya."

Jonathon obeyed, then quietly asked, "Who else?"

"Right behind the Camelsons came a cute young girl, Hillary. She was very worried 'bout cha. I had to tell her over and over that you was alright." Elaine leaned forward again, speaking softly, her lips curled in a tease. "Why haven't you said anything about her to me?" She raised her voice. "Anyway, she wanted to know if she could stop back by later today." Plopping back in her chair, she fingered her list some more.

"Well?" Jonathon asked.

"Well what?" His mom countered.

"What'd you tell her?"

"Tell who?" She unfolded her bulletin, looking further down the list, her glasses tilting on her nose.

Jonathon knew she had set the trap on purpose. "Mom, what'd you tell Hillary about coming back over?"

"Oh, that. Course I told her she could try back. Didn't ya wanna see her?"

He ignored his mom by sipping the coffee again, a long draw as he closed his eyes and leaned back. A tear formed at each corner of his eyes.

"Oh, Lord, now I've gone and done it," his mother sputtered softly. "Listen, Jonathon. I knows you're hurting. Something awful. I know ya lost your best friend in all the world."

The tears rolled out of his closed eyes, trickling down his cheeks. He debated returning to his room, but in his grief he didn't care. He'd just tune his mother out.

"But the world ain't stoppin' for ya, that's clear enough. You do your mournin'. I'll mourn with ya. Noelle was the sweetest." Her voice quivered, "— the sweetest girl, no doubt about it. And what's happened is just awful."

She stopped talking, which at first made Jonathon value the quietness. But after several seconds of silence he was compelled to crack his eyes.

His mother was bent over in her chair, chin to her chest. She held a tissue to her face, and for the first time he noticed a pile of wadded tissues on the end table beside her chair.

This was hard on her too.

She didn't move, except for a barely perceptible sway in her shoulders. He knew that position: she was praying.

He suddenly felt flushed, even embarrassed. She was praying for him, he knew. She was taking her son to the Lord, seeking God to comfort and support him. Recognizing her own inadequacy at helping her son, she turned to the Lord.

He, her son, was the object of this prayer.

The flush turned to a warm shiver across his flesh. Her praying heart was such an act of love. It was targeted to him at that moment. The God of all creation was being asked by his mother to come and console him, right there in that little room, on this unknown street in the meaningless town of Windwood.

Rising from his seat, Jonathon went to her chair and kneeled. Her folded hands broke apart to receive his hand, but she otherwise maintained her prayerful pose. He joined her, lifting up Manny and his parents before the Lord.

The doorbell interrupted their silent prayer five minutes later. Elaine got up, squeezing her son's shoulders before heading to the door. After answering it she stepped back, asking Jonathon, "Do ya know a Denise Harrison? She says she has something to show ya."

Denise Harrison, Henry Smitherton's daughter. Surprised, Jonathon motioned to his mother to invite her in. Denise came into the living room, her hair perfectly placed just like he remembered it from their short visit at the hospital when her father was so sick. She wore a red and black plaid dress with a wide black belt matching shiny black shoes. In her hands was a small cardboard box that she laid on the end table so she could extend her hand, accompanied by a sheepish smile. She greeted Jonathon like she knew him well.

"Jonathon, it's good to see you."

"Hello, Mrs. Harrison," he responded, gently shaking her hand while knowing little else to say.

"I can't stay long, but there's something I need to share with you."

Elaine interrupted, offering Mrs. Harrison a chair before sitting down herself.

"Thanks, Mrs. Thompson. Your son took great care of my father during several different hospital stays." She turned toward Jonathon, make-up and mascara highlighting her slim and attractive face. "I heard this morning what happened with Dr. Feddersen last night. A friend of mine at the police station filled me in. I am so very sorry about your friend." She paused in respect for the delicacy of her words. "When I heard of your involvement in the altercation, it reminded me of the time you spent with Dad during his last days of life. He spoke highly of you, Jonathon."

Nodding, Jonathon remembered well Henry Smitherton's fall out of bed, the nasty bruising, and Dr. Feddersen's feigned attempts at being Mr. Smitherton's friend. He wondered just how much Mrs. Harrison knew of her father's involvement with NanoMed.

She continued, "Before my father died, he recorded himself on a cassette tape. You know, my father's not the type to write messages or make recordings. He never communicated in those ways. If there was something to be said, he'd tell me. So I feared listening to the cassette, not wanting to hear what he didn't feel he could say to me directly. After I heard of Dr. Feddersen's experiments, it made me realize the possibility of what my father was wanting to say."

She reached for the cardboard box beside her and pulled out a cassette player. "The whole recording speaks of his involvement with Dr. Feddersen and NanoMed. I realize now that if I had only listened to this earlier, perhaps none of this…" Her voice trailed off, her gaze to the corner of the ceiling. "So much of what he did for NanoMed, he did for me. They paid him very well, and much of that my father passed to me." Fighting against tears, she lost her voice. After a few seconds with her eyes closed, she recovered, "I'm on my way to the police to share this with them. I'm sure it will give them some helpful direction. Before I give it to them, there's a part of the recording that Dad wanted me to share with you, Jonathon. If you don't mind, I'd like to play it for you." Her eyebrows lifted as she looked at both Mrs. Thompson and Jonathon for approval.

Jonathon answered, "It would be an honor to hear your father speak."

Pushing the play button, Mrs. Harrison held the cassette player on her lap and adjusted the volume. The recording picked up in mid-sentence, a gravelly, deep voice, unmistakably Henry Smitherton's.

"And tell Jonathon, the nurse up here. Tell him—he was right." There was a lengthy gap and then the same voice returned.

"Tell Jonathon his prayers were answered. His prayers to heal me—" Another gap of silence, "—his prayers are answered. My faith in God has become real." The voice weakened to a whisper, but the words remained clear. "I saw it...I saw that faith, in Jonathon. My sickness was not healed. No, death is upon me. But I have found my Lord, Jesus Christ. Tell Jonathon his faith showed me Christ. Tell him I am healed."

Mrs. Harrison dabbed her eyes with a tissue, turning off the player.

Jonathon's mother sobbed openly.

"That's the grandest testimony I ever did hear," Elaine mustered between her tears. "You've got a wonderful daddy there. He's surely smiling from heaven now."

Jonathon was thoughtful. "Those are incredible words. I can hardly believe them."

"Believe them, Jonathon," Elaine responded with composure. "I'm here to thank you for making all the difference that matters to my father. I love him and miss him, but your influence on his life has made a special difference." She placed the cassette player in her box. "Well, I must go. This tape will go directly to the police. I expect that the evidence here combined with what is discovered in NanoMed will lead the courts to convict Dr. Feddersen with a lengthy jail sentence."

"He deserves the 'lectric chair." Elaine said.

"My friend told me that Dr. Feddersen was complaining that he had pancreatic cancer," Denise added. "The same cancer that NanoMed had given my father. If that's true, Dr. Feddersen won't last in jail more than a year."

"That may be worse than the electric chair," Jonathon said.

"Well, Jonathon, you deserved to hear my father's words directly. I hope his words encourage you."

With that, she stood to leave, and Jonathon followed her to the door.

"Thanks, Mrs. Harrison. It must be a comfort to you to know that your father trusted Christ before his passing."

"I'm understanding more and more what that means." She pushed open the door herself, and Jonathon for the first time noticed her vacant eyes. "I hope I find the peace my father had in his final moments."

"Follow the faith of your father and you will," he called to her as she walked down the sidewalk in the brisk afternoon breeze.

Returning to the living room, his mother remained seated, eyes gleaming with pride at her son.

"Didn't know ya sparkled him, did ya?" She grinned broadly.

"Mom, I didn't heal him. I think I've lost that gift."

"Boy, didn't ya hear the dead man's words? You healed him alright. Better than that, ya healed his heart."

"I didn't even pray for him, really." He plopped back down in the easy chair.

"Didn't have to. He saw it in ya, Jonathon."

Jonathon pushed against the armrests to recline the chair, not allowing himself to meet his mother's eyes.

"Don't be so hard on yourself. It's God working through ya anyway. Just think, Jonathon. He used you."

Sitting silent, he closed his eyes again. *But what about Noelle? God, why did she have to die?*

He could hear his mother clinking cups beside him when she interrupted his thoughts. "Oh my, I forgot one." He opened his eyes to see her holding her folded bulletin.

"That nice man, Mr. Sunday, came by too." She pointed to a spot on her bulletin. "I knew I was going to forget, and then I even wrote it down and still forgot. I must be slipping faster than I thought."

She picked up her coffee cups again and started to leave for the kitchen.

"Mom, Michael Sunday came by?" he asked impatiently.

"Yes, boy, that's what I said." She went into the kitchen and he heard the sink faucet pour out water.

Rising from his chair he followed her, leaning against the side wall beside the stove. "So, did he say anything?" He tried to sound casual.

"Who?" Her back was to him as she washed the cups and yesterday's dishes.

"Michael Sunday, Mom. Don't do this to me. Did he say anything?"

"As matter of fact he did." She kept her hands buried in the water. "Something about how he'd heard ya called for him last night."

Jonathon walked forward to stand beside his mother. "Yes, I did call him. But he never answered." He leaned forward to look at his mother's face.

"That musta been what he was talking 'bout."

"What? What else did he say?"

She stopped washing and clasped her hands in a dry towel.

"He said he was sorry, Jonathon." She turned to look at him, her eyes glistening. "Sorry he didn't make it. Something about how he was held up by somebody else. I think he said he was fighting somebody else." Shrugging her shoulders, that part didn't seem to matter. She reached and grasped Jonathon's hand, her warmth from the dishwater was a stark contrast to his chilly fingers.

"But he said he got there in time to see Noelle be healed." Elaine's eyes glimmered with tears. "He said he was there, Jonathon."

"But she wasn't—"

"Oh, Jonathon. But she was. Just like that Denise lady's father. Noelle was healed in the heart. God is using ya all over the place."

Jonathon turned toward the window looking out over the sink, the sun streaming across the yet frosted lawn outside.

"And we know it for sure, Jonathon." Elaine put her hands back in the dishwater. "Mr. Sunday was there. Told me hisself."

Jonathon suddenly felt the warmth of the sunny day inside himself.

No, it was different.

His chest was burning, as if the sun was beaming straight into his heart. And a tingle tickled his neck, slowly migrating, wonderfully, right down his spine.

The incredible sensations brought a smile to his lips—until a dish cloth slapped him in the face.

"Don't cha just stand there dreaming." His mother smiled, dropping a wet cup in his hands. "Help me dry now, boy."

About the Author

Michael J. Huckabee has twenty years of experience in clinical medicine as a physician assistant. He resides in Nebraska with his wife and four children, and teaches at a private college. He serves as a public speaker on medical ethics to various community, religious and health professional groups. This is his second novel.